EFFECTIVE SCHOOL
MANAGEMENT

Bertie Everard read chemistry at Oxford and joined ICI in 1951 as a research chemist. He moved from the technical side in mid-career and became the Company Education and Training Manager, responsible for senior management training. Shortly before retirement in 1982 he was appointed a visiting professor at the Polytechnic of Central London and later a visiting fellow at the University of London Institute of Education, where he helped to design and run courses in school management. He undertook a year's research into the problems of school management, comparing them with those in industry, and published the results in another book, *Developing Management in Schools*. He was a consultant in the management of change to a project concerned with the Education Act 1981, and helped to write the training manual, *Decision Making for Special Educational Needs*.

He spent ten years as an external verifier for NVQs in management, training and development, and sport and recreation (including outdoor education). He was on the Education Management Development Committee of the British Education Management and Administration Society for several years. He now chairs his local YMCA, which provides early years education for 200 children and is a director of a leading educational charity, the Brathay Hall Trust.

Geoffrey Morris read modern languages at Cambridge and later also graduated in law. He is the managing director of EMAS Business Consultants Ltd. Before joining EMAS (European Management Advisory Services) in 1971, he was a senior manager in the Unilever Group, and prior to that he was a schoolteacher for ten years, five of them as head of modern languages and general studies.

In 1967 he obtained the backing of the CBI to run a course in management for schoolteachers – the first of its kind. Since then he has been active in promoting management in schools through courses at Brighton Polytechnic and Brunel University, with lectures and workshops for groups of inspectors, headteachers and administrators and consultancy and development activities within individual schools. From 1983 to 1986, he was a member of the CNAA Education Organization and Management Board. Since 1999 Geoffrey has been chairman of a charity, whose main focus is on building and equipping schools and training potential managers in Kosovo and Bosnia.

In his mainstream consultancy activities Geoffrey has worked across Europe and in the Far East with several multinational organizations, and for twelve months he acted as Head of Management Training for British Rail, during which time he was active in developing links between education and industry. He is a tutor and Executive Board Member of the European Master's Programme in Food Studies. He lectures and writes regular articles on Environmental Law and conducts 'Team-building and Organisational Behaviour' programmes for both industrial and educational clients.

Ian Wilson read mathematics at Cambridge and then obtained his PGCE at Chelsea College Centre for Science Education. He taught mathematics in two inner London schools before becoming, successively, Head of Mathematics at Clapton School and William Ellis School. He then became Deputy Head at Park Barn School Guildford. He was Headteacher of Woodcote High School in Croydon for eight years, during which time he was a Headteacher representative on Croydon Education Committee, and took part in an international research project on Effective Leadership. Since 2000, he has been headteacher of Rydens School, a mixed 11–18 comprehensive of 1,300 students in Walton-on-Thames.

Ian has written two mathematics textbooks and a guide to parents on ICT, as well as editing school versions of three of the plays of G B Shaw. He is a reviewer for the *Times Educational Supplement*. Ian is an associate consultant with Surrey LEA, and a member of the Education Committee of the Royal Society.

Effective School Management

Fourth Edition

K. B. Everard, Geoffrey Morris
and Ian Wilson

$SAGE

Los Angeles | London | New Delhi
Singapore | Washington DC

First published 2004
Reprinted 2006, 2007, 2009

SAGE Publications Ltd
1 Oliver's Yard
55 City Road
London EC1Y 1SP

SAGE Publications Inc.
2455 Teller Road
Thousand Oaks, California 91320

SAGE Publications India Pvt Ltd
B-1/I 1 Mohan Cooperative Industrial Area
Mathura Road
New Delhi 110 044

SAGE Publications Asia-Pacific Pte Ltd
33 Pekin Street #02-01
Far East Square
Singapore 048763

Library of Congress Control Number: 2003115416

A catalogue record for this book is available from the British
Library

ISBN 978-1-4129-0048-5
ISBN 978-1-4129-0049-2 (pbk)

Typeset by GCS, Leighton Buzzard, Bedfordshire
Printed in Great Britain by TJI Digital, Padstow,
Cornwall

FSC
Mixed Sources
Product group from well-managed
forests and other controlled sources

Cert no. SGS-COC-2482
www.fsc.org
© 1996 Forest Stewardship Council
Text pages are FSC certified

Contents

Preface

Improving the effectiveness of school management remains one of our fundamental concerns.

(School Teachers Review Body, 1995, para. 134)

The main purpose of this book is to help teachers with senior management responsibilities, and the schools and colleges that they work in, to become more effective. It is not a book by academics for other academics, but by practitioners for practitioners. Practitioners of what? Ian Wilson is a practising head and the two original authors, Bertie Everard and Geoffrey Morris, have both been senior managers in industry, and we have spent much of our careers helping others, both in industry and education, to learn to become more effective managers, as well as improving the effectiveness of organizations – commercial, industrial, educational and church. So it is not only in the practice of management and the workings of organizations that we claim some expertise but also in the methods by which both can be improved.

Of the two original authors, one of us (Morris), having taught and managed in schools and in Unilever, is managing director of a European management consultancy which has played a strong role in developing school management training since 1971; the other (Everard) has been education and training manager of ICI, and since 1982 has trained over 1,000 school heads in management, mostly as a visiting fellow at the University of London Institute of Education. We think this makes our book unique, because there are so few people who have had enough management responsibility and training experience both in school and in industry to bridge the cultural and terminological gap fully. We both became involved, through the former CNAA Education Organization and Management Board in validating award-bearing courses in education management, and have both taught on such courses. So we have a foot in the academic world and are broadly familiar with what is taught in higher education about management, and with the value system that pervades such educational institutions. Those, then, are our credentials.

Naturally these experiences have shaped our outlook on school and college management and leadership. They have convinced us of the value of building 'learning bridges' between educational and non-educational (but particularly commercial) organizations, so that successful management practice and organizational design can be transferred to and fro. However, because industry has a longer tradition of management and leadership development, and spends more on it than does education, most of the traffic across the bridge is towards education. We believe that only some of the available know-how should cross the bridge, and even that may need translating or adapting before it can be put to beneficial use.

It is our contention that those who do not believe that schools can learn from industry base their case on false premises and lack of first-hand knowledge of industrial management. They have a concept of industrial organizations and managers which we scarcely recognize as real – or, if real, as effective. We know of the charges of exploitation and the supposed taint of the profit motive, but we do not accept that the ethics of most businesses are malign. Our proposition is this:

> Some firms are effective, ethical and successful, partly because they are well led and organized, which is partly because their managers have learned management systematically.
>
> Equally, some schools and colleges are effective and successful, partly because they are well led and organized, which is partly because their heads and senior staff have learned management systematically.

Therefore heads and senior staff in schools and colleges can learn to manage better by studying what their counterparts do in successful firms and schools and across national boundaries such as the Atlantic Ocean and the North Sea.

Such learning takes time. We think nothing of investing four to six years in the training of a doctor, lawyer, chemist or vet, but how many managers get even as many *weeks'* training? Yet management can be just as complex and demanding as these other professions.

Just as doctors' and vets' mistakes may die, managers can kill their organizations. We can learn from others' mistakes, and industry has made many (as has education). So we need to be discriminating about what we allow to cross the learning bridges. Industry has had to be discriminating in the same way, for many of the new ideas about organization and management stem from institutions of higher education. Some work and some don't. This book is about those that work, and it warns the reader of some of the traps for the unwary.

For too long books and courses on education management have been considered by students as too 'theoretical', 'academic', 'impractical' or even 'irrelevant'; they do not deal with the real condition of the manager, but with some kind of idealized role. Since 1988 the concept of competence-based learning and criterion-referenced qualifications has proved to be a powerful countervailing force, stimulated by the former Employment Department's Standards Initiative and by the National Council for Vocational Qualifications (SCOTVEC in Scotland) – now superseded by the

Qualifications and Curriculum Authority. This development is probably the biggest single reform in vocational education and training since the Statute of Artificers was enacted in 1543. It is just as revolutionary as the introduction of the National Curriculum. Schools have already felt the impact with the arrival of GNVQs as alternative qualifications to GCSE and 'A' levels.

The CNAA used to adopt the following principle in assessing polytechnic courses (author's italics):

> The direction of the students' studies must be towards greater understanding and *competence*. Thus, while it may be appropriate for a programme to include the acquisition of techniques or skills, or the learning of data, these must lead to a higher level of intellectual and creative *performance* than that intrinsic in the learning of skills, techniques or facts themselves.

We subscribe wholeheartedly to this principle, and the whole thrust of the book is aimed at improving competence and performance. We do not disparage theory; Lewin's aphorism that there is nothing so practical as a good theory rings true for us, but we believe that too many books on education management are written from a theoretician's point of view. Our aim has been to redress this balance and to complement with something more practical the texts written by those academics who simply study management without practising it (excellent though many are).

Perhaps a clue to the different approaches lies in the words used to describe 'management'. It is different from 'administration' (though in North America this word comes nearer to what we mean by 'management') and 'leadership', but includes both. Consequently, we see a manager as someone who

(1) Knows what he or she wants to happen and causes it to happen;
(2) Is responsible for controlling resources and ensuring that they are put to good use;
(3) Promotes effectiveness in work done, and a search for continual improvement;
(4) Is accountable for the performance of the unit he or she is managing, of which he or she is a part;
(5) Sets a climate or tone conducive to enabling people to give of their best.

(Everard, 1984)

Since our third edition was published in 1996, there has been a gradual shift of emphasis from 'management' towards 'leadership'. This is exemplified by the creation of the National College of School Leadership (www.ncsl.org.uk) and by the rebranding of the MCI management standards as 'management and leadership' standards (www.management-standards.org.uk); Figure 1 is the new functional map on which these standards are based, and the latest key purpose is defined as:

> Provide direction, gain commitment, facilitate change and achieve results through the efficient, creative and responsible deployment of people and other resources.

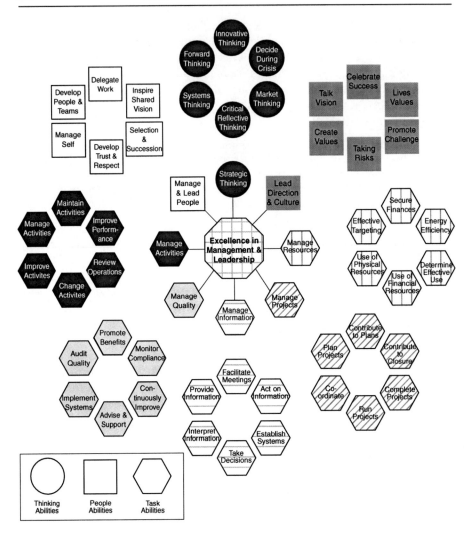

Figure I Integrated management and leadership

Most of our readers will recognize both definitions as describing the role of heads, principals, rectors and leaders in schools and colleges. Some will aspire to such posts or to the next rung down: deputies, assistant headteachers, heads of lower school, heads of faculties, principal teachers.

What we have to say is directed at primary, secondary and special schools, as well as early years education centres (though the parts that deal with the interdepartmental problems of large institutions will scarcely apply to a small village primary school); and it is as relevant to the independent as to the state sector.

We believe that much of what we say also applies to the management of colleges and universities and we hope that this will be borne in mind by readers in such institutions. However, in this stratum of education, it is more to the teachers of education management on long or short courses that we offer guidance – on what, in our experience, teachers as managers really want to learn. Although the book is based on studies of effective management and successful organizations, and is pitched at a practical level, it is underpinned with theory. If it fails to do justice to important schools of thought, this is because we have quite deliberately selected approaches that we ourselves have used, and found relevant.

We have included short tasks which the reader can relate to his or her own school situation. Some of these exercises could be used for group discussion – group learning is a useful method which can be set up in any school or for a peer group from different schools in a locality. Other issues for discussion have been added to the fourth edition. Wherever we can, we have included examples from schools.

Such conscious linking of the book to the reader's own situation helps the process of learning. We espouse the experiential learning model described by Kolb (1984, p. 33), which is based on earlier work by Lewin and Dewey. It postulates a cycle of improving competence by observing and reflecting on concrete experiences, then forming abstract concepts or generalizations, then testing the implications of these concepts in new situations. Thus learning combines the processes of experience, perception, cognition and behaviour; it is not simply the imparting and assimilation of knowledge. This book cannot supply the concrete experience, so it will not be as helpful to readers whose roles are not managerial; but we hope it will help perception, reflection and conceptualization, and we suggest ways of putting the results of these mental processes into practice.

We see the book being used for personal study at home or work; as part of the reading for a short or a long course; for informal group discussion; and as a reference handbook for the practising manager. We don't think that this multiplicity of aims is ambitious because that is how we have used similar books on management. Our main concern is that so many of those who could benefit from it simply can't find the time for reading; their priorities leave no space for self-improvement. It is worth reflecting whether such an ordering is in the best interests of the school, for it is impossible to change a school for the better without changing oneself.

The report of the School Management Task Force (1990), *Developing School Management – The Way Forward,* called for a 'new approach to school management development which focuses attention on the support which should be available in and near to the school and places less emphasis on off-site training'. It sees management development as a crucial process in helping organizations achieve their purposes, and quotes Everard's definition of it as 'an approach that supports, promotes and is harmoniously related to the development of the organization'. This philosophy pervades our book, which emphasizes almost every characteristic of effective schools which the report lists, and shows how each can be developed by schools themselves. We share the task force's view that schools should be moving towards an integrated corporate approach to the development of the workforce, led by the head, so that achievement of corporate goals and meeting the individual's needs become matters of mutual benefit rather than of competing demands. The report advises schools to draw on industrial expertise; our book packages this in an interactive form which schools can use by themselves, selecting whichever topics, techniques and exercises meet their needs.

In 1995 the Teacher Training Agency (TTA) became responsible for guiding nationally the professional development of teachers, including those in management roles, and launched the HEADLAMP programme for training newly appointed heads, now renamed the Headteacher Induction Programme (HIP), in which many have now participated. Two other programmes have since been added, and the work has now been taken over by the National College for School Leadership.

We admit to being, in the writing of this book, creative plagiarists, a condition rife among management trainers. In the distant past we have picked up from lectures, handouts, articles, internal reports, books and discussions with professional colleagues a whole host of interlocking ideas which we have built into our personal repertoires, as birds build a nest. Often the source of the original idea gets lost as it is embellished and refashioned to new use. We are conscious of our debt to many 'gurus'. As well as a general acknowledgement to all those whose ideas we have used, we have tried to give credit where we know the source. But there are some to whom we owe a special debt.

Bertie Everard had the privilege of working over several years with Professor Dick Beckhard of MIT, when he consulted with ICI, and with other ICI colleagues such as Arthur Johnston and Derek Sheane. Part III owes much to the insights developed during this experience. Professor Bill Reddin, the late Ralph Coverdale and his disciples, and Meredith Belbin have also helped to shape his ideas. Later there were colleagues in the University of London Institute of Education and in the BEMAS Education Management Development Committee, especially Janet Ouston.

Geoffrey Morris would like to express his thanks to his colleagues in EMAS (European Management Advisory Services) who have contributed to the development of ideas used in this book, and to Tom Lea, late of Brighton Polytechnic, with whom he worked on frequent courses over a period of twenty years; to Malcolm Mander of Brunel University and to Carmen Newsome, Head of Tockwith Primary School, Yorkshire, who provided an insight into Ofsted inspections and the changing primary school. He would also like to acknowledge the, usually positive, criticism of his wife (a former teacher), his daughter (a teacher) and his son (a manager), and to thank them for giving him temporary leave of mental absence from the family.

Ian Wilson would like to acknowledge the many useful discussions he has had with senior leadership teams at Rydens School and Woodcote High School. He has also been influenced by colleagues on the international research project on school leadership in which he participated. He is grateful for the support and encouragement of fellow heads, including Sandy Davies, Roy Blatchford and Keith Sharp and colleagues in Surrey, especially Judy Nettleton for information on special schools. His family have been, as usual, tolerant of his hours spent with a PC rather than with them.

All of us have been rightly chivvied by our editor, Marianne Lagrange, and by Berteke Ibbett and Irene Greenstreet, Morris's secretaries, who word-processed the script. To these and others unnamed, we express our thanks.

Bertie Everard
Geoffrey Morris
Ian Wilson

PERSONAL APPLICATION

Study the management and leadership functional map in Figure 1. How well does your own job map on to it (you may want to rephrase a few functions? How do the functions of a headteacher differ from those of managers and leaders in general? If you conclude that they are much the same, are you willing to accept the generic nature of such roles and therefore the relevance to your job of insights from non-educational settings?

Acknowledgements

Figure 9.4 is adapted from *The Learning Organization* (1987) by permission of the author, Bob Garratt and Profile Books. The learning styles description is reprinted from Honey and Mumford's *Manual of Learning Styles* (1986: 2nd edn) by permission of the authors.

Figure 10.2 and the definitions of team roles in Chapter 10 are reprinted by permission of Belbin Associates UK, and thanks are due to Dr Meredith Belbin for agreeing to the use of this material from his book, *Management Teams: Why They Succeed or Fail* (1981) and from the website, www. belbin.com.

The quotation from *Ten Good Schools* in Chapter 16 (Crown Copyright) is reproduced with the permission of the Controller of Her Majesty's Stationery Office.

The authors gratefully acknowledge their indebtedness to Professor Fullan and to Professor Beckhard and his colleagues in Part III, which freely quotes from their work; also to their publishers, Teachers College Press and Thomson Publishing, and Addison-Wesley Publishing Company respectively, for permission to use this material: Fullan, M.G., *Change Forces*, Thompson Publishing © 1993, Fullan, M.G. with Stiegelbauer, S., *The New Meaning of Educational Change* (2nd edn), New York, Teachers College Press © 1991 by Teachers College, Columbia University (all rights reserved), R. Beckhard and R. Harris, *Organizational Transitions: Managing Complex Change* © 1987 Addison-Wesley Publishing Company Inc.

Acknowledgement is made to the McGraw-Hill Book Company (UK) Ltd for permission to use material from V. Stewart's book, *Change: The Challenge for Management* (1983) in Chapter 16. The authors also thank HarperCollins Publishers, Inc. for permission to use selected excerpts from *In Search of Excellence: Lessons from America's Best-run Companies*, by Thomas J. Peters and Robert H. Waterman Jr. Copyright © 1982 by Thomas J. Peters and Robert H. Waterman Jr.; and 'Hierarchy of needs' from *Motivation and Personality* by Abraham H. Maslow. Copyright © 1970 by Abraham H. Maslow. The authors would also like to thank Frederick Herzberg for permission to use material from *Work and the Nature of Man* (1966).

Chapters 14–18 are illustrated from a case study of a highly successful change programme currently in progress: the Barrow Community Learning Partnership (BCLP). Our thanks are due to Mason Minnitt, Director, Rick Lee, Deputy Director, Professor Murray Saunders and Steve Lenartowicz, BCLP Action Forum, who provided internal reports and gave freely of their time in describing the programme and enabling us to relate it to this book.

Exercises 1–4 and 7–10 and some other material in this book are the joint copyright of EMAS Business Consultants Ltd and EMAS Consultants Ltd.

1

Introduction

Are good managers born, not trained? Does management come naturally to us? Before answering these questions, you may find it useful to complete the following brief questionnaire. Answer each question in turn, without hesitating too long, and without reading ahead.

Management principles questionnaire

Award a grade of 0 (totally disagree) to 4 (totally agree) to indicate to what extent you agree or disagree with each of the statements that follow. Please do not look at Questions 6–10 until you have answered Questions 1–5.

(1) One should ignore certain faults in the work of subordinates in order not to discourage them.

| 0 | 1 | 2 | 3 | 4 |

(2) I spend too much time sorting out problems that my subordinates ought to be able to deal with.

| 0 | 1 | 2 | 3 | 4 |

(3) I try to tell my subordinates exactly what they have to do and how I want it done.

| 0 | 1 | 2 | 3 | 4 |

(4) I know enough about my area of responsibility to be able to take most decisions quickly and without having to seek the views of my subordinates.

| 0 | 1 | 2 | 3 | 4 |

(5) I always tell my staff why we are making changes.

| 0 | 1 | 2 | 3 | 4 |

(6) If anyone finds any fault at all with my work I would rather he or she told me to my face.

| 0 | 1 | 2 | 3 | 4 |

(7) If I have a problem I like my boss to take over and sort it out.

                0   1   2   3   4

(8) I like to be told exactly how I am to do my job.

                0   1   2   3   4

(9) If my boss is going to take a decision affecting me or my department I like him or her to consult me first.

                0   1   2   3   4

(10) It is difficult to appreciate the logic behind many education office decisions.

                0   1   2   3   4

Interpreting the questionnaire

As you neared the end of the questionnaire you probably realized that there was a relationship between Questions 1 and 6, 2 and 7, etc. In fact, the first five questions all relate to the way in which we manage others or believe that we ought to manage others. Questions 6–10, on the other hand, are concerned with the way in which we believe we are or ought to *be* managed.

It seems logical that we should manage others in the way that we like to be managed. However, you will be among the vast majority of those who have answered this questionnaire if you have, by a '4' grading, firmly asserted that 'if anyone finds any fault at all with my work I would rather he or she told me to my face' (Question 6), yet have at the same time suggested by a '3' or a '4' that 'One should ignore certain faults in the work of subordinates in order not to discourage them' (Question 1).

Answers by a typical group of fifty headteachers of all types to the questionnaire gave the average results shown in Figure 1.1.

	0	1	2	3	4		0	1	2	3	4
1				X		6					X
2				X		7	X				
3				X		8		X			
4				X		9					X
5				X		10				X	

Figure 1.1 Scoring sheet for management principles questionnaire

In looking at your own scores or at the above scores, two objections may emerge:

(1) 'The questions are not exact matches.' This is true – but necessary in the interests of not making the correspondence too obvious during the answering of the questionnaire. The match is close enough to make the point.
(2) 'The way in which you manage or wish to be managed differs from level to level. Headteachers do wish to be told of their faults (and can safely be told of their faults as they will be too mature to be discouraged!), but this is not the case with less senior staff.' However, this questionnaire has been given to groups of school staff at all levels and the mean response has been almost identical.

    In the case of Question 10, the wording was changed to 'Many of my headteacher's decisions ...' The responses still clearly made the point that at any level we believe that we are keeping others informed of the reasons for change. However, in the vast majority of cases we are living in a fool's paradise.

INSTINCT, COMMON SENSE, SKILLS AND TECHNIQUES

From what we have seen above, it would appear that our 'instinct' for managing others may be less reliable than we think. We may, in fact, be rationalizing ourselves out of facing up to issues with our colleagues or subordinates when, in fact, this sort of evasiveness of real issues is frustrating, destructive and time-wasting for all concerned.

Most of what we shall say in this book may well appear to be common sense, as it indeed is once the issues have been thought through. Unfortunately, as we often see in others, people sometimes do not behave in accordance with principles which *should* be obvious to them. The remedy is to be clearly aware of

(1) the pitfalls;
(2) the guiding principles which will help us to avoid the pits – or to get out of those we do happen to fall into; and
(3) the early warning signs of trouble.

Practice at reacting in the light of these principles will develop our management 'skills'.

Finally, the book will suggest certain techniques and 'tools' that we can use to improve the effectiveness of the 'team' for which we are responsible or of which we are members.

WHAT IS MANAGEMENT? WHO IS A MANAGER?

As all teachers will know from their university days, a great deal of ink can be expended in defining one's terms. Definitions of management are so many and varied that we could spend the next twenty pages on this subject alone. Our aim, however, is not philosophy but practical guidance. Let us therefore be brief.

What management is not is carrying out a prescribed task in a prescribed way. As we discussed in the Preface, management in its broadest sense is about

(1) setting direction, aims and objectives;
(2) planning how progress will be made or a goal achieved;
(3) organizing available resources (people, time, materials) so that the goal can be economically achieved in the planned way;
(4) controlling the process (i.e. measuring achievement against plan and taking corrective action where appropriate); and
(5) setting and improving organizational standards.

As all teaching jobs contain at least some element of 'management' in this sense, one can argue that every teacher is a manager.

More restrictive definitions of management argue that a manager must additionally 'direct' the work of others. Again, in their classroom role, this definition could apply to all teachers and, indeed, almost all principles of management do have very direct application to 'managing' the classroom.

However, our prime concern will be with school 'managers' in the more conventional sense, i.e. those teachers who have some responsibility for planning, organizing, directing and controlling the work of other teachers.

THE MANAGER AND THE ORGANIZATION

The 'organization' – be it department, school, college, university, education authority or, indeed, the educational system *in toto* – expects of its 'managers' three things. These are that they will

(1) integrate its resources in the effective pursuit of its goals;
(2) be the agents of effective change; and
(3) maintain and develop its resources.

Integration of resources

The managerial role – as opposed to the teaching role – is to be the 'glue' in the organization, not, it is hoped, in the sense of 'gumming up' the works – though those whom you manage will inevitably see it that way at times – but in the sense of holding the organization together.

The first post in which a teacher has to plan, organize, direct and control the work of other teachers involves a fundamental change in the criteria for job success. Many learn the lessons the hard way.

Throughout the *educational* process, success as a student tends to depend on demonstrating and exploiting one's own ideas and talents. This may also be the focus in one's first teaching appointment. As a manager, on the other hand, success depends on using the ideas and talents of a team, on arriving at decisions and actions to which the team members feel committed and on ensuring that they are put into effect. Though you do not feel that someone else's idea is quite as good as your own, you may be wise to back that idea, particularly if the person who puts it forward has a key role in implementation.

The manager is less concerned with *being* a resource than with *using* resources. At most levels of school management, teachers are fulfilling both classroom and management roles, and the danger is that one forgets that behaviour which succeeds in the classroom is different from that required to motivate the team.

Geoffrey Morris has not forgotten the occasion when, in his first year as head of department, he made changes in textbook and curriculum without fully involving the members of his department!

Effective change

Change is an essential function of the managerial role. It may be initiated from within the school or imposed from without. It may take the form of making improvements in the way in which we achieve ongoing goals, or we may have to cope with new goals and challenges.

Over the last thirty-five years, schools have had to carry through a number of radical reorganizations caused by changes in politics, philosophies and birth-rates. In the years that lie ahead, the one thing that seems certain is that the rate of technological and social change will, if anything, accelerate, and the ability of our pupils to succeed – or, indeed, survive – in a changing environment will depend on our ability to adapt the content, methods and ethos of education to the new needs.

Change features strongly in the pages which follow. By definition, strategic decisions involve change. As managers, we are involving others in that change, and we need to bear in mind that the following phenomena tend to come into play, affecting both ourselves and those whom we manage:

'Not invented here'.   Next time you are in a meeting and hear someone propose a course of action, note carefully how many of the ensuing comments are positive and how many are negative. (NB 'Yes, but's' count as negative.) The natural tendency in people is to resist and even resent ideas which are not their own. The tendency is even stronger if a change is parachuted upon them. Listen to the comments when a memo from the headteacher is posted on the staff-room notice-board announcing almost any change – or when yet another government circular comes round.

'I haven't time'.   Implementing changes always takes time, and teachers' time is always in short supply. It is easier to apply a standard solution which has

worked in the past, to go over the same ground, to repeat the same syllabus using the same methods, than it is to prepare and implement a new approach. However good intentions may be, crises and routine will usually take priority over preparation for change. The only way to overcome the time barrier may be to set clearly defined action deadlines. However much time may be given for these, we will often find that the action is not taken – by ourselves or others – until the last minute, when it is promoted to the 'crisis' category because someone is 'breathing down one's neck'.

'A bird in the hand'.   Change means risks and unforeseen problems. Will there be timetable clashes? Will the pupils respond in the way that is hoped? Will we have the resources to cope? Can we handle the new situation?

Restricted vision.   Research has shown that the most important indication of high management potential and effective managerial performance is the 'helicopter' quality – the ability to take the broader view of one's activities and to see them in context.

   However, we all have a tendency, particularly in times of stress, to move our sights down a level instead of taking this broad view. Thus we may

(1) jealously conserve the interests of ourselves or our departments instead of relating to the interests of the total organization; and
(2) take decisions to deal with instant crises and forget that the decision may create a dangerous precedent which will itself provoke more crises (the history of management/union relations is littered with catastrophic short-term expedients).

Problems of reorganization, status, demarcation, authority.   As well as consuming time, such changes are seen by most people as containing 'threats'. Usually our first reaction is to concentrate on these threats instead of looking for the opportunities. A sign of individual confidence and organizational health is said to lie in the ability to reverse this trend.

Shortage of money. Change almost always costs money!

Maintaining and developing resources

The tangible resources of an organization can be classified as

(1) human (the people employed by the organization);
(2) material (buildings and equipment); and
(3) financial (the funds available to the organization).

If these resources are not maintained we simply do not have an organization to integrate or to change.

   Alongside these are a number of *intangible* resources, of which 'image' or 'reputation' are the most generally recognized. Without the right image, the survival of any commercial enterprise, including an independent school, is certainly in doubt and, even within the state system, image matters wherever choice comes into play, e.g. recruitment of staff, placement of pupils in jobs and parental/student choice of school or college. Reflect on what other intangible resources are possessed by a school and their relative importance: ethical standards? disciplinary standards? external relationships and support?

It is not enough to *maintain* resources. The process of change demands that managers focus a great deal of attention on *developing* resources to meet new challenges and needs. If the educational system is to progress and be relevant to society, it must be 'need driven' and not 'resource driven' – that is to say, resources must be adapted to meet needs and not vice versa. These needs will be derived from the interplay of the school's values, the trends within the environment and educational legislation.

Managerial activities particularly concerned with the maintenance and development of resources are

(1) *human* – selection, job design, performance management, career planning, training, project work, coaching;
(2) *material* – purchasing, stock control, asset management; and
(3) *financial* – budgeting, cost control, fund-raising, cost/benefit analysis.

While barriers to curriculum development are most often said to be financial, the real problems are often human. Do staff have the skills and knowledge needed to introduce new subjects and methods? Do they want to make the changes? The relationship between skill and knowledge on the one hand and desire to innovate on the other is a 'chicken and egg' situation. To support a new subject we need to understand it; to wish to learn about a subject, we may need to be convinced of its relevance.

A school manager needs to be able to plan, organize and control all his or her resources, but the most crucial skill is undoubtedly the development of human resources.

ETHICS AND THE MANAGER

As teachers we already play an important and influential role in the lives of our pupils. As managers we become, additionally, one of the most important influences on the working lives of the staff who report directly or indirectly to us. As heads we fashion the value system of the school.

On our actions and attitudes will depend to a large extent

(1) whether the staff are happy or unhappy in their work;
(2) their work priorities; and
(3) the standard which they observe and reflect.

As 'leader' of a group of staff, we have a potential 'power-base' which can be used to influence decisions. Unscrupulous managers can make life hell for those of their departments who do not support them in staff meetings, whether or not the issue under discussion has previously been discussed within their departmental groups. Words like 'loyalty' can be corrupted to mean slavish adherence to the party line.

As we shall see, good 'meeting management' can become 'manipulation'; objectivity, honesty and justice can be lost in the emotion of conflict; all sorts of games can be played.

Every manager should constantly reflect on the ethics of his or her conduct. Other people, especially more senior managers, are more perceptive of unethical manoeuvrings than ever the perpetrator imagines. People who fondly imagine themselves to be seen as brilliant young managers, or as shrewd and sympathetic handlers of people, may, in fact, be regarded as unprincipled rogues by their colleagues.

Standards of competence, for use in NVQs, are now required to capture occupational demands arising from ethics and values, and the practical consequences for performance of subscribing to a value base have to be incorporated into descriptions of outcomes (NCVQ, 1995). The new standards for management and leadership include a unit 'Ensure compliance with values, ethical and legal frameworks' (www.management-standards.org).

THE SCHOOL'S ROLE AND MISSION: ARE EDUCATION AND MANAGEMENT INCOMPATIBLE?

Most authors on this subject readily reconcile education and management. However, there are still those who passionately believe that the manager's role and mission, as we have described them, are incompatible with those of a school. It is argued that schools, with their deep-rooted educational values and academic professionalism, are not the kind of organizations that ought to be managed by a 'linchpin head' or even a senior management or leadership group – they ought to be self-managing communities with access to power dispersed equally among the staff. This case has been argued in a London Institute of Education Paper, *Education plc?* (Maw *et al.*, 1984), which reflects the views of a number of educational sociologists and other theorists in institutions of higher education and of teachers who have been trained to embrace their thinking. The main arguments adduced in support of this stance are given below. We set them out early in this book because, unless they are confronted, much of what follows may be rejected by readers who espouse similar views:

(1) 'Managerialism' is in conflict with the values and purposes of schools.
(2) Stress on means as against ends devalues professional competence.
(3) Hierarchically organized schools deprive teachers of involvement in fundamental educational thinking.
(4) Vertical accountability is debilitating; it leads to suspicion, resentment, divisiveness, problems of legitimacy and (in the case of appraisal) attendant psychological detriment to isolated individuals.

(5) The conception of authority relationships within an educational system is contrary to democratic principles and has a miseducative effect on pupils.

(6) Pupils should not be politically educated through belonging to an institution that is run by a 'linchpin head'.

(7) The contexts of educational and commercial organizations differ fundamentally; the latter ignore important moral considerations, whereas to an educational undertaking, morality is central.

(8) Recommended management practice ('contingency theory') is tantamount to expediency and manipulation; the abrogation of such words as 'participation' is especially insidious.

(9) Management theory is a pseudo-theory, tricked out as a form of 'behavioural science', but without scientific basis; it lends a spurious legitimacy to the manipulative practices of managers.

(10) A commercially inspired management imperative may betray rather than enhance the specifically educational nature of schools, because its values, focus and style of operation are destructive and alien to progressive educational thinking.

(11) Managers surreptitiously enjoy the exercise of power, kick away much conventional morality and subjugate employees to the demands of the organization. Therefore heads should be regarded not as 'managers' but as professionally first among equals.

We believe that these arguments rest on false premises and on a lack of understanding of what well-managed commercial organizations are really like (for example, those with the Investors in People accolade). Some postulate a classical model of an industrial organization which has long been superseded; some do not correspond with life in such organizations as we have experienced it as managers and managed. The fact is that there is great diversity in industry and commerce, and within this are to be found exemplary organizations and departments with whose managers most teachers would find some rapport. Only part of industry is concerned with the routine tasks of mass production: research, accounts and training departments resemble schools in being staffed mainly by skilled and articulate professionals, and are managed accordingly.

If we thought that the approaches we advocate in the rest of this book would have the effects that critics of 'managerialism' fear, then we should not have written it. We are more than ready to defend on moral and ethical grounds everything we have written. No less than the critics do we respect professional competence, individuality and the centrality of values in the (often hidden) curriculum of schools. One of us was a founder member of the National Association for Values in Education and Training (NAVET) and has contributed a chapter on 'Values as central to competent professional practice' to a book on *Managing Teachers as Professionals in Schools* (Everard, 1995b). For us management does not and should not imply the naked exercise of power, nor the subservience of the managed, nor insensitivity to individuals' needs, nor the renunciation of human values. It does, however, call for the knitting together of social and economic values, as warp and weft.

We readily acknowledge the cultural differences between schools and other organizations, with their different *raisons d'être*, and we are deeply aware, through bitter experience, of the pitfalls of using concepts and terminology that mean different things to people on different sides of the cultural divide. It may be that such pitfalls partly explain why we are able to accept the five conclusions about school management training with which Fielding ends his critique in *Education plc?* (Maw et al., 1984), while rejecting most of the arguments on which he bases them; and why we wholeheartedly subscribe to Mitchell's view of the headteacher's role, in the same booklet, quarrelling only with his stereotype of industrial managers.

However, this is not a book about educational and managerial philosophy and ethics: it is about effective practice. Hence all we need do at this point is to outline how we perceive the school as an organization, and what its mission is:

(1) The *raison d'être* of a school is to promote its pupils' learning, within a curriculum acceptable to its stakeholders, or as prescribed by the law.
(2) A school organization should meet these ends efficiently and cost-effectively.
(3) In such an organization tensions will arise between social and economic values, professional autonomy and managerial control, individuality and hierarchy, structural authority and participative decision-making, the head's dual roles of 'leading professional' and 'chief executive', the educational good of the many and the self-interest of the few, high principle and pragmatic expediency – and many other dilemmas that sometimes require a decision as to the lesser of two 'evils', e.g. being cruel in order to be kind.
(4) Striking the correct balance in these dilemmas entails difficult judgements, which have to be referred to a set of values outside of and greater than those of the individuals in the organization.
(5) At the highest level of abstraction, such values apply to, and often drive, all successful organizations, be they educational or commercial, and they act as bridges between the two.

In the remainder of this book we shall often revert to these fundamental issues in exploring how managers can best fulfil their personal roles and at the same time contribute to that of the educational institutions where they are set in authority.

FURTHER READING

Bush, T. and Bell, L.A. (2002) *The Principles and Practice of Educational Management*, Sage, London.

PERSONAL APPLICATION

Does your personal value system get in the way of your becoming a more effective manager? What are the main sticking points? Can you find a mentor to help you to reconcile your innermost beliefs with the inexorable demands that your job places on you? Do any of your staff need mentoring for a similar reason?

PART I
MANAGING PEOPLE

2

The Manager as a Leader

Leadership is a process of influencing others to achieve a goal.
(Dickmann and Stanford Blair, 2002)

INTERPERSONAL SKILLS

Before we can set about our managerial role and mission, we need some skill in relating to other people. We need to understand the various behavioural processes that may be at work, and use our knowledge to influence or 'lead' individuals or groups. In a meeting, as we shall see, decisions can be influenced far more effectively by using the behavioural 'process' of the meeting than by simply restating one's arguments, however sound they are. How we use our awareness of behavioural processes is a key aspect of managerial ethics. Do we use it to 'manipulate' or to 'facilitate'?

In order to help us to understand managerial behaviour and leadership, a large number of models have been created. Because of the commercial interest in management training, such models have proliferated to the point of confusion, and authors have at times promoted their own models by attacking those produced by others.

Our aim is to avoid adding to the lists, nor do we wish to spend time carrying out a review of the differing approaches of the many theoreticians. Instead we shall focus on some generally agreed principles and on a set of well-established models which we have found to be useful to managers in general and to school managers in particular.

Those of our readers who have attended courses on leadership and who have read other management literature, including Goleman's *Emotional Intelligence* (1996), are almost certain to have some acquaintance with the contents of this and the next chapter. Having cast an eye over the subheadings, they may therefore wish to proceed directly to Chapter 4.

MANAGEMENT STYLE MODELS

The best known of the management style models are based on the premiss that every manager has two main concerns. These concern

(1) to achieve results (i.e. he or she is 'task' oriented); and

(2) for relationships (i.e. he or she is 'people' oriented).

Earlier style models such as the Schmidt–Tannenbaum continuum
(Tannenbaum and Schmidt, 1958) suggested that these two concerns were in
conflict and that the more a person was concerned with results, the less he or
she would be concerned about relationships, and vice versa. The type of style
model shown in Figure 2.1 resulted.

Results   Relationships

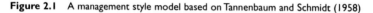

| Autocratic | Paternalistic | Consultative | Democratic |
| (Tell) | (Sell) | (Involve) | (Codetermine) |

Figure 2.1   A management style model based on Tannenbaum and Schmidt (1958)

However, it was not long before it was realized that a manager's concerns
for results and relationships were not necessarily opposed to each other, but
that it was possible to be concerned about both at the same time (how do I
best get results through people?) or, indeed, to be concerned about neither.
This is the concept recognized in a number of style models which put results
and relationships on two different axes of a graph and either name or number
the extreme positions, e.g. the Blake Grid (Blake and Mouton, 1994).

Figure 2.2 sets out such a model which gives both the Blake numbers and
verbal style descriptions. (NB The reader should note that the descriptions on
the model are used in a specific context as defined. Words such as 'political'
are used later in the book in a more positive context.)

Some attributes of each of the five named style positions are as follows:

Assertive
   • wants things done his or her way;
   • 'tells' rather than 'listens';

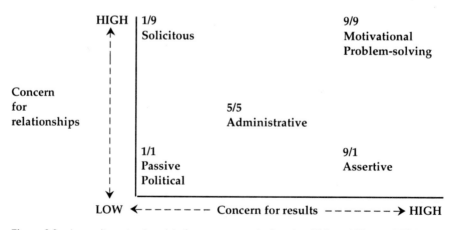

Figure 2.2   A two-dimensional model of management styles based on Blake and Mouton (1994)

- doesn't worry too much about other people's feelings or opinions;
- is aggressive if challenged;
- 'drives' things ahead; and
- checks up on staff.

Solicitous
- cares about people;
- wants to be liked;
- avoids open conflict – smooths and coaxes;
- 'if the school is "happy", that is all that matters';
- praises achievement to the point of flattering;
- glosses over slackness or poor performance;
- tends towards 'management by committee'; and
- is helpful.

Motivational/problem-solving
- agrees goals and expects achievement;
- monitors performance against goals;
- helps staff members to find solutions to poor performance;
- faces up to conflict calmly;
- agrees and monitors action plans;
- involves staff in decisions which affect them;
- delegates clearly; and
- takes decisions as and when needed.

Passive/political (NB People whose concern is neither for results nor for people are often frustrated, disillusioned or feel under threat. They may respond either 'passively' or by indulging in considerable 'political' activity):

Passive behaviour:
- does no more than is required;
- resists change;
- becomes 'slack' if not checked; and
- blames other people, the 'children of today', innovation, the government, etc., for creating intolerable conditions.

Political behaviour:
- is very concerned about status;
- is quick to criticize; and
- draws attention to the faults of others.

Administrative
- goes 'by the book';
- maintains the existing system;
- is conscientious rather than creative or innovative; and
- is steady.

ORIENTATION AND BEHAVIOUR

It is extremely important to realize that any such model operates at two different levels:

(1) Basic orientation (or 'dominant style'), i.e. the way in which a person most naturally behaves or wants to behave.
(2) Behaviour, i.e. the way in which a person actually does behave on any particular occasion.

Basic orientation – sometimes known as 'management approach' – will remain relatively constant. We can all think of people who tend to be 'assertive' in all they do, who are concerned to explain to their subordinates exactly what is wanted and how it is to be done and who tend to be intolerant of – or not to listen to – ideas other than their own. On the other hand, we have met basically 'solicitous' people who want above all to maintain good relationships.

Behaviour, however, will vary – and should vary – according to circumstances and people. As we shall see later, one of the characteristics of those who truly have a high concern for both people and results is that they should be able to adapt their behaviour according to the needs of the person with whom they are dealing.

DOMINANT AND BACK-UP APPROACHES

Under stress people may move automatically from their so-called 'dominant' approach into a quite different approach, which is often referred to as their 'back-up' approach. For example, heads who are in the habit of doing what they want without regard for the opinions of the staff may, if confronted, fall into profusions of apology using phrases like: 'Why didn't you tell me?', 'I had no idea you felt strongly about this', 'My door is always open.' Such a swing from assertive to solicitous is fairly common. Of course, once the crisis has passed, such heads may well go on doing what they want, but discerning members of staff will have noted the reaction for future use.

One should not count on this sort of reaction. In some cases, the dominant approach grows even harder under challenge or stress. Furthermore, just as in one individual an assertive approach may, when challenged, give way to a solicitous or even passive back-up, some helpful and caring individuals can turn into roaring lions if pushed too far.

SUITING BEHAVIOUR TO CIRCUMSTANCES

If we are to manage our relationships with parents, governors, colleagues, superiors and subordinates, the important skill is to be able to suit our behaviour to circumstances and individuals. This calls for 'situational sensitivity' and 'style flexibility' (Reddin, 1971).

If there is a fire or other emergency, an assertive style by the leader is probably highly appropriate – there may not be time to consult or to let people 'do their own thing'. On the other hand, if a person is in distress, a highly solicitous approach is probably best – 'Forget your work, go home, sort things out, and come back when you can.' Such an approach may bear rich rewards in terms of future loyalty and work.

RECOGNIZING INAPPROPRIATE BEHAVIOUR

While it is true that there are times when any of the range of behaviours may be equally appropriate, we must remember that there are other times when a particular behaviour is quite inappropriate. It is vitally important that we increase both our

(1) skill in recognizing when a particular form of behaviour is wrong; and
(2) ability to use alternative forms of behaviour.

Remember that as well as 'concern for results' and 'concern for relationships', everyone has a third concern – 'concern for self' or, more positively, for 'personal effectiveness'. People – and organizations – will adapt very quickly to whatever patterns of behaviour are seen to 'pay off' and will avoid patterns which do not 'pay off'. Thus there is a very interesting interaction of management styles. If it is clear in an organization that 'those who shout loudest get most', a lot of people will start to shout loudly. If esteem or salary depends on having a large number of subordinates, empires will be built.

While it is impossible to provide for every contingency, there are a number of rules of thumb which the individual manager can use in spotting an inappropriate use of behaviour on his or her part. Remember that these rules only apply to *inappropriate* uses of the different types of behaviour, and that while assertive behaviour, for example, may have a negative effect on some people, there are others who like to be dealt with in an assertive way and who will not respond to anything else.

Different individuals need to be handled in different ways. While some people may be slow to take action if not 'chased', for example, others will be sufficiently self-motivated to produce the best results when left alone.

In dealing with pupils, the technique of 'acting' an emotion is one that most of us have used. Our response to staff may need the same degree of control. The danger always is that of getting 'hooked into' behaviours which may be counterproductive.

LEADERSHIP AND JOB EXPERIENCE

In dealing with subordinates the appropriate leadership style may vary according to how long they have been in the job (Hersey, Blanchard and Johnson, 1996). In the early days they may look for high task behaviour from their boss, i.e. for him or her to tell them what is expected and teach them how to do it in detail. At a second stage a more overtly 'motivational' behaviour may be called for, i.e. agreeing what is expected but leaving the subordinate more freedom to decide *how* to carry it out and giving feedback on results. At the third stage, the employee may simply need positive or negative feedback on results (a demonstration of genuine interest). Finally, a self-motivated employee may for most of the time be left to get on with his or her job, though this approach may never be right for certain subordinates.

Signs of inappropriate use of assertive behaviour

To a subordinate
(1) The subordinate may adopt a passive role: 'If my boss will not listen to my ideas, I will not contribute unless specifically asked or told to do so.' If you have a passive subordinate, you should always ask whether this is a basic orientation or whether you have caused it! A head of department once said to us: 'I am paid to take decisions and I do so. My worst problem as head of department is that I have "turned off" teachers in my department and I can't seem to motivate them.'
(2) The subordinate may react politically, and start to bypass you by giving his or her ideas and suggestions to others who are more interested – thus competing rather than contributing.
(3) There may be a direct rebellion or protest. (As we have seen, some assertive bosses when faced by this move sharply into a solicitous role. This solicitous approach is usually short lived.)

To an equal
(1) Some equals will respond in equally assertive terms and a win–lose conflict may quickly develop (Chapter 7).
(2) Other colleagues of a 'solicitous' disposition may 'smooth' the situation by not responding strongly. However, they may then undermine your position in less obvious ways.

Signs of inappropriate use of solicitous behaviour

To a subordinate.   Contrary to the expectations of many 'solicitous' managers, most people are not motivated by flattery or a style which overlooks infringements. 'If the boss does not care about my results, why should I bother?' Hence there may be slackness and low task motivation.

To an equal.   A colleague who always agrees with you on the surface (but may undermine you in your absence) loses your respect!

PASSIVE/POLITICAL ORIENTATION

While passive/political *behaviour* may sometimes be appropriate, an *orientation* which is directed neither towards results nor towards relationships is unlikely to be of much real value to an organization or school except in the accomplishment of purely manual tasks under strict supervision. Remember, of course, that it *may* be the school 'culture' or managerial behaviour which has produced this orientation!

Behind many a 'nine-to-four' schoolteacher is a history of being frustrated or overlooked. Some of these individuals show surprising enthusiasm and ability outside school as leading members of local societies or even councillors. What went wrong?

STYLE AND THE SCHOOL MANAGER

On any day we will see a rich variety of behaviour exhibited by our professional colleagues, our pupils, the administrative and ancillary staff and other people with whom we come into contact. In each situation the basic style orientation of the individual will be modified to a greater or lesser extent, deliberately or unthinkingly, in response to the situation with which he or she finds him or herself confronted.

Experience over the years helps us to learn to respond more effectively to many of the situations with which we are faced – to control our instinctive reactions so as better to achieve a desired result. However, there are certain behavioural patterns which we may never try unless we make a deliberate effort. Furthermore, we may become locked into assumptions about the way in which others will react.

An understanding of management style should reopen the options, cause us to challenge our assumptions and consequent behaviour and, as a result, make us more effective leaders.

PERSONAL APPLICATIONS

(1) Think about your colleagues and try to classify them according to their dominant management style. What back-up style(s) does each of them have?
(2) What do you believe to be your own dominant and back-up styles? Ask your colleagues for their views.

DISCUSSION TOPIC

To what extent is it desirable to modify our management style? What are the dangers and how do we overcome them?

CATEGORIES OF LEADERSHIP

There are two main categories or models of leadership – transformational and transactional – but other epithets have also been used, such as invitational, distributed and charismatic. Transformational leadership is about the ability of an individual to envisage some new social condition and to communicate this vision to followers (Stoll and Fink, 1996). Sergiovanni (1996) adds to this definition a moral dimension, connected with the meaning of work and life in general. Transactional leadership is based on the exchange relationships between the leader and the follower (Leithwood, 1995).

Invitational leadership focuses on the humanistic side of education, mediated through interpersonal interaction, institutional policies and practices and values such as optimism, respect, trust and care (Stoll and Fink, 1996).

Distributed leadership is characterized by widespread delegation of responsibility, encouraging leadership behaviour to emerge from below as well as above; any individual will take the lead for a limited time and/or within a limited specialist field. Its success depends, as always, on ability to relate approach and information to the issue and to the other group members, and also on a culture in which it is encouraged and accepted by the appointed leader. By contrast, charismatic leadership focuses strongly on the personality of the person at the top of the organization.

In so far as effective school leadership will ultimately be tested by its ability to prepare teachers to meet the challenges of change, which may impact on the organization anywhere, heads would do well to practise transformational leadership themselves, while seeking to distribute transactional leadership to all levels in their school organization.

STANDARDS FOR MANAGEMENT AND LEADERSHIP

As part of a government initiative, national occupational standards of competence for managers were introduced in 1992 and national vocational qualifications based on them were made available to school heads by the then College of Preceptors (now Teachers). During 2002–3 these standards were reviewed to take account of the emergence of leadership as a key aspect of competence and to incorporate best practice from other countries. This work, carried out first by the Council for Excellence in Management and Leadership (www.managementandleadershipcouncil.org) and subsequently by the Management Standards Centre (www.management-standards.org), has resulted in a number of 'maps' which show the relationship between management and leadership functions, as well as descriptions of the functions, to be used as a basis for a qualifications framework. Figure 1 in the Preface is an example of such a map. The upper items are in the 'leadership' category, whereas the remaining items describe the functions of operational management. Some 'fine-tuning' may be needed to make the map fit school management; nevertheless, this approach to describing the functions of heads and the knowledge, skills, personal qualities and styles that they employ is to be commended.

Despite its title, this book's authors have always regarded leadership as an indispensable part of management, and we do not think it helpful to create an impermeable boundary. For those who prefer to differentiate, however, West-Burnham (1977) sums it up succinctly (Figure 2.3).

LEADING is concerned with:	MANAGING is concerned with:
• vision	• implementation
• strategic issues	• operational issues
• transformation	• transaction
• ends	• means
• people	• systems
• doing the right things	• doing things right

Figure 2.3   The differences between managing and leading

PERSONAL APPLICATION

Think about how you do your job. In relation to what your school requires of you, have you got the balance right between leadership and management? To which functions in Figure I (see the Preface) do you need to give more attention?

CHARACTERISTICS OF HEADTEACHERS AND DEPUTY HEADTEACHERS

Under the auspices of the National College of School Leadership, Hay McBer have researched the characteristics of high-performing school leaders in different settings. They identified the following characteristics each of which they have defined in some detail (see www.ncsl.org.uk/index.cfm?pageID=haycompletechar).

- Analytical thinking
- Challenge and support
- Confidence
- Developing potential
- Drive for improvement
- Holding people accountable
- Impact and influence
- Information seeking
- Initiative
- Integrity
- Personal convictions
- Respect for others
- Strategic thinking
- Teamworking
- Transformational leadership
- Understanding the environment
- Understanding others.

Hay McBer stress that these characteristics may be combined and applied in different ways according to the setting and the individual. It is not a case of 'one size fits all'.

In order to illustrate the need for variety, Hay McBer have created four 'models of excellence' for:

- Headteachers in medium and large schools
- Headteachers in small schools
- Headteachers in special schools
- Deputy headteachers

See www.ncsl.org.uk/index.cfm?pageid=haycompletechar.

PERSONAL APPLICATION

Consider the list of 'characteristics' in the above section. Score each characteristic on a scale of 0 to 5 to reflect its importance to the running of your own school. Consider to what extent you possess and apply these characteristics.

FURTHER READING

Adair, J. (2002) *Inspiring Leadership*, Thorogood, London.

Bennett, D., Fawcett, R. and Dunford, J. (2000) *School Leadership*, Kogan Page, London.

Caldwell, B.J. and Spinks, J.M. (1992) *Leading the Self-Managing School*, RoutledgeFalmer, London.

Caldwell, B.J. and Spinks, J.M. (1998) *Beyond the Self-Managing School*, RoutledgeFalmer, London.

Dickmann, H. and Stanford-Blair, N. (2002) *Connecting Leadership to the Brain*, Corwin Press, Thousand Oaks, California.

Edwards, G., Winter, P.K. and Bailey, J. (2002) *Leadership in Management*, Leadership Trust, Ross-on-Wye.

Gillen, T. (2002) *Leadership Skills for Boosting Performance*, Chartered Institute for Personnel and Development, London.

Goleman, D. (2002) *The New Leaders: Emotional Intelligence at Work*, Little, Brown, London.

Hay, W. (2003) *Leading People and Teams in Education*, Open University, Milton Keynes.

Tomlinson, H. (2004) *Educational Leadership: Personal Growth for Professional Development*, Sage, London.

Sadler, P. (2003) *Leadership*, Kogan Page, London.

3

Motivating People

MOTIVATION

'Motivation' can be defined as 'getting results through people' or 'getting the best out of people'. The second definition is slightly preferable, since 'the best' which people can offer is not necessarily synonymous with 'the results' which we might initially want from them, though it should be in line with the overall goals and ethos of the school or college.

As Peters and Waterman (1995) say: 'Management's principal job is to get the herd heading roughly west.' A head of an English department may, for example, have fairly strong feelings about the choice of set books. However, if he or she wishes to get the best out of the teacher responsible for taking the class, he or she should at least allow his or her own choice to be modified by the teacher's preference. Both should be asking what is in the best interests of the pupils.

In motivating people we should be concerned with the needs and potential of three parties:

(1) The group which we are managing or in which we manage.
(2) The individuals who make up that group.
(3) The 'clients' (pupils, parents, etc.) of the school, college or other organization in which we all work.

A fundamental mistake is to forget that people are best motivated to work towards goals that they have been involved in setting and to which they therefore feel committed. If people do not feel committed towards a given result or activity, the only motivations at our disposal are those of the carrot and stick – reward and punishment. We therefore have to be prepared to modify our own initial perceptions of what is required. Some people have a strong 'internal' motivation – a sense of purpose or drive. Others do not.

WHOM DO WE NEED TO MOTIVATE?

In a hierarchical organization, subordinates are obvious candidates for 'motivation'. However, it is even more important to be able to motivate equals and superiors. In the last resort, we can tell a junior member of our department what he or she is to do, but we have no such power with a schoolteacher who is our equal and even less with the headteacher, chair of governors or local education officer. Here we are in much more of a 'selling' role and, like all good salespeople, must be very aware of the benefits that will accrue to our customer.

A cynical – but often true – maxim is: 'There is nothing I cannot achieve provided that my boss gets the credit for it!'

SATISFYING NEEDS

People work in order to satisfy some need. The need may be to achieve fame or power, to serve other people or simply to earn the money to live. It may even be the rather negative need to avoid punishment.

Most motivational theorists have therefore concentrated their attention on

(1) examining human needs; and
(2) considering how the needs are met and can be better met in work.

People work at their best when they are achieving the greatest satisfaction from their work.

MASLOW'S HIERARCHY OF NEEDS

Maslow (1943) suggested that it was useful to think of human needs as being at different levels in a hierarchy – see Figure 3.1. The principle behind the hierarchy is that, starting from the bottom, the needs at each level have to be satisfied to some extent before we think about needs at the next level up.

SELF-REALIZATION	Achievement Psychological growth
EGO	Status Respect Prestige
SOCIAL	Friendship, group acceptance Love
SECURITY	Freedom from danger Freedom from want
PSYCHOLOGICAL	Food, drink, shelter, sex, warmth, physical comfort

Figure 3.1   A hierarchy of needs, based on 'Hierarchy of needs', in Maslow, A.H. (1970) *Motivation and Personality* (2nd edn), copyright © by Abraham H. Maslow

The physiological needs. Undoubtedly physiological needs are the most basic of all needs. For the person who is missing everything in life, it is most likely that the major motivation will be the physiological needs. A person who lacked food, security, love and esteem would probably hunger for food more strongly than for anything else.

The security needs. If the physiological needs are gratified, there then emerges a new set of needs, which are categorized roughly as the security needs. Robinson Crusoe's first thoughts on reaching his desert island were to find water, food and shelter. His second was to build a stockade and to get in reserves of food and water.

The social needs. If both the physiological and the security needs are fairly well satisfied, then there will emerge the needs for love and affection and belongingness. Now the person feels keenly the need for friends, a special relationship with one partner, or children. There is a hunger for affectionate relationships with people in general, for a place in the group.

The ego needs. Having established a base of friendship, acceptance and affection, most of us want to prove our worth within whatever group or groups we belong to. We seek to demonstrate to ourselves and others that we are as good as, or better than, other members of the group. We pursue promotion, influence, status, power, reputation, recognition, prestige, importance, attention.

The need for self-realization. Even if all these needs are satisfied, we may still be discontented and restless if we feel that we have talent and potential within us which we are not fully exploiting.

Why do people write poetry, plays, books and music, play sports, act in plays, take up hobbies, climb mountains? We have a need to achieve, fulfil ourselves, become what we are capable of becoming, meet new challenges.

In his later writings Maslow identified an even higher need, self-transcendence, to describe the inner grace of a person who feels called to serve a cause above and beyond him or herself, such as a deity.

THE RELEVANCE OF THE HIERARCHY

There are a number of important points to be made about the hierarchy:

(1) If an individual is really deprived at a lower level, he or she may lose interest in the higher-level needs. How often do we hear someone who suddenly finds him or herself in pain in hospital make a remark like: 'To think that I was worrying yesterday because I hadn't been invited to... This puts things in perspective'? Serious financial hardship or threats of redundancy can take the mind off thoughts of achievement.

(2) On the other hand, a 'satisfying' job at the higher levels will raise the level of tolerance or deprivation at the lower levels. Teachers, doctors and

nurses are prepared to tolerate conditions of employment which would not be acceptable to someone with a boring job – though even they have their limits.

(3) When a need at a given level is satisfied, the law of diminishing returns sets in. When I have eaten a meal, I do not wish to eat another immediately. While I may like friends and parties, too many become a nuisance. Even prestige can pall and those who courted publicity on their way to promotion and fame may seek, when they have 'arrived', to avoid the limelight.

(4) 'Oversatisfying' of a need may produce a sense of guilt and/or deliberate self-deprivation. Drop-outs are often the children of well-to-do families, and young people will undertake ventures which involve frugal living and risk in order to prove themselves.

(5) Different people will feel needs with differing intensity. One person's social needs may only be satisfied when surrounded by friends, whereas another will be content simply to have the companionship and love of his or her partner. Very exceptionally, an individual will shun all company, but such 'hermits' are extremely rare. They may, like saints, have reached the level of self-transcendence.

The interesting thing is that when dealing with people with whom we work, *most of us have a tendency to behave as though the needs of others, particularly our subordinates, are at the lower levels.*

'I look for satisfaction in my job but the rest of the staff are concerned only about physical conditions, being treated kindly, not being asked to work hours which are unreasonable, being given appropriate recognition of their status.' This is the same sort of phenomenon as was illustrated by the questionnaire on page 1. Furthermore, the staff themselves often reinforce our beliefs by complaining about precisely those things we have just mentioned.

The two views of work – one asserting that people seek fulfilment through work, and the other suggesting that they seek only to satisfy lower-level needs – are neatly described by Douglas McGregor (1985). McGregor called the two conflicting assumptions about the nature of work Theory X and Theory Y.

THEORY X AND THEORY Y

Those managers who adopt 'Theory X' believe that

(1) work is inherently distasteful to most people;
(2) most people are not ambitious, have little desire for responsibility and prefer to be directed;
(3) most people have little capacity for creativity in solving problems;
(4) motivation occurs only at the physiological and security levels; and

(5) most people must be closely controlled and often coerced to achieve organization objectives.

'Theory Y' managers, on the other hand, believe that

(1) work is as natural as play, if the conditions are favourable;
(2) control of one's own work activities is often indispensable in achieving organizational gains;
(3) the capacity for creativity in solving organizational problems is widely distributed in the population;
(4) motivation occurs at the social, ego and self-realization levels as well as at the physiological and security levels; and
(5) people can be self-directed and creative at work if properly led.

FREDERICK HERZBERG

Herzberg (1975) put to the practical test, through a series of experiments conducted with widely differing groups of workers, the sort of thinking developed by Maslow and McGregor.

One of his best-known experiments consisted of asking people to think of three occasions when they had felt very satisfied in their work and three occasions when they had felt dissatisfied. He then asked them to categorize the causes of satisfaction and dissatisfaction under a number of headings. Finally he recorded for all the individuals in the group the frequency with which each category had been noted as a cause of satisfaction or dissatisfaction. A typical result is shown in Figure 3.2.

From these findings, Herzberg drew some important conclusions:

(1) The things which make people happy at work are not simply the opposites of the things which make them unhappy, and vice versa. The two sets of things are different in kind. You will not make people *satisfied*, therefore, simply by removing causes of *dissatisfaction*.
(2) The things that make people dissatisfied are related to the job environment. The things that make people satisfied on the other hand are related to the job content.
(3) While those who have a satisfying job may have a higher tolerance of dissatisfiers, the dissatisfying factors can be so strong that the job becomes intolerable.
(4) Managers must therefore be concerned with ensuring both that causes of dissatisfaction are removed and that opportunities for satisfaction are increased – that, in Herzberg's terms, the job is 'enriched'. It is in this latter respect that managers usually fail. Instead of using the real 'motivation' which comes from a satisfying job, they use rewards and threats.

Herzberg calls the environmental factors which are capable of causing unhappiness the 'hygiene' factors because he believes that these have to be reasonably well 'cleaned up' as a prerequisite for satisfaction. Among the hygiene factors are

(1) organizational policies and administration;
(2) management;
(3) working conditions;
(4) interpersonal relationships; and
(5) money, status and security.

The work content factors which lead to happiness Herzberg calls the 'motivators', and these are as follows:

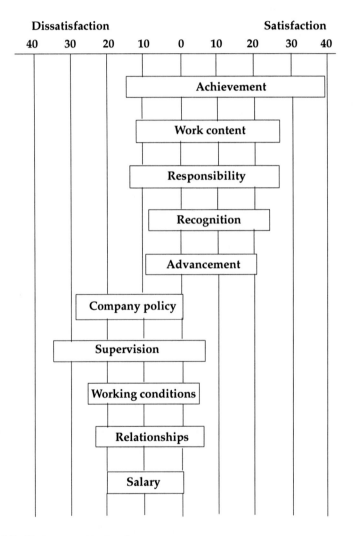

Figure 3.2 Motivators and hygiene factors
Source: Herzberg (1975)

- *Achievement.* This is a measure of the opportunities for you to use your full capabilities and make a worthwhile contribution. It includes the possibilities for testing new and untried ideas.
- *Responsibility.* A measure of freedom of action in decision-taking, style and job development.
- *Recognition.* An indication of the amount and quality of all kinds of 'feedback', whether good or bad, about how you are getting on in the job.
- *Advancement.* This shows the potential of the job in terms of promotion – inside or outside the organization in which you currently work.
- *Work itself.* The interest of the job, usually involving variety, challenge and personal conviction of the job's significance.
- *Personal growth.* An indication of opportunities for learning and maturing.

At this point you may like to look at how 'motivating' your own job is, in Herzberg's terms, by completing and scoring Exercise 1 at the end of this chapter.

Educators' jobs usually score fairly high in Herzberg's terms, though low scores on 'Recognition' are not uncommon. This is less a particularity of the teaching profession than a British or European cultural norm. We hesitate to tell people how they are getting on, though this knowledge is not only an element in job satisfaction but also essential for improvement and adjusting to the needs of the job. This should be the purpose of staff appraisal.

The relationship between the Herzberg 'motivators' and the top two levels of Maslow's hierarchy is self-evident.

INVOLVEMENT

Where staff at any level are 'involved' in decisions taken by their superiors, peers or even subordinates, all the motivators are brought into play. This is particularly the case where the decision under discussion will affect the person involved.

Involvement should produce the commitment to goals on which a sense of achievement depends. By involving people we show them recognition and increase their sense of responsibility. The interest of their job should be increased and we are providing them with the broader view which provides both a learning opportunity and experience which may be of use in seeking advancement.

ACHIEVEMENT NEEDS

Motivational theorists are almost unanimous in giving a special place to the need for achievement. In his book, *Every Employee a Manager*, Myers (1991) neatly specifies that a sense of achievement arises when an individual clearly perceives a goal and is then able to

(1) *plan* how to achieve the goal;
(2) *implement* his or her own plan; and
(3) *control* (i.e. 'monitor') the results.

In this sense, whatever the other issues involved, public and internal examinations provide a motivational loop in that teachers and pupils know more or less what is expected; can plan how to achieve the required standard with freedom to choose textbooks and other means; can carry out the teaching/learning in line with the plan; and, finally obtain a result. In the absence of examinations, learning goals and measures of achievement may be less clear, and we may have problems in finding motivational substitutes.

Fundamental to the concept of achievement is the perception by the individual to be motivated that the goal is relevant to him or her. In a world where traditional learning is no longer linked to career prospects – GCSE or GNVQ results do not guarantee a job – teachers and pupils have a further motivational problem.

THE SELF-MOTIVATED ACHIEVER

As with all needs, the intensity of the need for achievement varies greatly from person to person. In some pupils, particularly at secondary level, we may feel that it has almost disappeared! McClelland's (1985) interest is in those with very strong achievement needs who offer great potential, but can also pose problems where their own perception of goals may be different from our own.

McClelland would claim that most of us have a motivation to achieve something. He would also claim, however, that only in 10 per cent of the population is this a highly developed motivation. According to McClelland, the most convincing sign of a strong achievement motivation is the tendency of a person who is not being required to think about anything in particular, that is, who is free to relax or to let his or her mind wander, to think about ways of accomplishing something. On a car journey the self-motivated achiever will typically set him or herself time-targets or fuel-consumption targets. On the way to work he or she will try out new routes to cut mileage or time. He or she will work to achieve a standard in a sport, to take on new challenges in his or her job, to produce a play, to organize a new function.

Such tendencies emerge at a very early age. In a series of experiments McClelland provided young people with an upright pole and quoits. Some would throw the quoits aimlessly around, build towers, drop them with ease on to the pole or quickly lose interest. However, certain individuals would set themselves a challenge by attempting to hit the pole or throw the quoits over it from a distance chosen by them such that success would not come too easily nor be impossible or subject to pure luck. Following his subjects' careers, McClelland found that those who showed a strong achievement motivation in childhood tended to manifest the same drive in adult life.

Although only about 10 per cent of people are strongly motivated, the percentage in certain occupations is likely to be much higher. This is especially true of people in managerial positions, and independent entrepreneurs. A person with a strong achievement motivation is likely to surpass the accomplishments of equally able but less strongly motivated people, especially in one of the above occupations.

McClelland's studies have identified three major characteristics of the self-motivated achiever, and why supervisory tactics, which may be appropriate to other kinds of people, are often inappropriate when applied to a man or woman with a strong achievement motivation.

First, achievers like to set their own goals. They are nearly always trying to accomplish something. They are seldom content to drift aimlessly and let life happen to them. They are quite selective about which goals they commit themselves to and for this reason they are unlikely automatically to accept goals which other people, including their bosses, select for them. Neither do they seek advice or help except from experts or people who can provide needed skills or information. Achievers prefer to be as fully responsible for the attainment of their goals as it is possible to be. If they win they want the credit, if they lose they accept the blame. Either way they want the victory or defeat to be unmistakably theirs.

Second, achievers tend to avoid extremes of difficulty in selecting goals. They prefer moderate goals which are neither so easy that winning them would provide no satisfaction nor so difficult that winning them would be more a matter of luck than ability. They will tend to gauge what is possible and then select a goal that is as tough as they think they can fulfil, i.e. the hardest practical challenge. This attitude keeps them continually straining their abilities to their realistic limits, but no further. Above all else they want to win and, therefore, they do not knowingly commit themselves to a goal that is probably too difficult to achieve.

Third, achievers prefer tasks which provide them with more or less immediate feedback, i.e. measurements of how well they are progressing towards their goal. Because of the importance of the goal, they like to know how well they are doing at all times.

The effect of a monetary incentive on an achiever is rather complex. Achievers usually have a fairly high opinion of the value of their services and prefer to place a fairly high price tag on them: they are unlikely to remain for long in an organization that doesn't pay them well. But it is questionable whether an incentive payment actually increases their output since they are normally working at peak efficiency anyway.

McClelland notes that monetary incentives are actually more effective with people whose achievement drives are relatively weak, because they need some kind of external reward to increase their effort. The main significance of additional income to achievers is as a way of measuring their success. McClelland emphasizes that the achievement motive, as he defines it, is not the only source of success attainment. Other drives can also lead to high levels of attainment, but achievers have a considerable advantage.

Can the level of achievement motivation be increased in people whose achievement drives are not usually strong? McClelland believes this may be possible and indeed there are considerable reserves of latent untapped achievement motivation in most organizations. The key is to build more achievement characteristics into the job – personal responsibility, individual participation in the selection of targets, moderate goals and fast, clear-cut feedback on the results each individual is achieving, etc.

For achievers themselves, McClelland believes that many standard supervisory practices are inappropriate and in some cases may even hinder their performance. Work goals should not be imposed on achievers. They not only want a voice in setting their own goals but they are also unlikely to set them lower than they think they can reach. Highly specific directions and controls are unnecessary; some general guidance and occasional follow-up will do. But if the job does not provide its own internal feedback mechanism regarding the achiever's effectiveness, as is the case, for example, in some professional or administrative jobs, then it is vitally important to achievers that they be given frank, detailed appraisals of how well they are performing in their jobs.

MOTIVATION THEORY AND THE SCHOOL MANAGER

The key to effective management is the ability to get results from other people, through other people and in conjunction with other people. If the underlying psychology is wrong, the most carefully constructed system and techniques will fail. Efficient headteachers are not necessarily effective headteachers. But if relationships and motivation are good, people will readily accept and overcome some administrative or environmental flaws (but see Herzberg, 1975, p. 29).

Three basic rules should underlie management relationships and the application of any technique:

(1) We should remember to use the 'motivators', i.e. people's need for achievement, recognition, responsibility, job interest, personal growth and advancement potential. We tend to underestimate the needs of other people in these areas. Involving others in decisions which affect them is one way of meeting all or most of these needs. This principle is as valid for the caretaker or the dinner lady as it is for teaching staff.
(2) The relative intensity of psychological needs will vary greatly from person to person and from time to time. There are people who simply are not interested in motivators, or who do not wish to have these needs satisfied at work. If a teacher's spouse loses his or her job, security needs may well be the most important need. If there is a marriage break-up,

both security and social needs may surface, though these may be followed later by a need to find renewed interest and achievement in the job.

These are predictable and often recognizable behavioural phenomena. However, when symptoms and causes are less obvious, the risk is that we misjudge the needs of colleagues or friends. Some of us have a tendency to assume that the needs of others are the same as our own; others tend to assume the opposite.

As a fairly light-hearted exercise in judging your ability to assess the motivation of others, you may like to try Exercise 2 at the end of this chapter with a group of colleagues or friends.

(3) We should try to suit our management behaviour to both the personalities and the needs of the situation. Our automatic behavioural reaction may not be the right one. Think about the alternatives.

Despite every effort there will remain individuals who have no wish to be 'motivated' and who view with suspicion any attempt to increase their responsibilities, job interest or involvement. Such attitudes may typically be found in caretakers, ancillary staff or teachers who are frustrated. However, the danger is always that we give up too easily. The right approach may prompt a surprisingly warm response.

PERSONAL APPLICATIONS

(1) (a) Invite the members of your department to complete the Opinion Questionnaire of Exercise 1, making it very clear that this is not a test of their competence but of the environment in which they work.

(b) Discuss the results either on a one-to-one basis or in a departmental group. Try to find and agree for each person one thing that would increase job satisfaction. Put it into practice.

(2) Try to identify some 'self-motivated achievers'. Consider to what extent the standards by which they judge their achievement are compatible with the school's goals.

DISCUSSION TOPIC

How can we apply the motivation theories in this chapter to the motivation of parents, children and governors?

FURTHER READING

Adair, J. (2003) *The Inspirational Leader: How to Motivate, Encourage and Achieve Success*, Kogan Page, London.

Fraser, L. (1992) *Maximising People Power in Schools: Motivating and Managing Teachers and Staff*, Corwin, London.

Stewart, V. and Stewart, A. (1988) *Managing the Poor Performer*, Gower, Aldershot.

EXERCISE 1: Opinion Questionnaire

The aim of this exercise is to discover your reaction to your job.

Instructions

Answer each question to show how you feel. Do this by circling the number of the statement which best describes your opinion. The only correct answer is your frank opinion.

Questionnaire

(1) Think about the specific duties of your job. How often have you felt unable to use your full capabilities in the performance of your job?

Almost always	Very often	Fairly often	Not very often	Very seldom	Almost never
0	1	2	3	4	5

(2) How many functions do you perform on your job which you consider relatively unimportant or unnecessary?

Almost all of them	Most of them	Quite a few	A few	Very few	None of them
0	1	2	3	4	5

(3) As you see it, how many opportunities do you feel you have in your job for making worthwhile contributions?

Almost none	Very few	A few	Quite a few	A great many times	Unlimited
0	1	2	3	4	5

(4) How often do you feel that your job is one that could be dropped?

Almost all the time	Most of the time	Quite often	Very seldom	Almost never	Never
0	1	2	3	4	5

(5) How much say do you feel you have in deciding how your job is to be carried out?

None	Almost none	Very little	Fairly large amount	Very large amount	Unlimited amount
0	1	2	3	4	5

(6) How frequently have you felt in your job that you could achieve more if you could have complete freedom of action to accomplish your objectives?

Almost all the time	Most of the time	Quite often	Not very often	Very seldom	Almost never
0	1	2	3	4	5

(7) How frequently in your job have you received some type of recognition for your accomplishment?

Almost never	Very seldom	Not very often	Quite often	Very often	A great many times
0	1	2	3	4	5

(8) How often does your job give you the opportunity for personal recognition?

Almost never	Very seldom	Not very often	Quite often	Very often	A great many times
0	1	2	3	4	5

(9) How do you feel about your present post as a job where you can continually learn?

Nothing more to learn in it	Practically nothing to learn	Can learn something but not much	Can still learn a little	Can still learn a lot in it	Can still learn a vast amount
0	1	2	3	4	5

(10) How do you feel about your general association with the school as an opportunity for learning?

Provides no chance for learning	Provides almost no chance	Can learn something but not much	Can learn a little	Can learn a lot	Can learn a vast amount
0	1	2	3	4	5

(11) Leaving aside any regular measurements of your job (indices or performance standards), how often have you inwardly felt you have achieved something really worth while?

Very seldom	Once in a while	Fairly often	Often	Very often	All the time
0	1	2	3	4	5

(12) To what extent is it possible to know whether you are doing well or poorly in your job?

No way of knowing	Almost no way of knowing	To some extent	To a large extent	To a great extent	Entirely possible
0	1	2	3	4	5

(13) To what extent is it possible for you to introduce new (untried) ideas on your job?

To no extent	Almost no extent	Very little extent	Fairly large extent	Large extent	Very great extent
0	1	2	3	4	5

(14) How often have you found the kind of work you are now doing to be interesting?

Never	Very seldom	Not very often	Quite often	Very often	Almost always
0	1	2	3	4	5

(15) Based on your past experience in your present job, how often have you thought that you would like to resign or change jobs?

Very often	Often	Fairly often	Once in a while	Very seldom	Never
0	1	2	3	4	5

(16) To what extent do you consider your present post helpful for a person who wants to get ahead?

Almost no extent	Very little extent	Not very helpful	Fairly helpful	Very helpful	Extremely helpful
0	1	2	3	4	5

(17) If you wish to make any comments about your job, your chance for achievement, recognition and personal growth, use the space below.

Scoring sheet

Mark your score for each question in the appropriate space, add the total for each group and divide as indicated.

Question	Score	Group total		
1				
3				
11			÷ 4 =	(ACH)
13				
5				
6			÷ 2 =	(RY)
7				
8			÷ 3 =	(RN)
12				
16			=	(AD)
2				
4				
14			÷ 4 =	(WI)
15				
9				
10			÷ 2 =	(PG)

Grand total

Interpreting your score

The scoring sheet has interpreted your responses to give a rating to your job under the following headings:

Achievement (ACH)	Advancement (AD)
Responsibility (RY)	Work interest (WI)
Recognition (RN)	Personal growth (PG)

Note that the rating is not of *you* but of the extent to which you feel, according to your answers, that *your* job provides you with opportunities for achievement, responsibility, etc.

The headings listed are the factors which, according to Herzberg, are the 'motivators' in work.

In the grand total you have a score which reflects the relative weighting which Herzberg gives to each motivator in determining overall job satisfaction.

You may like to compare your own score against the European norm:

	ACH	RY	RN	AD	WI	PG	Overall
UK and European norm	3.1	3.0	2.9	3.2	3.6	3.5	51.8

As a rule of thumb, a score of 3.5 or above for any heading indicates a thoroughly satisfying job. A score of between 2.5 and 3.0 suggests that there may well be room for enrichment of your job. If your score is less than 2.5 for any heading, you and your manager should be asking why. There may be a simple explanation (e.g. a head of a large school may well score 0 on opportunity for further advancement!), but the likelihood is that there is an area of frustration here.

An overall score of 55+ would indicate total job satisfaction. However, between 45 and 55 should not give any cause for concern.

Note, finally, that the first three areas – 'achievement', 'responsibility' and 'recognition' – are particularly within the control of your superior and the way your work is organized.

NB All the above remarks are equally valid if you give the test to your subordinates. It can provide the basis for a discussion which can make their jobs more interesting and your life easier and more efficient.

EXERCISE 2: Assessing the Motivation of Others

The exercise that follows should be carried out with at least three (preferably five) friends or colleagues. The friends need not be connected with work – indeed, the exercise can provide a semi-serious hour's entertainment for you, your spouse and a few dinner guests. While it is essential that all the people involved in the activity should have met several times previously and spent some time together, they do not need to have a particularly close social or working relationship.

Before conducting the exercise, you are advised to familiarize yourself thoroughly with the two forms (pp. 42–43) and with the exercise instructions, but you should *not* read the 'Interpretation'.

When you have completed the exercise, develop a personal strategy to remedy any problems you may have either in assessing the needs and wants of others or in ensuring that others know your own needs and wants. Put it into practice.

Instructions

Form 1, column 1.   Each of the participants in the exercise should be given a copy of Form 1. On this form are listed a number of 'needs' or 'wants' which are felt to a greater or lesser extent by most people.

In the first column of the form each participant should rank the needs in order of importance to him or her by writing the figure '1' against the most important, '2' against the next most important, and so on.

Usually people will find it relatively easy to rank the most important and the least important but may have some hesitation in the middle rankings. If this happens, the order probably does not matter and a choice should be made fairly quickly either way. Others may feel that two needs 'overlap' for them. If so, they should ask which is the really driving purpose for them and which is the means to the end.

The golden rule is not to spend too long in contemplation – first instincts are often the most accurate.

Form 1, column 2, etc.   Having ranked the needs in order of importance for themselves, each participant should write at the head of column 2 the name of the first person to his or her right, at the head of column 3 the name of the second person to his or her right and so on.

The next step is for each participant to fill in, *outside the brackets*, under the appropriate column what he or she thinks the person concerned will have written in column 1 of his or her own table, i.e. participant A tries to assess how important each need is to participants B, C, D, etc. This must obviously be done without reference to any of the other participants.

We now have the raw data to be processed.

Form 2. At this stage Form 2 should be given to each participant. Each person heads the columns with the same names as on Form 1. The purpose of Form 2 is to enable each participant to find out how each other participant perceived his or her needs.

The most efficient way of transferring the information is to

(1) ensure that each participant has written his or her name clearly at the top right-hand corner of Form 1; and
(2) circulate the Form 1s and let each person enter on his or her Form 2, under the column bearing the name which is in the top right-hand corner of the

Form 1 (Exercise 2) – your own views of your own needs and those of other group members

Your name ....

Motivation	1 Yourself	2	3	4	5	6	7
		(Names of other group members)					
(a) To be liked	( )	( )	( )	( )	( )	( )	( )
(b) To make a lot of money	( )	( )	( )	( )	( )	( )	( )
(c) To serve other people	( )	( )	( )	( )	( )	( )	( )
(d To have a good time	( )	( )	( )	( )	( )	( )	( )
(e) To be secure	( )	( )	( )	( )	( )	( )	( )
(f) To be an expert	( )	( )	( )	( )	( )	( )	( )
(g) To become well known	( )	( )	( )	( )	( )	( )	( )
(h) To be independent	( )	( )	( )	( )	( )	( )	( )
(i) To make the most of your talents	( )	( )	( )	( )	( )	( )	( )
(j) To maximize status	( )	( )	( )	( )	( )	( )	( )
(k) To be a leader	( )	( )	( )	( )	( )	( )	( )
(l) To achieve something worth while	( )	( )	( )	( )	( )	( )	( )

Form 2 (Exercise 2) – your motivation as seen by others

Motivation	1 Yourself	← Ratings of your needs by other group members →						Row total (excl. row '1')	Ranking or totals
		2	3	4	5	6	7		
(a) To be liked	....	....	....	....	....	....	....	....	....
(b) To make a lot of money	....	....	....	....	....	....	....	....	....
(c) To serve other people	....	....	....	....	....	....	....	....	....
(d) To have a good time	....	....	....	....	....	....	....	....	....
(e) To be secure	....	....	....	....	....	....	....	....	....
(f) To be an expert	....	....	....	....	....	....	....	....	....
(g) To become well known	....	....	....	....	....	....	....	....	....
(h) To be independent	....	....	....	....	....	....	....	....	....
(i) To make the most of your talents	....	....	....	....	....	....	....	....	....
(j) To maximize status	....	....	....	....	....	....	....	....	....
(k) To be a leader	....	....	....	....	....	....	....	....	....
(l) To achieve something worth while	....	....	....	....	....	....	....	....	....

Form 1 which has been passed to him or her, the ranking which on that Form 1 appears under the column bearing his or her own name.

Form 1, inside the brackets. When all participants have transferred the information from all Form Is on to their Form 2, you can begin the next process, which is to let each person discover how accurate was his or her judgement of how others would rank themselves.

This is best done by having each person in turn read out the figures in *column 1* of his or her own form (e.g. how they ranked their own needs). Each other participant can then enter what is read out *inside the brackets* under the appropriate column on their own Form 1.

When this is done you can go on to the interpretation.

Interpretation

You now have data on at least two important subjects. These are your ability to

(1) assess the needs and wants of others and therefore to have a clue as to how to 'motivate' them by meeting these needs and wants; and
(2) project your own needs and wants to others.

The first set of information is obtained by comparing the figures inside and outside the brackets under each column on Form 1. (NB The first three and the last three rankings are the most important.) The second set of information is obtained from Form 2.

In the discussion and comparisons which will inevitably arise from this exercise, it may be interesting to look for the occurrence of certain common phenomena:

(1) It often happens that the 'quieter' individuals are the best at perceiving the needs of others and vice versa.
(2) On the other hand, the needs of these quieter individuals are not so easily perceived *by* others.
(3) Certain people have a tendency to assume that all other people have the same needs as themselves.
(4) Other people display the opposite tendency and assume that their own needs are quite different from those of others.

The moral of this exercise is obvious. From the first moment we meet any other person we are making assumptions about their needs, their temperament and their reactions, and we are acting on these assumptions. We modify our superficial assumptions very quickly as we receive back certain clear signals. For example, if we start to talk to someone about football we will learn quickly whether or not they are interested. If we start to try to impress someone with our knowledge we may be quickly cut down to size. However, even with people we know quite well, the deeper needs may remain hidden and we may therefore 'get it wrong' – if, for example, we offer a make-or-break opportunity to someone who is looking for security.

It is, finally, worth noting that the priority which people attach to needs will vary over time according to circumstances. In times of economic crisis and unemployment, 'security' rises sharply in the rankings of most people.

4

Taking and Implementing Decisions

MAKING THINGS HAPPEN

Whether we are setting goals, planning how to achieve them, or coping with the issues which arise in organizing and carrying out day-to-day activities, making things happen as we wish them to (and preventing unwanted events!) depends on our ability to take and implement decisions. To accomplish both the taking and implementing of decisions consistently well is no mean task. Ingredients for success include self-discipline, perception, creativity, dynamism and considerable skill in handling both individuals and groups.

TAKING DECISIONS

Decision-taking can be a painful process since it usually involves

(1) change;
(2) conflict;
(3) the risk of being wrong and being called to account; and
(4) having to cope with a bewildering number of facts and alternatives.

The result is that many people would rather do almost anything than actually take a decision of any importance, though:

(1) the failure to take a decision is often worse than most of the alternatives; and
(2) colleagues and subordinates are often frustrated and virtually paralysed by lack of decision.

In a survey at all levels of one organization, people were asked what change they would most like to see in their boss. The most frequent reply by a clear margin was 'that he should take decisions'. Several added remarks, such as 'more clearly', 'more rapidly', and there was the frequent comment that 'It often doesn't matter which decision as long as he takes one or the other'.

A problem in any organization can be that the culture is such that people are blamed heavily if a decision is proved to be wrong, whereas no blame is attached for inertia. In fact, failure to take decisions, or 'management by default', often has the same effect as a decision and is often worse than any considered alternative.

The risk of not deciding is often the greatest of all risks to the organization. This is obvious when a commercial organization slides into bankruptcy through failure to respond to market changes. Unfortunately, it is not quite so obvious if schools fail to make the adjustments in curriculum and attitude necessary to prepare their students for a changing society.

LOGICAL STEPS IN DECISION-TAKING

Whether a decision is taken by an isolated individual or in the context of a meeting, common sense suggests a series of logical steps. These are summarized in Figure 4.1.

In taking run-of-the-mill decisions we will often run through the steps subconsciously and, indeed, time constraints dictate that we do no more. However, the risk is that in big as well as small decisions we lose creative input, and therefore quality, by short-circuiting unduly. It is all too easy to jump for the first solution that comes to mind without considering alternatives or possible side-effects.

Step 1: statement of situation

Decisions are made either to correct a situation or to improve it. Therefore the situation must be understood and its causes explored. We can often usefully compare the situation 'as is' and the 'ideal' that we should like to see. We can also ask questions such as when, where, how and why the problem occurs, or when, where, how and why there is a situation that could or should be improved. What has changed? Relevant data (facts, attitudes, events, figures) can be adduced and the total should be seen in a context of what the school is trying to achieve.

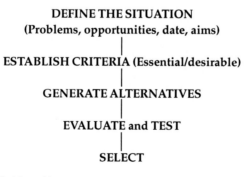

DEFINE THE SITUATION
(Problems, opportunities, date, aims)
|
ESTABLISH CRITERIA (Essential/desirable)
|
GENERATE ALTERNATIVES
|
EVALUATE and TEST
|
SELECT

Figure 4.1 Steps in decision-taking

Often it can be useful to restate the problem in as many different ways as possible. The more specific we can be, the better. 'A lot of parents are complaining that their children's property has disappeared' may be able to be restated as 'Ten parents have complained that valuable items (six pens and four calculators) have gone from form rooms over the lunch-hour' or even that 'Children have no secure place to leave valuable items over the lunch-hour'. Such restatements often suggest possible solutions.

Similarly, a problem which appears as 'Parents are complaining that they have to wait around between appointments to see staff on parents' evenings' can be restated as 'Parents get bored between appointments'. This quickly suggests the solution of introducing displays of work, refreshments, opportunities to try the computers, etc., rather than playing with appointment schedules.

Step 2: establishment of criteria

When a problem has been defined and its causes identified, the needs of the situation can be determined. These should be expressed in terms of ends not means. To help establish priorities, it is useful to split the needs into two categories:

(1) *Essential ends* – those which, unless they are achieved, will mean that the situation has not been put right or improved.
(2) *Desirable ends* – those which are wanted but are not essential to putting right or improving the situation.

Pursuing the example of lunch-hour losses, we may feel that the criteria for a satisfactory solution are as follows:

Essential
(1) Lunch-hour thefts from form rooms will not occur.
(2) Parents will have no grounds for complaint against the school in this matter.

Desirable
(1) Children should not have to carry their possessions at all times, in particular during lunchtime.
(2) Staff should not be burdened with extra duties.
(3) Children should be able to leave their possessions anywhere on the premises at any time without risk of theft.
(4) Any thieves will be caught and dealt with.
(5) Would-be thieves will be deterred.

Step 3: generation of alternative courses of action

The fact that we have to take a decision implies that at least two alternative courses of action are available, even if one alternative is to do nothing. In the simplest cases, there are often several alternatives. The risk is that we do not think of them. It is very true that there is nothing more dangerous than a good idea – if it is the only one you have!

When working as an individual the task of seeking alternatives can often be helped by 'sleeping on it' or seeking other inputs in discussion or from texts. When decisions are being made in a group or team setting, all too often one, or perhaps two, people will make suggestions and the discussion will then be limited to whether or not to accept these, instead of calling for other ideas.

A flip-chart is a wonderful tool for collecting alternatives. People cannot think of other ideas until they know that their first idea has been recorded. Once this has happened, they have no grounds for repeating their idea until others have also had their say. Another good mechanism for collecting ideas is the 'silent meeting' in which participants record their ideas on 'Post-its' and stick them on the chart. Discussion on the alternatives should be forbidden until this step is complete. The best solution may combine two or more alternatives.

Step 4: evaluation and testing of alternative courses of action

Evaluation consists of comparing the alternatives generated at Step 3 with the criteria from Step 2.

Any alternatives which do not satisfy the 'essential' criteria can be weeded out immediately. Thus, in our lunch-hour losses example, we could immediately rule out doing nothing or simply 'having a word in Assembly'.

Some other alternatives before us might be as follows:

(1) Carry out an investigation to discover the thief.
(2) Set a trap.
(3) Establish a lunch-hour security duty for staff supported by prefects.
(4) Lock the form rooms at lunchtime and unlock them five minutes before the start of afternoon school.
(5) Tell the children that they must keep valuable and attractive items such as pens and calculators on their persons at all times during the day.
(6) Provide a secure area in which children can leave their belongings before lunch and recover them after lunch.
(7) Provide lockable personal lockers.

Each of these alternatives will to a greater or lesser extent satisfy or not satisfy our 'desirable' criteria. Solutions 3, 4 and 6 may well put an extra burden on staff. Solution 5 would partially break the criterion of children not having to carry possessions around with them. Solutions 1 and 2 applied alone might not satisfy the 'essential' criteria but could be used in combination with other actions. They would, of course, take up staff time.

Finally, we need to 'test' the proposals for 'side-effects', i.e. for the fact that they might bring new problems and disadvantages. Thus Solution 5 could bring the risk of loss or damage at lunch-hour play. Solution 7 could cost money. Solution 6 could bring organizational and space problems.

Step 5: selection of a course of action

Few alternatives will meet all the 'desirable' criteria and be without disadvantages. Our choice should in the end be a balanced judgement in which we are aware of the potential snags and in which we weigh the relative priority which we give to each of the desirable criteria and the extent to which each alternative satisfies each criterion.

PERSONAL APPLICATION

Before moving on to the next section, think of some problem with which you are currently faced and work through the decision-making steps systematically.

THE IMPLEMENTATION OF DECISIONS

The road to Hell is paved with good intentions, and the road to managerial and organizational ruin is paved with decisions that have not been implemented – or, worse still, that have been implemented halfheartedly. There are managers who are sufficiently foolish or immodest to believe that whatever they have decided will automatically be done. The wise head knows better.

Apart from the obvious consideration of practicability, whether or not a decision is effectively implemented depends **on two** things:

(1) A clearly defined and communicated structure for implementation.
(2) The commitment of those responsible for implementation.

A STRUCTURE FOR IMPLEMENTATION

This is by far the simpler part of the process though it is too often forgotten in the joy of having reached an individual or group decision. Basically the structure consists of

(1) determining (agreeing?) *who* will do *what* by *when* (the *action plan*);
(2) *communicating* the action plan to the parties concerned; and
(3) *ensuring* that reviews take place.

To avoid ambiguity it is usually advisable for the action plan to be communicated in writing either as a memo or as part of the minutes of a meeting. Additionally it may be necessary to speak to the people responsible for action to ensure that they have actually read the paper and that they understand exactly what is intended.

The review procedure may take the form of a special meeting, or bringing up the action plan on the agenda of a more general meeting.

Where actions involve more than one person it is important to state – and to repeat – to all those involved in implementation that anyone who at any stage feels unable to fulfil his or her part of the action plan on time should immediately inform whoever is responsible for co-ordinating the action plan. An 'update' of the plan may then prove necessary. The most vulnerable decisions are often the simplest, where, for example, one or two people agree informally that they will 'let each other have a copy of …' or that one of them will 'ring X and sort it out'. The discipline of jotting down any such action to which you have personally committed yourself is a good beginning to establishing a reputation for 'reliability'.

If you do not already have on your desk an 'action book' in which you systematically read and work through 'things to be done', you should at least try that discipline. Each morning you should review the book to ensure that actions agreed the previous day are added and that 'things left undone' are brought forward.

STYLES IN DECISION-TAKING

Four types of decision-taking can be identified:

(1) *Autocratic:* the decision is taken without consultation, then others are informed of what is to be done and what is expected of them.
(2) *Persuasive:* the decision is taken before consultation and then 'sold' to others.
(3) *Consultative:* the views of others are sought and taken into account before a decision is taken.
(4) *Codeterminate:* decisions are taken on either a consensus or majority basis.

The appropriate style will depend on people and circumstances.

Autocratic decision-taking

This style is acceptable for routine matters which do not deeply concern people one way or the other. It will also be accepted more easily where the decision-takers have a considerable track record of success, where they are acknowledged to be the expert or where they have 'charisma'. Though people may grumble, they may also grudgingly accept that the decisions taken at a much higher level must sometimes be handed down without opportunity for consultation.

In such situations (e.g. when the head or the LEA has issued an edict) commitment may be built by creating an opportunity for frank questions to be put and honestly answered, and by 'consulting' on how the edict will be implemented.

Persuasive decision-taking

This differs from the autocratic style in that the manager uses his or her powers of advocacy to explain and justify his or her decision to his or her staff, subsequent to the decision being taken. It is not open to negotiation. This can be perceived as dishonest, in so far as staff are manipulated by slick 'sales talk' into accepting *un fait accompli*. It would, indeed, be dishonest if such a decision masqueraded as 'consultation'; but if it is presented as what it really is, and not fudged, it is an acceptable type of decision-taking in the right circumstances, and all of us use it in our daily lives. The secret of persuading people effectively without consulting them is to try to demonstrate understanding and sincere respect for their points of view; it also helps to explain why the manager thought consultation was inappropriate (see pp. 224–5).

Consultative decision-taking

This method combines the advantages of obtaining the ideas, suggestions and commitment of those involved, with vesting decision-taking responsibility in one person who should be able to assure consistency of decision-taking and conformity to established guidelines. It combines motivation with effectiveness.

Codeterminate decision-taking

This approach runs the risk of inconsistency and, while having the virtue of 'collective responsibility', it may thereby avoid individual responsibility. It is the only method available when no one party has clear decision-taking authority. Negotiation and 'management by committee' are forms of codeterminate decision-taking. Many joint decisions between heads of department are of this form.

Whatever form of decision-taking is used, the important things are that:

(1) the form of decision-taking should be 'open' and clear to all concerned;
(2) it should be consistent with reality; and
(3) the decision-takers should understand and establish the conventions of the particular form of decision-taking.

If these conditions are not met, we may find ourselves confronted with situations like these:

(1) A group 'votes' for a decision which is unacceptable within the school context (e.g. too expensive).
(2) A decision-taker who is trying to operate in 'consultative' mode comes under attack because the rest of the group expect that the majority view should be accepted.
(3) A decision-taker seeks people's views but ignores all that is said.

(4) Having agreed in a meeting or group to do something, the decision-taker finds that what has been agreed does not take into account the interests of some other person, or some other relevant fact.

CONSULTATIVE DECISION-TAKING – THE 'MANAGEMENT CONTRACT'

Consultative decision-taking imposes behavioural obligations on both the decision-taker and those who are invited to participate. There is a 'contract' to observe clear roles and conventions in going through the steps in decision-taking.

The terms of the contract are as follows:

(1) The decision-taker will share his or her perceptions of the situation and the criteria.
(2) The other persons involved will ask questions (and give answers) and put forward perceptions, problems and facts relevant to the situation. At the 'alternatives' step they will contribute proposals for action. (A wise decision-taker will ensure that these are recorded on a flipchart for all to see!) There can be some evaluative discussion of the various alternatives.
(3) The decision-taker will *listen* (i.e. not merely keep quiet), bearing in mind that his or her job is *not* primarily to *produce* the ideas but to use the best ideas whatever their source. (If one thinks someone else's idea is nearly as good as one's own it is probably better!)
(4) *After* the meeting (or individual discussion) the decision-taker will *decide* after due consideration of the proposals and any other factors. He or she should then *communicate and explain* the decision, being prepared to answer any questions.
(5) Finally there is an implied contract that, having been given every opportunity to contribute to the decision, the 'doers' will each play their full part in making it work.

It should be borne in mind that this 'contract' between the decision-maker and the 'doers' can easily be broken by either side. Typical breaches of contract to be avoided are as follows:

(1) The decision-taker suppresses key information or consults only when it suits his or her purpose.
(2) The 'doers' attack and criticize rather than make constructive proposals.
(3) The decision-taker goes on the defensive or feels that it is his or her duty to have all the ideas. Phrases like 'Yes I had thought of that but...' are not helpful in encouraging people to make suggestions.
(4) The decision-taker does not really listen to the ideas of others but has clearly made his or her mind up in advance. This is 'playing' with people.
(5) The decision-taker unreasonably refuses to explain his or her decision. (NB (a) The words 'on principle' often indicate 'I have run out of logical

reasons'; (b) to tell someone that you are not prepared to disclose your reasons implies a parent–child relationship.)

(6) The 'doers' do not give their full commitment to implementation.

Managing the process of consultation is not easy. It is a comparatively slow way of coming to a decision, and it brings with it a perceived risk of early confrontation. However, it has the following advantages:

(1) People who have been involved will be likely to be more committed to the decision taken. They will understand it.
(2) You have benefited from the ideas of others before taking the decision and are therefore less likely to have to back off and lose face because you failed to take into account some important consideration.
(3) For the above reasons, though decision-taking is slower, implementation is likely to be much more effective and faster.

Skill in managing the consultative process depends on the following:

(1) Being very clear on the terms of the 'contract', making them explicit ('*I* should like your views before *I* decide what to do about…' not '*We* have to decide…') and carrying them through.
(2) Dealing politely but firmly with 'breaches'. If discussion starts to become negative, you should ask very deliberately, and repeatedly if necessary: 'What do you suggest we do then?' If people are not implementing a decision, take them up on it quickly: 'Is there some problem?'
(3) Refusing to become emotionally 'hooked' on attack/defence. If people shoot at you ('If you had done what I suggested three months ago' or 'The problem started when you…'), lie down till the bullets have passed, and then come back with a remark such as 'All that is as may be, but what do you suggest we do now?'
(4) Asking questions and collecting in ideas rather than making statements.
(5) Practice.

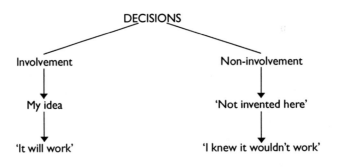

Figure 4.2   The choices between involvement and non-involvement

COMMITMENT

While not all staff like to be involved in decision-taking, there is overwhelming evidence that *most* people would like a greater share than they have in decisions which affect them but which are the responsibility of others. A simple model putting the choices between involvement and non-involvement is shown in Figure 4.2.

If people make such remarks as 'Don't ask me, you are paid to decide', you should ask yourself whether this reflects a real reluctance to be involved or whether, on the other hand, your own behaviour where there is such 'involvement' is seen as a charade masking an inbuilt resistance to the ideas of others. It is not enough to ask for opinions and ideas, you should also use them when reasonably possible.

PERSONAL APPLICATION

Think of some decisions that you have taken recently and for each say whether your approach was autocratic, persuasive, consultative or codeterminate. Do you consider that your approach was the right one in each case? Did you have any problems in implementation and why?

DELEGATION

Commitment based on the 'My idea – it will work' principle becomes even stronger if we delegate as much as possible of the decision-taking to the implementers. This is the thinking which underlies 'management by objectives'.

Ideally heads or heads of department will involve their subordinates but take the decisions themselves in determining

(1) common policies;
(2) common systems;
(3) school or departmental objectives (these could derive in part from a higher level); and
(4) what each individual is expected to achieve.

How individuals achieve their objectives can then be left to them, subject always to a respect for the objectives of others and to staying within the agreed policies and systems. As we saw earlier, this puts the individual into an 'achievement loop' of planning, implementing and controlling against meaningful goals. If the goals have been agreed with the head or head of department and colleagues, and if there is a review process, recognition of achievement is also built automatically into the process.

Effective delegation depends on

(1) clearly defined objectives with a timetable;
(2) clearly defined criteria which should be borne in mind in achieving the objectives; and

(3) review procedures or check points.

Let us suppose that the head delegates to a member of staff the task of organizing a school fair on a given date. The teacher who has been made responsible will need also to know what essential and desirable criteria apply, as follows.

Essential
(1) We must invite X, Y and Z.
(2) Areas A, B and C must not be used.
(3) *We must not incur a budget of more than £x and we must not lose money.*
(4) There will be no alcoholic drinks on sale.
(5) We must provide for the possibility of bad weather.

Desirable
(6) We shall raise at least £x.
(7) We shall avoid clashes with competing activities.
(8) We shall get subscriptions from local businesses.

The list is not, of course, comprehensive for even an imaginary fete. Many other items may be quite clearly implied from the school's culture or from previous experience. However, especially if there is a new head or a new organizer, a thorough briefing meeting can save a lot of wasted effort.

Job descriptions (see p. 75) are an important tool in permanently delegating authority and responsibility for decisions and actions.

KEY PRINCIPLES

The effective taking of decisions depends in short on a logical process which ensures in particular that we

(1) gather as many as possible of the relevant facts and opinions;
(2) consider the alternatives; and
(3) take into account the criteria which we need to meet and choose accordingly.

Effective implementation depends on

(1) a plan;
(2) reviews of progress; and
(3) the involvement of the right people at the right time and through a well controlled process.

PERSONAL APPLICATION

Plan to delegate a task or activity for which you are responsible (e.g. parents' evening, school trip, sports day). Consider who should be involved, the objectives and criteria that you need to communicate, and how you can achieve clear and accepted delegation so that all know who is to do what by when. Put your plan into practice.

DISCUSSION TOPIC

Do teachers have time to
(1) take decisions in a consultative way?
(2) implement autocratic decisions?
(3) take any decisions?

FURTHER READING

Adair, J. (1985) *Effective Decision Making: A Guide to Thinking for Management Success*, Pan, London.

Burns, R. (2002) *Making Delegation Happen. A Simple and Effective Guide to Implementing Successful Delegation*, Allen and Unwin, London.

A good general text explaining how decisions are taken in the public sector is

Lawton, A. and Rose, A.G. (1994) *Organisation and Management in the Public Sector* (2nd edn) Financial Times Prentice Hall, London.

5

Managing Meetings

MEETINGS AND THE MANAGER

Though we tend to think of a meeting as a formal gathering at a prearranged time and place, many meetings to discuss and progress the work of the school or college are casual, informal affairs consisting of only four, three or even two people. Such meetings can have just as important or even more important outcomes for the organization. Meetings come in all shapes and sizes. They may be highly structured and highly formalized with members speaking to each other 'through the chair' and observing a rigid agenda, or there may be no formal agenda and no acknowledged chairperson. They may have many legitimate purposes, but – as we shall see – they all too often wander aimlessly and have no productive outcome. They consume a high proportion of the non-classroom time of all teachers.

TEAMWORK

Meetings are of critical importance in co-ordinating effort and effecting change, and a very important part of the manager's role is to ensure that they are vehicles for communication and action rather than for confusion and frustration. This will be achieved by 'helicoptering' above the hurly-burly of the discussion, asking what we wish to achieve, being aware of the behavioural processes at work and trying to structure the meeting in such a way as to channel positively the energies of those involved.

TESTS OF AN EFFECTIVE MEETING

The key criteria for judging a meeting's effectiveness are

(1) Did the outcome of the meeting justify the time spent on it?
(2) Could there have been a better outcome for the same investment?
(3) Will the outcome be acted on?

In order to analyse whether or not these criteria have been met, further questions should be asked:

(1) Was the purpose of the meeting clear to all those who attended?
(2) Was the attendance correct for the subject under discussion? (Who else should have been there? Who was not really needed?)
(3) Were the participants adequately prepared for the meeting?
(4) Was time well used?
(5) How high was the commitment of the participants?
(6) Did the meeting achieve its purpose?
(7) What was the quality of the outcome?
(8) Was there a clear definition of
    (a) action to be taken following the meeting?
    (b) responsibility for taking the action?
    (c) a mechanism for review of the action?

Some of the above questions need no further discussion. Below are some considerations which are relevant in answering the others.

PURPOSE OF THE MEETING

The main purpose of some meetings – particularly of regularly held meetings – appears to be to fill Monday morning, the first afternoon of term, etc. In others, there is often a hidden conflict between, for example, those participants who believe that they are there to take a decision (possibly forcing it by a majority vote) and others who see the meeting as a vehicle for giving and receiving information and airing views in order to enable 'the boss' to take his or her own decisions.

Among the possible reasons for holding a meeting are to

(1) take decisions (e.g. on the organization of parents' evenings, fetes, curriculum changes);
(2) collect views, information and proposals in order to enable an informed decision to be taken by an individual (e.g. on a submission to the LEA in response to a circular);
(3) brief the meeting on, for example, policy;
(4) exchange information (e.g. on the progress of various aspects of a common project);
(5) generate ideas by use of a 'brainstorm', 'spidergram' or other creative method (these techniques are discussed later in the chapter); and
(6) enquire into the nature and causes of a problem, such as the behaviour of a particular child or group.

Any one of these purposes is legitimate and it is quite possible that different agenda items will have different purposes. What is important is that the purpose of the discussion at any time should be clearly stated and agreed. An important function of a formal or informal chairperson is to ensure that this is done, and to 'remind' the participants whenever the discussion appears to be losing relevance. Where there is no chairperson, or where the discussion is straying wildly, any participant can often make a very telling and constructive contribution simply by asking: 'What are we trying to achieve?'

Attendance

All that needs to be said here is that attendance should be determined not by status or convention but by relevance:

- Who has the information we need?
- Who can give a responsible undertaking?
- Who will have to act on the outcome?

Participants may change according to the agenda item. For some items it may be appropriate to have a fairly junior person 'sit in' or make a presentation.

It is important to ensure that the people needed at a meeting actually can and do attend. To miss a meeting can waste the valuable time of the other members, particularly if the missing member's agreement is needed to some key action. If a meeting can be missed fairly regularly the question should be asked whether the person concerned ever needs to attend. Should he or she just receive the minutes, or attend when specific items of interest to him or her are discussed?

Preparation

Some schools and colleges develop a vicious circle whereby people are too busy attending meetings to be able to prepare for a meeting and therefore have to attend a further meeting to present what should have been prepared for the first meeting.

Ability to prepare will depend on the circulation in good time of an agenda for the meeting. Key items for inclusion in the notice of a meeting are

(1) date, time, place and intended duration of meeting;
(2) people attending and roles (e.g. chairperson, secretary);
(3) purposes of meeting (e.g. decision-taking, information-giving, information exchange, brainstorming);
(4) preliminary documentation, preparation, etc.;
(5) agenda items with, for each item, relevant documents, etc., and a note of the persons responsible for introducing the item (NB An early agenda item should always be minutes of the last meeting, if any, and action taken); and
(6) particulars of procedure for adding any items to the agenda.

For small, informal meetings it may be enough to say 'I should like to discuss... Could you bring X, Y and Z with you?'

The use of time – meeting structure

Efficient use of time will largely depend on having and keeping to a structure which is suited to the purpose and membership of the meeting.

An invaluable piece of equipment at any meeting is a flipchart or whiteboard on which key ideas, information or proposals can be recorded for all to see. Advantages to be gained from this common-sense but underused item are the following:

(1) The discussion is focused.
(2) Ideas are not 'lost' (accidentally or otherwise).
(3) Flipcharts are a useful record on which minutes can be based (and against which minutes can be checked).
(4) Time is not wasted while individuals repeat ideas which they feel have not been heard or considered by the meeting.
(5) Recorded ideas (e.g. alternative proposals) can be dealt with in sequence, and those who have put forward an idea can take a full part in all discussions in the confidence that their own view will in due course be considered. Most people are incapable of listening to anyone else until they are sure their own view has been or will be heard. If, as often happens, there are two or more people in a meeting who feel this way, a 'dialogue of the deaf' is guaranteed.

Given the structure which is naturally created by a written record visible to all, other structural considerations will be determined by the circumstances, such as the size of the meeting.

LARGE MEETINGS

The only thing which is accomplished efficiently in a large meeting is the giving of information (preferably, of course, with the help of visual aids and handouts).

If the audience is to respond with ideas or ask questions which are meaningful to more than the questioner, the meeting should be split into discussion groups (each with its own room and flipchart). Each group should be asked to formulate ideas and questions which a representative can present to the reconvened main meeting.

A typical programme for such a meeting would be as follows:

Chairperson's introduction
(Purpose and structure of the meeting)   5 minutes

Presentation(s) of key facts, considerations, criteria by
the decision-taker with handout   10 minutes

Questions of clarification   5 minutes

Group meetings
*(Groups, each containing a mix of departments, develop
ideas and proposals. The decision-taker will visit groups
to answer any questions)*   40 minutes

Group presentations
(Each group will make a 3–5 minute presentation with
key points on flipchart)   20 minutes

Questions
(After all groups have presented, questions of clarification
will be put by the decision-taker and other groups)   15 minutes

Arrangements for follow-up   5 minutes

End of meeting

The study-group concept can be effective with as few as eight members in a meeting (i.e. two groups of four) and should certainly be seriously considered if meaningful participation is expected from more than twelve people.

DECISION-TAKING

As we discussed in the last chapter, 'participative' decision-taking has many advantages, and 'management by committee' does not, for the very simple reason that committees present problems of consistency and accountability. Even within the 'democratic' process of British government, the Prime Minister may overrule the Cabinet and, on major issues, voting within the House of Commons is effectively controlled by the government and opposition party machines rather than by the judgement of the individual member. In the same way, most company boards operate on a basis of giving the final word to one person, whether the chairperson or the managing director.

Meetings at any level should therefore be clear on whether a decision is really being taken *by* the meeting or whether, on the other hand, there is, for each decision, one person who has the responsibility for taking the decision *with the help of* the meeting.

Whichever is the case, the meeting should follow a clear structure which is stated at the opening of the meeting. If the meeting is to split into groups after an initial presentation and questions, this should be made clear. If we are seeking to achieve 'involvement' in decisions, the steps described at Figure 4.1 can be followed, with key points, especially the criteria and alternatives, listed on a flipchart for all to see.

There is, however, one very important warning. In the atmosphere of the meeting, it is very easy for the decision-taker to be swept along and to forget or minimize constraints and pressures from outside the meeting. Will there be funds available? Will the governors agree? Wise managers will let it be known at the start that they do not intend to make the final choice during the meeting. They should state clearly how and when the decision will be made known and explained, and they should hold to their promise.

The aim of the decision-taker during the meeting should be to explore fully the alternatives presented by comparing them with the criteria and asking questions of the meeting to help understanding of what each proposed alternative implies.

INFORMATION EXCHANGE

The important structural message under this heading is that where a series of people are to report overlapping information to a meeting (e.g. a report back from groups or progress reports on a project), questions on each report should be limited to 'clarification' until all reports have been given. Then and only then should a full discussion take place within the full meeting or in groups. If this principle is not followed, much time is wasted after early reports in discussing issues which may be covered in later reports. Also, later reporters suffer considerable frustration when their 'thunder' is 'stolen', and they are apt either to abstain from discussion or to take over the answering.

GENERATION OF IDEAS

Generation of ideas can be the purpose of a total meeting or of a part of a meeting. In the decision-taking process we look to the meeting to contribute ideas during each of the first three steps, i.e.

(1) statement of the situation;
(2) establishment of criteria; and
(3) generation of alternatives.

Less familiar to many schools – though increasingly being used – are pure 'brainstorming' meetings in which the aim is to promote creative solutions to problems.

Whether in a brainstorming session or a lower-keyed session for the generation of ideas, the key to success is to gather in ideas systematically and not to allow any evaluative comments during the process. The person leading the meeting should make it clear throughout that even the merest 'Yes, but… ' is unacceptable during the 'gathering' phase. All ideas must, of course, be recorded on a flipchart.

Once the ideas have been listed, then, and only then, should questions be asked to clarify what is meant or implied or involved in each suggestion. The irrelevant should be discarded; the relevant suggestions should be debated one by one in depth.

Brainstorming

In normal meetings the process of gathering ideas, prior to discussing them, will be relatively calm and rational. Sometimes, however, we may want a completely uninhibited generation of ideas and comments. Brainstorms, as we call such sessions, are particularly appropriate when we want to unleash creativity or frankness. The aim is to get as many ideas in as short a time as possible. Guidelines given to the group are as follows:

Suspend judgement. Never evaluate the ideas being produced in a brainstorming session, whether they are yours or other people's. Never use the phrases 'That won't work' or 'That's silly' or 'We've had that before'. Laugh *with* the wild ideas, not at them. No one likes being laughed at, but laughing with the wild ideas encourages further ideas.

Let yourself go and freewheel. This means drifting or dreaming, and brings into play the subconscious levels of the mind. Don't be worried about putting forward wild or silly ideas. In fact, the wilder the better.

Quantity. Quality implies evaluation. Suspend judgement. Go for quantity, the more the merrier. All ideas are good.

Cross-fertilize. This is where the group comes in. Always be prepared to pick up somebody else's idea and suggest others leading from it. Don't leave it to Charlie to develop his own – after all, he's going to pick up yours!

Use verbal shorthand. Don't hold things up by explaining your idea at length. Just shout out the one or two words that will convey your thinking. (You can explain later!)

Brainstorming is both fun and highly productive. Used with a group of school heads of department to answer the question 'How does the staff judge a timetable?', a list of over sixty criteria was produced within 15 minutes, reflecting interests which ranged from educational to purely personal. Some examples of the output were

(1) good mix of subjects for children;
(2) double periods;
(3) no double periods;
(4) free periods Friday afternoon;
(5) free periods Monday morning;
(6) one free period per day;
(7) children move as little as possible;
(8) staff move as little as possible; and
(9) specific criteria, such as no French after PE.

In a half-hour discussion which followed the brainstorm, the member of staff responsible for timetabling was quickly able to come to grips with her colleagues' preferences, some of which they might have hesitated to admit in a more inhibited discussion. Some guidelines on mix of subjects for the children also emerged, not to mention a review of period length and daily structure.

With two or three colleagues 'brainstorm' possible uses for a paper clip or an elastic band.

Spidergrams

Another approach to generating ideas is the 'spidergram' or 'mind pattern', a technique which can also be used in a group, or individually, for organizing or recalling ideas. It is an excellent basis for planning an essay or report. The technique consists of setting down the subject as a central point and adding on the other ideas around this point as they emerge. Normally the first thoughts will be immediate associations or main branches from the word but this will not always be the case, and additional main branches may emerge as we proceed.

Thus, if we start with the subject of curriculum development, the first ideas that emerge may be illustrated in Figure 5.1. We may then be 'triggered' by one of the main branches – see Figure 5.2.

Next a subject such as 'funds' may be linked with a number of other issues such as 'retraining' and 'teaching materials' – this we can illustrate by a link line between the subjects in another colour.

The value of the method is that it enables the individual or group to collect ideas and organize them as they spring to mind, rather than hold them back until the relevant subject comes up in sequence. Furthermore, by letting our eyes wander over the chart we constantly restimulate our brains in each area. Whereas brainstorming can be used effectively in groups of up to twenty people, spidergrams are best used in smaller groups. For further reading see Buzan (2003).

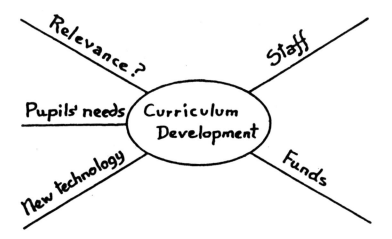

Figure 5.1   Spidergram: first ideas

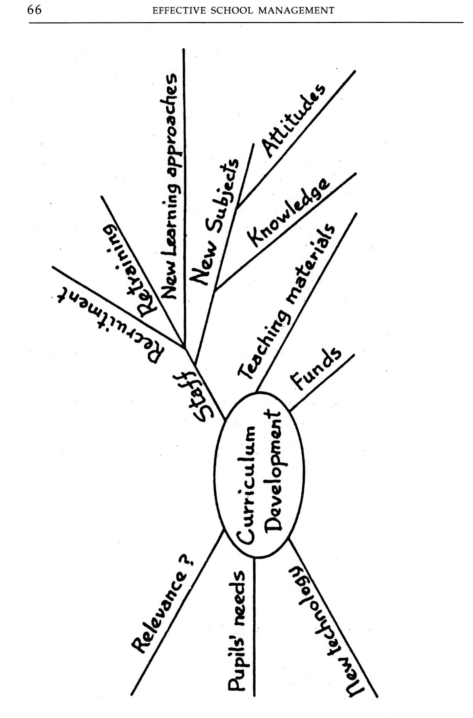

Figure 5.2   Spidergram: branches

PERSONAL APPLICATIONS

(1) Draw a spidergram linking the subjects in this or any other chapter.
(2) Apply the above principles to the next meeting you run, not forgetting to annotate your own agenda with target times and purpose against each agenda item.

GROUP DYNAMICS

A valuable exercise is to watch a video recording of a meeting, preferably one in which you have taken part. If this is not possible, you will have to rely on sitting back and observing. Among the phenomena which you may notice are

(1) repetition by the same person of the same point;
(2) failure of people to take up each other's points except to attack them with a 'Yes, but...';
(3) 'not invented here' reactions;
(4) lack of interest manifested by 'body language';
(5) arguments about the structure of the meeting: 'Wouldn't it be best if we first...', 'I don't see how we can decide that before...', and constant changes in approach to the problem;
(6) people trying to 'score' off each other;
(7) several people talking at once;
(8) 'blocking out' of certain people and alliances between others; and
(9) possibly some skilful manipulation of the meeting.

Meetings can take place in which the results are less the result of logical and constructive debate than of skilled games play. You may have come across examples of the following:

Clique-forming. In this activity certain members of the meeting have an implicit or explicit understanding that they will support each other whatever the rights and wrongs of a particular issue.

Selective support. This game may be played by the chairperson who carefully selects for consideration those ideas which approximate to his or her own while ignoring those which do not. A variant is played by the ordinary meeting participant who does not express his or her own opinion but waits until other people have spoken before making a remark like: 'I think that Mr X hit the nail on the head when he said ... and Mrs Y had a good point. Couldn't we build on these by ...?' There is a fair chance that any idea which follows will be supported by X and Y, who are flattered that someone has actually listened to them.

Selective minute writing. Careful selection has been known to destroy the true impact of a meeting!

Failure to listen. This is the game of asking people for their views in order to ignore them.

While we don't suggest that you should use manipulative tactics, it is important that you should be able to recognize them and counteract them. Commitment to the results or decisions will depend on the apparent honesty of the decision process and conduct of meetings.

Process review

Exercise 3 at the end of the chapter is a 'group performance checklist' which can be used to 'score' a meeting which you have attended. It highlights eight areas which are key to a meeting's success and asks you to judge to what extent various behaviours are shown.

Such checklists can be used to powerful effect in a training context, where the various participants to a meeting first record their individual scores, and then compare scores, discuss the reasons for the scores, and in particular for any discrepancies, and finally decide how they will improve their effectiveness as a group in subsequent meetings.

Following the use of such a procedure for training purposes, some groups build a review into their normal meeting procedure, at the end or after the first 20 minutes of a lengthy meeting, or at any time when the meeting appears to be losing its effectiveness. This can become a relatively short procedure in which a practised and 'open' group will immediately bring forward perceptions such as 'We completely ignored Mrs X's point' or 'We are each defending our parochial interests again'.

There is further discussion of group dynamics in Chapter 10.

Whether or not they have a formal role, the aim of each meeting participant should be to move the meeting towards the positive behaviour outlined by the (a) items in the group performance checklist. This can be done by, for example,

(1) drawing in someone who is being ignored or is remaining silent;
(2) asking quite deliberately for other views and stressing that it is 'Speak now or for ever hold your peace';
(3) asking people to talk one at a time;
(4) drawing attention to the use of time;
(5) asking exactly what decision is being minuted;
(6) summarizing the stated opinions as you now understand them.

Good questions which a consultant, an observer or an observant participant may usefully ask are as follows:

Question	When to use
What do you understand to be the goals of this meeting?	Whenever they have not been stated.
What order of priority should these in?	When the agenda looks items be too long.
What do you understand 'X' to have just said?	When someone has not listened.

Where is the discussion aiming now?	When you do not know.
Where are we in the systematic approach?	When the discussion rambles formlessly.
What has just been decided?	When it is not clear what has been decided.
How exactly did we reach that decision?	When it was not reached systematically.
Who is to do that?	When an action is not assigned.
When is this to be done by?	When no time has been set.
For instance?	When airy-fairy generalizations are made.
What was your purpose in saying (or asking) that?	When an unhelpful contribution has been made.
Have you followed your plan?	When they have not.
How is the time going?	When everyone has forgotten its passage.
Are we helping you?	When discussion on someone's point makes slow progress.

PERSONAL APPLICATIONS

(1) Carry out a process review following your next meeting using the Group Performance Checklist.
(2) Arrange to video or observe a meeting and carry a process review alone or, preferably, in conjunction with the other participants. Be prepared for discrepancies in the way you and others rate the meeting and explore them.

PREPARING FOR A MEETING

Whether you are to chair a meeting or participate, you will greatly enhance the chances of achieving the sort of outcome you want if you spend a short time in preparation. The checklists which follow may help.

Chairperson's checklist

Planning the meeting
(1) purpose(s) of the meeting;
(2) main agenda items (subject possibly to additions);
(3) essential and desirable participants for the whole meeting;
(4) participants for parts of the meeting;
(5) date and time, bearing in mind
    (a) availability of essential and desirable participants;
    (b) degree of urgency; and
    (c) need for preparation;
(6) place.

Notification and circulation of agenda
(1) time, place, date and expected duration of meeting;
(2) purpose;
(3) proposed agenda;
(4) procedure for adding other items to the agenda;
(5) circulation list indicating who is to attend the full meeting, who will attend part only, who is being informed but will not attend.

Preparation for meeting
(1) main meeting room;
(2) group rooms if needed;
(3) visual aids (e.g. overhead projector, screen, slides);
(4) flipchart(s) and dark-coloured markers that work;
(5) seating;
(6) pads and pencils;
(7) masking tape, tacky putty or adhesive pads to stick up flipchart sheets.

Content of meeting
(1) clear objectives (inform, involve, generate ideas?);
(2) appropriate structure;
(3) clear ground rules;
(4) 'honest' procedure;
(5) use of flipcharts or whiteboard;
(6) commitment.

Follow-up
(1) Who will do what, when, where?
(2) Written minutes circulated with action responsibility.
(3) Control and review procedures.

Participants' checklist

Preliminary work
(1) What are the items on the agenda to which I shall be expected/would wish to contribute?
(2) Are there any 'hidden' agendas for which I should be prepared?
(3) Do I wish to introduce any topics? If so, how? For example:
    (a) add them to the agenda before the meeting;
    (b) add them at the beginning of the meeting;
    (c) make sure that they are considered as part of one of the agenda items; and
    (d) put down a proposal.
(4) In the light of the above:
    (a) What information should I study, prepare for circulation as a handout, prepare to present?
    (b) Do I need to request any facilities such as flipcharts or overhead projector?

(c) Do I need to talk to anyone before the meeting in order to gather information or to lobby?

Meeting content
(1) What sort of outcomes should the meeting have (e.g. a decision, an exchange of ideas, factual information, a plan of action)?
(2) Is there any outcome that I particularly want?
(3) Is there any outcome that I particularly do not want?
(4) Are there any conditions that I should like to see built into certain outcomes?
(5) What alternatives can I propose?
(6) What arguments should I use?
(7) What arguments can I expect to be used in opposition to my ideas?
(8) When and how should I present my ideas?
(9) Am I really thinking in the best interests of the organization?
(10) How will my views be perceived?

Follow-up
(1) To what action am I prepared to commit myself/my department?
(2) What time/cost is involved and is this reasonable in the light of other commitments?

DISCUSSION TOPIC

What are the main problems we experience in our staff meetings? What practical steps should we take to remedy them?

FURTHER READING

Dobson, A. (1999) *Managing Meetings: How to Prepare for Them, How to Run Them and How to Follow up the Results,* How To Books, Oxford.
Forsyth, P. (1996) *The Meetings Pocketbook*, Management Pocket Books, Arlesford.
Timm, P.R. (1997) How to Hold Successful Meetings: 30 Action Tips for Managing Effective Meetings, Career Press, USA.

EXERCISE 3: Group Performance Checklist

According to the group's performance, distribute 100 points among the statements under the first heading below. Then do the same for the statements under the other seven headings.

1. *Objectives*
(a) Objectives were clear, and understood and accepted by all group members.
(b) There was no clarity or agreement on what the group's objectives were.
(c) Though the objectives were clear, full commitment to these objectives by group members was lacking.

(d) A significant amount of time was spent on secondary issues or unimportant detail.

(e) Personal goals weighed more heavily than group objectives.

2. *System*

(a) A logical procedure or method of approach was agreed and adhered to unless deliberately changed; the meeting ran smoothly.

(b) The meeting was overorganized or rigid; following 'proper procedures' was more important than dealing effectively with the issues.

(c) The meeting was chaotic and undisciplined.

(d) The meeting went round in circles.

(e) Important ideas and information took longer to emerge than they should have done.

3. *Participation*

(a) All members participated actively; everyone contributed and all contributions received thoughtful attention; humour was a constructive element of the meeting.

(b) Several members dominated a group of relatively passive members.

(c) Members tended to interrupt one another; two or more people talked at once.

(d) Silences fell as members seemed not to know where to go next; initiatives were lacking.

(e) Frivolity, joking and irrelevant comments crept in.

4. *Relationships*

(a) Group members showed confidence in and trust and respect for each other.

(b) Relationships were formal and guarded.

(c) Members were not open to each other's ideas; listening was poor.

(d) Cliques or subgroups developed.

(e) Maintaining a spirit of good fellowship and friendliness was more important than dealing effectively with the issues or problems.

5. *Decisions*

(a) Decisions were well considered, based on facts and reason and reached by consensus.

(b) Decisions were forced by individuals; not everyone's point of view received equal attention.

(c) Decisions were reached by majority vote.

(d) Decisions were compromised rather than fully reasoned out.

(e) Few or no decisions were made; issues were left hanging; it was frequently not clear whether a decision had been made.

6. *Disputes*

(a) Points of disagreement were thrashed out logically until all parties were satisfied.

(b) Disagreements were smoothed over; keeping the peace was more important than getting the best decision or solution.

(c) 'Win–lose' power struggles were fought out; personal victory seemed to matter more than getting the best solution.

(d) Compromise positions were taken; 'workable' solutions were accepted rather than 'best' solutions.

(e) Differences were side-stepped or ignored.

7. *Leadership*

(a) There was a sense of shared responsibility for the quality of the meeting; individuals took leadership initiatives as required.

(b) A leader was agreed at the start and provided leadership initiatives as he or she saw fit.

(c) Two or more members of the group seemed to be engaged in a battle for the leadership of the group.

(d) The group's needs for leadership were not met.

(e) Leadership was overdone; the meeting was too tightly controlled; spontaneity and flexibility were lacking.

8. *Use of resources*

(a) The group made the best possible use of the resources available to it (e.g. time, special knowledge, special skills, equipment).

(b) Time available to the group was not used to the best advantage.

(c) Ideas or relevant information emerged too late or failed to emerge at all.

(d) The group did not make full use of the skills of its members.

(e) The group did not make the best use of the equipment available (e.g. by failing to capture information on a flipchart).

6

Recruiting, Employing, Appraising, Developing and Dismissing Staff

PEOPLE AS A RESOURCE

In Chapter 13 we shall discuss in some depth the management of resources – financial, physical and human. In the educational system, it is human resources which consume the most investment. In many ways we should treat people as any other resource, selecting the best for the purpose we wish to accomplish, and maintaining, improving and adapting the resource as we would a building or piece of equipment to ensure that it meets our needs. However, there is one important difference: people are *thinking* resources who, whether we like it or not, will decide jointly with their managers and colleagues on how their time, energy, knowledge and skill will be used. Indeed, the true human resource is not the whole person, but his or her efforts which will be jointly managed by the individual himself or herself and the 'management' of the organization in which he or she works. The final arbiter in the use of a person's efforts will always be him or herself, since he or she has merely contracted to supply some of his or her services over a given period of time.

Teachers are often shocked at the idea of describing staff as 'human resources', yet on a continuum of attitudes towards employment (Figure 6.1), where does the average school or college management stand? Do we accept that in selecting a new member of staff we are working *with* the candidate to find out how his or her skills and personality will blend with the needs of the school and the existing skill and personality mix? Do we believe that we can sit as equals with our staff to discuss their performance *and our own performance* in order that both of us can develop as individuals and as members of a team, albeit with different roles in the team? Or do we feel that relationships are such that appraisal of our colleagues will be seen by them as 'judgement', and that it would be 'improper' for them to pass a view on the

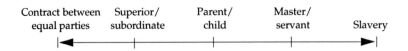

Contract between equal parties	Superior/ subordinate	Parent/ child	Master/ servant	Slavery

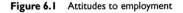

Figure 6.1   Attitudes to employment

performance of their 'superior'? How do we view the caretaker and ancillary staff? Should our relationship to them be different from our relationship to our professional colleagues and, if so, how?

It is important to know where we stand and to behave in a coherent way which is consistent with the realities of power. In the teaching profession it is sometimes more difficult than elsewhere to invoke sanctions against the incompetent. We are therefore almost entirely dependent on the recruitment of good staff, and the creation of open relationships in which staff at different levels will work together to make themselves, each other and the organization more effective.

RECRUITMENT OF STAFF

Standard elements in the recruitment process are

(1) the job description;
(2) the personal profile;
(3) attracting suitable candidates;
(4) application forms;
(5) references; and
(6) the interview.

The person under whose immediate direction the new recruit will work should be involved in all stages of the process. Increasingly, it is also the practice to take the views of those with whom the recruit will work and also of those whom the recruit will lead. At the earlier stages this allows for creative input (e.g. a readjustment of roles within a school or department) and at the interview stage it builds staff commitment and helps the candidate to assess the environment in which he or she will have to work. It is also common for candidates to be asked to teach a lesson, or to undertake an in-tray exercise or similar task. Some schools also find that the views of a specially convened pupil panel offer additional useful information.

The job description

A vacancy is an opportunity to rethink roles, and one should therefore be wary of automatically adopting the job description of a teacher who has departed. Whatever job description is developed, it should also be open to revision after appointment as a candidate may emerge with unforeseen talents that one may wish to use. This is particularly true in relation to out-of-school activities, general studies or subjects such as information technology.

Traditionally, a job description will contain

(1) job title;
(2) brief description of the purpose of the job;
(3) reporting relationships; and
(4) description of duties.

A further very useful concept is that of

(5) competences, i.e. abilities and attitudes (as opposed to qualifications) that the occupant of the post will need to possess (see Chapter 8).

However, the most helpful element of all, both to the candidate and the person or committee charged with the appointment decision, is a sixth element, namely

(6) criteria for effectiveness.

Criteria for effectiveness, which can often usefully be expressed as questions, tell us how performance in the job will be assessed. For a head of French, for example, criteria might be as follows:

(1) Are oral standards maintained and improved?
(2) How many pupils have visited France on exchanges, school trips or as paying guests?
(3) Is there a thriving French club?
(4) Are examination results satisfactory?

Additionally there will be criteria which will apply to all heads of department, for example:

(1) Is the atmosphere in the department enthusiastic and harmonious?
(2) Does the department work well with other departments?
(3) Is administration accurate and timely?
(4) Have objectives been achieved?
(5) Has the performance of pupils been satisfactory in public examinations and assessments?
(6) Does the department meet Ofsted criteria?

PERSONAL APPLICATION

As an exercise draw up a set of effectiveness criteria for the school caretaker; the school secretary; a lunchtime supervisor.

Personal profile

Starting from the job description, the next step is to define the characteristics of the sort of person able to meet the criteria. Certain of these characteristics will be 'essential' and others 'desirable'. A useful checklist is

(1) personal characteristics;
(2) achievements and experience: general education, degrees, etc., jobs, special projects, awards;
(3) competences: abilities, aptitudes, skills, knowledge and effective application;
(4) motivation: ambition (direction?), social, intellectual, level of 'drive'; and
(5) personality: leadership, relationships, emotional stability.

It will be immediately apparent that while the first two categories are 'factual', the last three contain judgemental elements. Some of the characteristics will – or should – depend on looking for an approach which will complement that of other members of the team. If the team is creative, mercurial but disorganized, perhaps we should look for an 'administrator' input, and vice versa. If we do not define this need, the risk is always that the appointer will be attracted by someone whose approach is similar to his or her own, whereas the need is often for a dissimilar person who will complement him or her. The people we choose as friends are often similar to us; the people with whom we can most easily work (or live) are usually complementary in character (see Chapter 10).

Attracting suitable candidates

The relationship between supply of and demand for candidates for teaching posts has varied over the years and will presumably continue to do so. There is also, of course, a background of variation by subject. Specialists for example in maths, sciences and modern languages have tended over many years to be in relatively short supply.

In this shifting situation the need remains always to attract the right number of the right candidates. Ideally we should probably like about twenty application forms from which to select five candidates for interview.

There are a number of ways in which we can increase or decrease the number of applications we receive. We can

(1) tighten or slacken the essential and desirable characteristics in the personal profile and advertise accordingly;
(2) limit or extend our choice of advertising media;
(3) target groups other than existing teachers, redundant teachers or newly qualified teachers; and
(4) build the image of the school as an attractive place in which to teach and/ or offer or make known fringe benefits.

Taking each of these in turn:

Adjusting the personal profile
A critical examination of the personal profile is always well worthwhile before advertising a post. As we have already said, it is not always – even usually – wise to appoint someone in the image of the previous incumbent. We want to encourage a creative approach. Furthermore, we need to beware of anyone who demonstrably possesses all the qualities and more needed to perform in the job and has perhaps moved or been made redundant from a similar post. The problem with such people is that the job may present them with insufficient challenge and motivation. The ideal candidate is usually the one who has potential to grow into and develop a job – and possibly move through it to an even more challenging job.

For the above reason we should be careful not to make the essential characteristics (the 'musts' in the advert) too tight. However, we do want them tight enough firmly to rule out unacceptable candidates and particularly so in a buyer's market. Tightening the personal profile is a particularly good way of reducing applicants since it decreases the quantity by insisting on standards of quality.

The personal profile will, of course, form the basis of the job advertisement.

Use of advertising media
Choice of advertising media as a means of increasing or decreasing the number of applicants for a post has the advantage that the strength of the advertising can be increased if the first attempt does not provide enough candidates. Whether further advertising increases the quality as opposed to quantity of applicants will depend on whether the format and location of the advertising are only such that they reach those who are desperately seeking employment or whether they will also reach others who are not so engaged but might be drawn by a really attractive opportunity.

Targeting of non-conventional groups
Understandably, teachers feel considerable concern lest the profession should be diluted by the introduction of staff who have not been formally trained to teach. Proposals for 'licensing' or 'on the job' training have therefore met with union resistance. This resistance has been reinforced by justified resentment at failure to provide adequate training places or incentives and the perception that recruitment of untrained staff threatens the job prospects of unemployed trained teachers. The use of untrained or informally trained staff is therefore a practical option only in subjects, locations or times of dire shortage or in the independent sector.

Whatever the politics of the situation, the school manager can only broaden scope of choice – and therefore increase chances of recruiting better staff – by looking outside the conventional target groups of newly qualified probationers, existing teachers, unemployed teachers and married women returners. Far from diluting quality, the experience and competence of unconventional recruits might well enrich and broaden the profession.

Publicity has been given to the recruitment of teachers from other countries. Other groups that deserve special attention are

(1) early retirers of all kinds;
(2) industrial managers, especially those who have worked in the training and personnel functions;
(3) local authority officers;
(4) parents who may have no previous teaching experience, but who have relevant competences; and
(5) social workers.

People in the above and other categories may or may not have thought of teaching as a possible second career, but it is unlikely that they will have regular access to *The Times Educational Supplement* or to other lists of teaching vacancies. If they do read these lists, it is unlikely that the advertisements will encourage them to apply. A well-designed website, with a section devoted to vacancies which encourages such people to apply, can be a very useful additional source of applicants.

It is important therefore both to place targeted adverts in the 'job-hunting' journals read by these groups and to build up suitable contacts who will help in finding people through their own organizations. While personnel managers will not thank you for poaching their key staff, they may be very pleased to point redundant, retiring or change-seeking executives in your direction or to encourage their partners to move into or return to the teaching profession. At least one school in the South East of England relies very heavily for its staff on the wives of employees of a local computer company.

In times of teacher surplus the target group for recruitment can be narrowed by, for example, advertising only locally as opposed to nationally.

Building an image of the school as an attractive place in which to teach
One head in an area where recruitment is notoriously difficult asserts that he never has any problems because staff are 'queueing up' to come to his school. Part of this popularity can be attributed to an overall 'quality' image which attracts parents, pupils and staff alike – good academic results, good sports record, high standards of behaviour. However, specific attention has also been paid to feeding the press with articles and talking to local interest groups about the attractions of working at the school – though only the best staff will be accepted!

Image must not, of course, belie reality, and active steps have to be taken to ensure that staff conditions, facilities and, above all, motivational factors (see Herzberg, 1975) are to a high standard. We need to consider what possibilities exist, if any, to provide child-care or housing assistance where appropriate.

PERSONAL APPLICATION

Draw up (or revise) a job description, personal profile and advertisement to fill a real or imagined vacancy in your department. Consider how and where you would publicize the vacancy and whether you would vary the wording for different media.

Application forms

Most educational institutions have a standard form and most of these forms are well designed to bring out all the factual information needed, and also to elicit data which may give us a clue to behaviour (the 'judgemental' elements in the profile). A good application form will make it clear, in asking for references, whether or not these will normally be taken up before interview.

In reading application forms, we should remember that the most relevant data are often those that are missing. An unexplained break between periods of employment, particularly in a teacher's career, may mean imprisonment, dismissal for misconduct or a clash of personalities which has led to resignation from one job before getting the next. On the other hand, it may mean illness, or having a family. Absences from work (a key question in an application form) may mean a period of illness which has been cleared up or an ongoing health problem (physical or psychological) or family problems (ongoing or past) or undue willingness to take advantage of minor ailments. Whether the circumstances are acceptable to us or not, the point is that we want to know. A note should be made on the form to bring the matter up at interview.

We should, of course, be comparing each form with the 'essential' and 'desirable' criteria in our profile, and assuming that 'essential' really does mean that we will reject any applications which do not conform. We may also reject some which do not meet enough of our 'desirable' criteria.

References

As we have said, the reference procedure should have been made clear in the application form. In the teaching profession it is usual, subject to a request to the contrary, to take up references for the shortlist before interview.

Although a reference – unlike a testimonial – is a confidential and legally privileged document, many referees will hesitate to refer directly in writing to shortcomings in the candidate. Therefore the questions are 'What is missing?' 'Do I have a positive statement about the characteristics which I see as essential in this candidate?' If not, a telephone call to the referee can be of help. This will usually elicit a much franker view of the candidate and, in the case of the chosen candidate for a key appointment, many would argue that a telephone call to referees is a 'must' before making a final offer.

Planning the interview

The purpose of an interview is to find which of the shortlisted candidates best fits our needs. We are not looking for the most likeable person or even the one with the best track-record in his or her last job. First-class honours graduates do not necessarily make the best teachers, and first-class teachers do not necessarily make good school or college managers. Above all we want to check on those 'essential' and 'desirable' criteria about which we are not completely sure as a result of the application form and the references. Certain of these criteria will be biographical or factual; others will be behavioural or judgemental; most will be a mixture of the two, e.g. we may be able to judge a person's 'drive' by exploring in depth the results of some project he or she has undertaken, asking about the problems that occurred and whether and how these were dealt with and by whom.

Proficient interviewees will, if they can, steer us away from areas of weakness. Inexperienced candidates, on the other hand, may not know how to make the best of themselves at an interview. For both reasons it is essential that we are systematic in listing the areas we wish to explore and thinking about the questions we wish to ask. It is particularly important to think about the sort of facts and interview reactions that will help us to come to a meaningful conclusion on the behavioural/judgemental criteria.

It is essential that we make notes on each candidate as the interview progresses and that we take time at the end of each interview to consolidate these. The whole process is greatly helped if we prepare for each candidate a selection sheet (preferably on A3 paper) similar to that shown in Figure 6.2. The use and retention of such sheets can be valuable if any candidate alleges discrimination on racial, sexual or other grounds.

The interview

Educational interviews tend to be by a formal panel, possibly preceded by a 'tour' of the establishment and an informal preliminary meeting or series of meetings with the individuals with whom the successful candidate will have to work most closely, as well as teaching a lesson or undertaking other tasks. These informal preliminaries are to be encouraged, as they help the candidate to decide whether he or she wishes to select the job as well as providing potential behavioural input to the school's side of the selection procedure. Increasingly, schools are following the example of industry in using attitude

---

SELECTION SHEET

Position..   Candidate..

Job Description and Criteria For Effectiveness (attached)

Personal profile

E = Essential

D = Desirable	Application form	Reference	Interview question	Notes on candidate's response
Personal and physical				
....(E)				
....(E)				
....(D)				
Achievements and experience				
Abilities				
Motivation				
Personality				
Overall summary				

Interviewer..

Figure 6.2 Selection sheet

and profile questionnaires which can provide interesting insights for subsequent follow-up in interview. This input can usefully be collected by the head or head of department before the formal panel meets.

The formal panel members should each be given a copy of the 'selection sheet' for each candidate and taken through it beforehand by the head or head of department. A decision should be taken on how the procedure will be structured. How will the candidate be welcomed, introduced and put at ease? Who will lead the panel? Who will cover what areas of questioning? How shall we allocate time?

Questioning technique is important. Some useful 'do's and don'ts' to bear in mind are as follows:

Do not
(1) Start with intimate, personal, aggressive or argumentative questions. (These can come later when rapport has been established.)
(2) Use 'closed' questions which will lead to a 'yes' or 'no' answer unless there is a need to establish a clear fact which is uncertain (or about which the candidate is 'hedging') or unless you are going to follow up by an open-ended supplementary.
(3) Use multiple questions, loaded questions, trick questions or jargon.
(4) Lead – for example 'I suppose you …', 'I think … What do you feel?', 'No doubt you enjoy good relations with …' (Even if the candidate would be willing to tell you about problems, you make it almost impossible for him or her to do so.)
(5) Indicate disapproval or show that you are shocked.
(6) Worry about silences.
(7) Allow your prejudices (accent, dress, men with beards, women with earrings, as well as colour, sex, etc.) to affect your judgement.

Do
(1) Use 'open' questions which allow the candidate to express him or herself, to demonstrate knowledge, to add to the picture (you do not want them to repeat information that you already have).
(2) Probe tactfully, using 'Why?' 'What?' 'How?' questions, or

- 'Tell me about …?'
- What did you enjoy most about …?'
- What was your role in …?'
- How does our job compare with …?'
- 'What did you enjoy least about …?'

(3) Reassure a nervous candidate by 'congratulating' on achievements, smiling, making reinforcing noises, etc.
(4) Listen for at least two-thirds of the time.
(5) Guide tactfully into the areas you wish to explore.
(6) Close down one area and open up another with remarks such as 'OK, I think we've covered that; now, could you tell me about …'

(7) Come back to areas a candidate tries to avoid.
(8) Get his or her views on the job on offer and encourage criticism of the school.
(9) Observe behaviour (tenseness, etc.).
(10) When the candidate has had time to settle down, investigate relationships by covering social and work life. Look for clues of difficult adjustments, loyalty, etc. (NB The inability to relate well to other people is the most frequent cause of dissatisfaction with staff members of all kinds.)
(11) Give the candidate a chance to ask about the job, and check whether he or she is still interested and whether there are any reservations (family moves, etc.).
(12) Make sure the candidate knows what the next steps are.
(13) Close when both you and the candidate have enough information.
(14) Record your overall impressions before you meet the next candidate (otherwise you will forget).

Confirming the appointment

Every employee must by law be given a written statement of terms and conditions of employment. This statement must cover a number of specific points including salary, periods of notice, holiday entitlement and grievance procedure. It is good practice to incorporate these into a written offer to the chosen candidate.

Induction

As soon as candidates have accepted the appointment, they should be sent a copy of the 'departmental document' (schemes of work, departmental responsibilities, etc.), invited for an induction day and given the job description. The criteria for effectiveness should be agreed and preferably recorded in writing. An objective is seldom meaningful unless it is qualified in such a way that all parties will know whether it has been achieved. Time is the most important measure. Thus 'to put on a linguists' evening in the spring term' and 'to arrange an exchange visit to each of France and Germany next summer' are far more meaningful objectives than 'to increase out-of-school activities in modern languages'.

A pack of information, textbooks, school rules, standard forms, etc., should await the new recruit, and a guided tour and meetings should be planned. Form room, locker space, pass key or other physical details should be discussed. (It is useful to establish for each school an induction checklist.) Preferably the induction day will start and finish with the recruit's immediate manager who will also become the reference point for further enquiries.

EMPLOYING STAFF

Since this book first appeared, employment legislation has become much more complex. Most heads will have to rely on professional advice to avoid some of the pitfalls lurking around. Society is becoming more litigious as the 'blame culture' flourishes. Dealing with grievances and tribunals can devour precious management time. Problem avoidance is better than cure, which makes motivation and 'hygiene' so important (Chapter 3). Never let emerging human resources problems fester; they usually get worse! On the other hand, avoid caving in to buy peace, otherwise your management authority and freedom of action will be eroded. The following things help and hinder:

Help	*Hinder*
Keep your ear to the ground	Let work issues oust HR issues
Have explicit policies and procedures on important issues and communicate and keep to them	Sweep difficult problems under the carpet
Be consistent in your HR decisions and recognise when you are creating a precedent	Spring surprises on staff without prior consultation
	Make strategic decisions in the heat of a crisis
Gain explicit agreement from staff about anything potentially contentious	Play everything close to your chest
Document clearly key HR decisions	
Take advice from your LEA HR section	

Examples of the pitfalls that have been created by legislation such as the Children Act 1989 and the Employment Act 2002 are as follows:

Staff protection. The horror of an allegation about child abuse has haunted many a teacher. The Act underplays the propensity of children to tell fibs; false accusations are sometimes made with malicious intent. Heads should emphasise that child protection measures have an important secondary purpose of protecting staff.

Maternity, paternity and adoptive rights. The exercise of such rights can play havoc with the smooth running of a school and impair children's education. Because heads have a duty to all stakeholders, they have a difficult balancing act. Providing adequate cover for an absent senior teacher is problematic. However, it can be an opportunity to develop and test young teachers by giving them more responsibility.

EU Working Hours Directive (48 hour week). There are occasions when staff have to work long hours, e.g. on a residential trip. It helps if your management style enables you to draw on a bank of goodwill, but take care not to exploit this, especially if there may be a risk to health. (See the section on the workload agreement.)

Disability Discrimination Act. Employers have a duty to make reasonable adjustments to employment and working conditions so that anyone disabled does not receive less favourable treatment. Discrimination of various kinds can be challenged.

Employment tribunals. The important thing to remember is to keep written evidence demonstrating that the school has complied with statutory procedures though minor procedural errors can be disregarded. Unfair dismissal is one of the main sources of grievance.

Dispute resolution in the workplace. Written disciplinary and grievance procedures must be in place and be known to staff. Employment contracts must refer to them and be up-to-date.

Fixed term employees. Any staff employed on a fixed term contract (limited to four years) have been given new rights, e.g. to training and sick pay, based on the principle that such staff have the right not to be treated any less favourably than permanent staff.

Public Interest Disclosure Act 1999. It is the duty of all staff to take action if they think they have grounds for suspecting colleagues of fraud, corruption, malpractice, abuse, harassment, discrimination or legal or health and safety non-compliance. There need to be open channels of communication with management for dealing with such concerns, and a whistle-blowing policy and procedure communicated to staff. This should include a means of by-passing management to gain access to school governors. By law, there must be no victimization or recrimination: the information that whistle-blowers impart, even if inaccurate, tells a story. Concerns must be thoroughly and dispassionately investigated and remedial action taken if required.

Pending legislation. Watch out for new legislation on discrimination (e.g. on religious, age or sexual orientation grounds), pension rights, consultation, temporary workers (e.g. supply teachers) and dignity at work.

THE WORKLOAD AGREEMENT

In January 2003, the DfES and the Welsh Assembly announced that they had reached agreement with the teacher unions (with the exception of the NUT), and those representing support staff, on implementing a programme which will reduce teacher workload. The intention is to phase in changes to the teacher contract and to employ support staff in greater numbers and in extended roles. The first phase of the agreement will last until 2006, but it is likely that there will be further developments beyond that.

School leaders should produce a development plan for the changes to the workforce which the agreement will necessitate. A major change is the inclusion in the conditions of service requiring heads to ensure that teachers have a reasonable work–life balance. Teachers will, over time, no longer be required to undertake many routine tasks such as bulk photocopying, collecting money and minuting meetings. They will be required to cover for absent colleagues for a maximum of 38 hours per year, and will receive guaranteed planning, preparation and assessment time (PPA). Invigilation of exams will also cease to be the responsibility of teachers (although, in practice, many schools currently employ others to invigilate).

The progress of these changes will, of course, depend on sufficient funding being available to schools to allow them to employ the additional support staff who will be needed, but it is clear that school leaders in their dealings with staff will need to take account of a significant change in the assumptions of what constitutes a teacher's job. The agreement emphasizes the need to raise standards by allowing teachers to concentrate on the core tasks of teaching and learning. Employing larger numbers of support staff also raises issues about their training and development and we would suggest that their needs should be given an equal priority with those of teaching staff.

Developing staff

Fortunately the era is passing when it was assumed that a person equipped with a university degree or a teaching certificate or diploma was equipped for lifelong service as a teacher. Yet appraisal and development procedures, standard practice in most walks of life now, are still not fully understood and are sometimes treated with suspicion in parts of the educational profession. With appraisal now compulsory in maintained schools (through performance management policies), staff development should become gradually more systematic and effective.The NCSL is developing standards for continuous professional development (CPD).

Types of development need

The purposes of staff development may vary, and Figure 6.3 provides a useful clarification. Some needs will be specific to the individual, though two or more individuals may have a similar need; others – usually those related to change – will concern groups of people or even the total organization. Organizational change programmes are dealt with at some length in Part III. In the remainder of this chapter we shall be concerned with the development of individuals and groups.

APPRAISAL AND PERFORMANCE MANAGEMENT

Although appraisal is now mandatory in maintained schools, it is not always effective; indeed in some schools the process has been undermined.

However, a survey (Barber *et al.*, 1995) shows that appraisal has made a major contribution to identifying staff development needs and targeting resources effectively, leading to better focused INSET, in 70 per cent of schools. It has contributed to improved school management and the

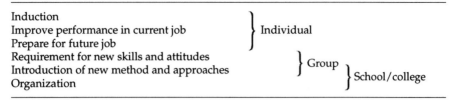

Induction
Improve performance in current job   } Individual
Prepare for future job
Requirement for new skills and attitudes   } Group
Introduction of new method and approaches   } School/college
Organization

Figure 6.3 Type of development need

development of a positive climate, with 70 per cent of teachers regarding it in a very positive light. At least 90 per cent found their appraisal interview to be fair, balanced and effective, but more needs to be done to link appraisal to the school development plan, and to set time-bounded action plans.

Performance management is, or should be, an opportunity for the individual to meet with his or her manager in order to take stock of their individual and joint achievements. As a result of the discussion, there should be agreement on action needed to

(1) improve the performance of the individual;
(2) improve working relationships; and
(3) develop the individual's career.

Well developed performance management systems are of considerable benefit to both the individual and the organization and, indeed, industrial staff will complain if their appraisal interview is overdue. At their best such systems are highly motivational to employees since they

(1) enable them to measure their achievement;
(2) recognize their achievement;
(3) prepare them for advancement;
(4) open up opportunities for personal growth; and
(5) 'clear the air' of problems and build their relationship with their manager.

This has been shown to be true of teachers no less than of employees elsewhere. However, because of the suspicion that appraisal has aroused, it is more than ever necessary in schools to prepare thoroughly for the process of appraisal, especially for classroom observation, the prospect of which is often experienced as threatening.

A new or badly conceived performance management system can be distrusted for many reasons. The appraisal can, for example, be – or be seen as – a judgement on the individual rather than a means to future improvement. Or both parties may be afraid that criticism or differences of view will lead to conflict (see Chapter 7). Or the normal resistance-to-change phenomenon may come into play. For example, arbitrary ground rules may be applied which limit discussion to trivia.

Essentials for effective appraisal

We can identify a number of features of constructive appraisal:

Objectivity. The basis for a constructive discussion is prior agreement on the criteria for effectiveness. A preliminary to appraisal is therefore a job description with criteria and clear objectives of the type discussed in the 'induction' section of this chapter. The focus should then be on results achieved against the criteria and objectives.

Willingness to listen. The manager's approach should not be to tell the staff member what is right or wrong but to ask for his or her views first. Indeed, many good systems will ask the employee to draft his or her answers to the appraisal form on to a separate form before the interview and to use this as a basis for the discussion.

Openness to criticism. Not just the subordinate but also a mature manager will listen very carefully to any criticism and use it as a basis for improvement. To silence criticism is to demonstrate insecurity.

Counselling not judgement. What can we do to improve the *situation* or the *results?*

Action planning. New objectives and development plans carried forward, progressed and reviewed systematically at the next review meeting.

The appraisal record

Headings for an effective appraisal record are as follows:

(1) Development planned/carried out over the last twelve months or since the last appraisal and results.
(2) Results achieved against job criteria and objectives.
(3) Notes on 2. (NB There may be very good reasons for failure to achieve a result.)
(4) Particular strengths.
(5) Areas in which improvement could be made.
(6) Action needed by the individual, his or her manager and/or others to achieve improvement.
(7) Staff member's wishes for the future and action that will be taken to prepare him or her.
(8) Objectives or targets (quantified as far as possible).

It is of course essential that the development actions are followed through.

PLANNING RECORD

Teacher:_____   Team Leader:_____

Date of meeting:_____

Objectives:

1.

2.

3.

Development and training

Resources to support the objectives

Teacher's comments

Teacher:_____(signature)

Team Leader:_____(signature)

Date:_____

ANNUAL REVIEW STATEMENT

Date of Review Meeting:

Teacher:

Team Leader:

	Met	*Further development*
Objectives	(□)	(□)

1.
                                        Yes

2.
                                        Yes

3.

Areas of particular strength (specify)

Areas to be developed

Support and resources to be provided by school (specify)

Teacher's comments

The content of this record has been agreed by:

Teacher:_____(signature)

Team Leader:_____(signature)

Date of receipt of the completed review statement by the teacher:_____

DISCUSSION TOPIC

How can we ensure that

(1) Appraisals are taken seriously?
(2) They lead to real improvements in the school?

MEETING DEVELOPMENT NEEDS

There are many ways of meeting development needs, and courses, if only because they are the most obvious, should be the last that we consider. Other methods are

(1) counselling, coaching and consultancy;
(2) planned reading;
(3) self-development;
(4) projects (e.g. organizing a school event);
(5) change in responsibilities (good for all concerned);
(6) sitting in on meetings (or e.g. being seconded to the Senior Leadership Team);
(7) producing a research report; and
(8) visits.

THE RE-ENTRY PROBLEM

Individuals emerging from any development programme in which they learn techniques, behaviours or approaches new to themselves and/or the school are likely to feel some degree of frustration when they try to apply what they have been taught. The re-entry problem is particularly apparent after an intensive programme away from the school. Ex-autocrats who return determined to be participative managers are often surprised to find that their subordinates do not respond with 'Hallelujah' but are more disposed to say 'He's obviously been on a course; how long will this last?' People feel uncomfortable if one of the 'norms' in their environment appears to change. They are suspicious. Unfortunately, this response may cause the returned trainee to doubt the validity of what he or she has learned and the development effort will have been wasted.

The re-entry problem will be eased if:

(1) Trainees are aware of it, bide their time a little (though not too much!) and make an effort to discuss their intended change with their team and involve them in helping to implement it.
(2) The trainee's superior who, it is hoped, has been a key party to initiating the development, provides support and counselling on and after re-entry. This guidance should be a natural consequence of a pre-event

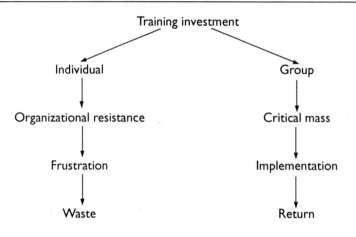

Figure 6.4   Training – investment and return

discussion on why the trainee is undertaking the development and a post-event debriefing. Sadly, these meetings do not always take place and this is a serious dereliction of managerial duty involving waste of training investment and demotivation of staff.

GROUP TRAINING

Many of the re-entry problems are overcome if staff are trained in groups or as a total team, thus creating a common understanding and a 'critical mass' for implementing the learning. School managers should be viewing all their decisions in terms of investment and return; a diagrammatic comparison is given in Figure 6.4.

In-service training days provide a valuable opportunity to

(1) introduce new concepts to a critical mass of staff;
(2) work through cases and exercises to ensure active learning;
(3) debate the concepts and discuss their application;
(4) make plans to implement; and
(5) plan to review implementation at a specified staff meeting or at the next in-service day.

A valuable contribution to school effectiveness can be made by going through such simple exercises as having individuals or departments specify what they

(1) expect from other individuals or departments; and
(2) feel able to offer to other individuals or departments.

This can then be followed by reaching agreement or 'contracts' as to how exactly individuals or departments can improve the service that they provide to their 'internal customers'.

A COHERENT APPROACH

Recruitment, appraisal and training are three activities which should not be seen in isolation from each other but as part of a comprehensive approach to developing a proficient, well motivated and effective staff – the key to a good school. Staff recruitment and development should be largely determined by the values, objectives and curriculum development plans of the school (see Chapters 11 and 13). The means of translating school objectives into individual staff responsibilities are job descriptions, and the techniques for obtaining and developing staff to fulfil the job descriptions effectively are those of selection and appraisal, followed up by development actions including training.

The procedures advocated in this chapter, are not easy to introduce into those schools where they do not already exist, for reasons which include

(1) resistance to ideas which appear to come from America and/or industry and are *ipso facto* (in the view of some) repugnant to the professional world of education, which is 'different';
(2) fear of being labelled incompetent;
(3) dislike of 'paperwork';
(4) discomfort at the idea that learning acquired at university may not be sufficient for a modern teacher;
(5) a feeling that teachers are by their nature people who have an instinct for choosing and developing staff;
(6) 'professional performance should be above judgement' (a misconstruction of what appraisal is about); and
(7) a feeling, perhaps caught from pupils, that training and learning are unpleasant things associated with children rather than mature adults.

For all these reasons, and others which you may like to add, each step forward has to be taken carefully but purposefully and using the strategies to which Part III is devoted. Organizations (and this includes some educational institutions) that have achieved the Investors in People kitemark must demonstrate that their staff are undergoing CPD. 'Learning for life', of which CPD is an example, is being promoted by government agencies. Progressive schools will have noted these national trends and will be building appraisal and development firmly into their management systems.

Finally, it should not be forgotten that a 'comprehensive' approach should include administrative and ancillary staff as well as teachers. Though the recalcitrance of some school-keepers can be attributed in part to local union stances, it should never be forgotten that a show of strength is a fairly normal reaction to being underestimated or taken for granted.

DISMISSING STAFF

It is with some sadness that we have felt it appropriate to add this section to our book. However, whether for reasons of redundancy, incompetence or misconduct, staff dismissals are becoming an increasingly common occurrence in the life of a school and, as responsibility for education is increasingly devolved to governors and heads, particularly of foundation schools, their involvement in dismissals becomes more direct.

The legal position (Employment Protection (Consolidation) Act, 1978)

All employees who work for more than eight hours per week, have not reached retirement age and have been continuously employed for more than two years are protected against 'unfair dismissal'. If such employees are found to have been unfairly dismissed they will be entitled to compensation.

Furthermore they will be deemed to have been unfairly dismissed unless the employer can show that he or she acted for one of the following five reasons:

(1) Incapability or lack of qualification.
(2) Misconduct.
(3) Redundancy.
(4) The continuation of work would have contravened a statute (e.g. a driver who loses his or her licence).
(5) Some other substantial reason.

And that the employer acted *reasonably* in all the circumstances. The burden of proof is on the employer.

Proving that an employer has acted reasonably depends almost entirely on whether the employer has followed the guidelines laid down in the ACAS Code of Practice on Disciplinary Practices and Procedures and whether the school has followed the procedures set out in the contracts of employment issued to its staff.

The decision to dismiss

If a school is contemplating the dismissal of any member of staff, it follows therefore that the head, the chair of governors and whoever else represents the 'employer' in the particular school should first check that the procedures set out in the contract of employment have been, are being and will be followed.

They should then be clear whether the reason for dismissal is misconduct, incapability or redundancy (other reasons are unlikely) and, subject to the contract of employment, should ensure according to the reason for dismissal that the following basic conditions have been met:

(1) *Misconduct:* that the employee has been warned in writing of previous cases of misconduct or has committed an act of gross misconduct. (Even then, suspension is a good idea while the facts are explored.)
(2) *Incapability:* that this has been drawn to the employee's attention in appraisal and other interviews and that he or she has been given all reasonable help to improve performance.

(3) *Redundancy:* that the post occupied by the employee has genuinely ceased to exist as a result of reorganization or that one post from a number of similar posts has ceased to exist and that the particular employee has been chosen for redundancy in accordance with established criteria.

Each school should have policies covering discipline of staff, capability procedures and redundancy. The LEA can provide model policies, often based on nationally negotiated policies, and the headteacher associations also produce model policies.

In cases of redundancy there will be an entitlement to, at least, a statutory payment according to the years of service or an agreed 'early retirement' package. In all cases there may be an entitlement to a period of notice or payment in lieu of notice.

Redundancy is the most common reason given for dismissal, though 'incapability' has become more common as weaknesses are revealed by Ofsted inspections and appraisals. The two can be neatly and humanely combined if the criterion for selecting for redundancy is quality of performance, though proof may be difficult unless very good records have been kept. Unfortunately, 'last in, first out' may have been established, and we may be constrained to lose the very people whom we least want to lose unless we make a stand. The governing body will need, in consultation with staff and the recognized trade unions and teacher associations (whether or not they have members in the school), to determine the criteria to be used when selecting staff for redundancy. The principle to be applied is that of achieving a balance between the needs of the school and the need to be fair in dealing with staff. Designing objective criteria is not enough to guarantee fair and reasonable selection; the criteria must be consistently and fairly applied.

When the above process has identified staff, a clear decision should be taken as to who will inform the employees. We would strongly suggest that the communication that someone is likely to be made redundant should be delegated to one person (e.g. the head), and that if another person requires or is required to be present, that person should intervene as little as possible and certainly be careful not, in any way, to undermine the 'messenger'.

Occasionally a potential redundancy or early retirement package may bring welcome relief. More usually dismissal (or suspension) will cause a trauma rivalled only by bereavement and marital breakdown. In all three situations we can expect the potential victim to move in turn through the phases of

(1) disbelief and refusal to accept;
(2) anger, frustration and despondency;
(3) acceptance (it is hoped!); and
(4) a positive attitude to getting on with life.

These are normal reactions and it is important that the deliverer of the message should expect and be prepared to deal with them by responding to the following guidelines:

(1) Choose a time and place so that there will be no interruptions, no one will be 'in a hurry' and the recipient of the news will have no further commitments that day. (The end of the afternoon is often a good time but, if it has to be earlier, make sure someone is standing by to take over any remaining teaching duties for the day. Friday is ideal as it allows a weekend for the employee to come to terms with the situation.)

(2) Work out and write down the details of any likely financial settlement, when exactly the employment is to terminate if agreed by the governors, when and how, in the case of misconduct, keys are to be handed over, the premises vacated and personal items removed, the nature of any appeals procedure and follow-up.

(3) Summon the person to the appointment at fairly short notice – not more than three hours.

(4) The tone of the interview should be one of helpful formality and should certainly not be preceded by questions about the family or interspersed with pleasantries.

(5) Don't torture the victim by beating around the bush. Come to the point as quickly, simply and firmly as possible, e.g. 'You will be aware that we have to make staff cuts this year and, after careful consideration, we have decided reluctantly to propose to the governors that they make you redundant with effect from...' Pause to allow the message to sink in.

(6) Responses from the 'victim' may be silence (Why me?), anger (What about my family?), tears or other expressions of disbelief, non-acceptance or grief. Do not get involved in lengthy explanations. Do not, above all, suggest that the decision to recommend dismissal is open to review or use phrases like 'We'll see what we can do!' Simply reaffirm slowly, simply, sympathetically ('I know that this must be a blow to you') that the decision to make the recommendation has been very carefully considered and is irreversible as far as you are concerned.

(7) At an appropriate moment explain the details that you have written down about payments, likely termination date, etc., and hand over the piece of paper, having, of course, kept a copy for your files. Explain that a formal letter of confirmation of the decision to recommend dismissal will be sent, that no further work will be expected today, that you or some other appropriate person will be happy to talk again and advise when there has been an opportunity to think things through.

(8) Conclude the interview by offering an opportunity to sit quietly somewhere, preferably with a cup of tea, offer the use of a phone, etc. Generally try to do whatever is helpful in cases of bereavement or trauma, bearing in mind possible dangers of driving home in a highly emotional state.

(9) Make sure that you and other help are available to help the identified person through the stages of acceptance and positive action.

Effecting the dismissal

Governing bodies must give any person whose dismissal is being considered the opportunity to make representations (orally, if requested) to the committee which has been convened to consider the dismissal. A friend or trade union representative may also accompany the member of the staff. There is a right of appeal to an appeals committee, which must comprise governors who have taken no part in the original process.

PICKING UP THE PIECES

You also need to consider the effect of a dismissal on the rest of the school staff, so that you can manage the 'fall-out'. Bad news travels fast and often becomes unhelpfully embellished. The victim will naturally want to shift blame, probably on to you, and to curry sympathy. Although relieved that the axe has not fallen on them, people will wonder who is next, and a mood of apprehension and depression is likely to spread.

If you have played down the prospect of dismissals, the staff will not have had time to adjust to reality. They will need to know enough of the background to be able to understand the rationale for your decision, even if they cannot at first accept it emotionally. They will want to ask questions – especially the union representative. You must provide them with adequate opportunities for access. Although a staff meeting about the matter may daunt you, you will have to face it. Try to resist any attempts to personalize the issue; the reactions you can expect are less a reflection on your personal competence than a natural response to a trauma befalling the school's social system (see the four phases above). Let the anger play itself out but, as soon as you can, move people towards the fourth phase, 'getting on with life'. Practical measures must be taken to fill the gap caused by the victim's departure; just as the arrival of a new recruit provides an opportunity to take stock of existing roles and responsibilities. Can it help to improve something that needed changing anyway?

Your task is to restore morale as soon as possible, and not allow a mood of discontent to take root. Try to direct attention to superordinate objectives: e.g. the need continually to provide the best quality of education with whatever resources are available. If there are precedents in which a former colleague passed through the slough of despond ultimately to reach a higher peak, quote them.

Advising governors as to which close colleagues to make redundant is one of the most stressful situations you are likely to face as a manager. You will probably need a support system to protect your own emotional well-being. A supportive senior management team can provide this, or you may have to turn to someone outside the school.

The positive leadership that you offer the school during its adversity will help to dissolve the negative feelings that usually accompany redundancy situations. This is what the school will look to you for.

PERSONAL APPLICATION

Role play informing a colleague that she/he will be recommended to the governors for dismissal. Then reverse the roles. In each case act as though you or your colleague is being made redundant from the actual job you now hold. You will be surprised how realistic the role play becomes.

DISCUSSION TOPIC

Compare and contrast the functions of recruitment, employment, appraisal, development and dismissal of *staff* with the corresponding functions applied to *pupils*. What does this tell you about ways in which staff management and pupil management could each be improved?

FURTHER READING

Armstrong, M. and Baron, A. (1998) *Performance Management*, Chartered Institute of Personnel and Development, London.

Blandford, S. and Welton, J. (1999) *Managing Professional Development in Schools*, RoutledgeFalmer, London.

Dukes, C. (2002) *Easy Step by Step Guide to Recruiting the Right Staff*, Rowmark, Hayling Island.

Everard, K.B. (1986) *Developing Management in Schools*, Blackwell, Oxford.

Fidler, B. and Cooper, R. (eds) (1992) *Staff Appraisal and Staff Management in Schools and Colleges: a Guide to Implementation*, Longman, Harlow.

Greene K. *et al.* (2002) *Administrative Support Staff in Schools: Ways Forward*: NFER Research Report RR331 for the DfES, NFER, Slough.

Hartle F., Everall K., and Baker C. (2001) *Getting the Best out of Performance Management in your School*, Kogan Page, London.

Horne, H. and Pierce, A. (1996) *A Practical Guide to Staff Development and Appraisal in Schools*, Kogan Page, London.

Kalinauckas, P. and King, H. (1994) *Coaching: Realising the Potential*, Chartered Institute of Personnel and Development, London.

MacKay, I. (1995) *Asking Questions and Listening Skills* (2nd edn), Chartered Institute of Personnel and Development, London.

Montgomery D. and Hadfield N. (1989) *Practical Teacher Appraisal*, Kogan Page, London.

Mumford, A. (1997) *Management Development* (3rd edn), Chartered Institute of Personnel and Development, London.

Parsloe, E. (1995) *Coaching, Mentoring and Assessing: A Practical Guide to Developing Competence*, Kogan Page, London.

Reeves, J., Smith, P., O'Brien, J.P., Tomlinson, H. and Forde, C. (2002) *Performance Management in Education*, Sage, London.

West-Burnham, J. (1998) *Leadership and Professional Development in Schools*, Financial Times Prentice Hall, London.

7

Managing Conflict

A KEY SKILL

The ability to handle conflict is a key factor in managerial success. Whenever we wish to make changes, there is potential for conflict. Furthermore, we not only have to handle situations in which there is conflict between ourselves and one or more other members of staff but may also at times have to resolve conflicts between our subordinates or, most difficult of all, to plot a course through the minefield of 'politics' when two of our peers or superiors are locked in struggle. In the last case, it often happens that one party will deliberately block anything which appears to be the initiative of, or have the backing of, the other, and progress may be difficult. On the other hand, one may have more freedom of action while the opposing parties are locked in battle: a head who is 'at war' with a local authority, his or her governors, a parental committee or a pressure group may be only too pleased if the staff just get on with running the school. The worst situation occurs when no one fills the vacuum caused by his or her preoccupation.

This chapter deals with the nature of conflict, how it builds up, its positive and negative effects and some guidelines for handling conflict situations.

THE VALUE OF CONFLICT

Conflict in the sense of an honest difference of opinion resulting from the availability of two or more possible courses of action is not only unavoidable but also a valuable part of life. It helps to ensure that different possibilities are properly considered, and further possible courses of action may be generated from the discussion of the already recognized alternatives. Also, conflict often means that the chosen course of action is tested at an early stage, thereby reducing the risk of missing an important flaw which may emerge later.

Alfred Sloan, a former president of General Motors, would always refer for further consideration at the next meeting any proposal on which his board members were unanimous. A large proportion of such proposals were, it appears, eventually rejected! (Sloan, 1986).

The absence of conflict may indicate abdication of responsibility, lack of interest or lazy thinking.

REASON AND EMOTION IN CONFLICT

Most conflicts have both rational and emotional components and lie somewhere along a spectrum between genuine conflict of interest on the one hand and personality clash on the other.

Examples of genuine conflict of interest occur, for example, where the vendor of a house seeks the highest price, while the purchaser wishes to pay as little as possible. There is also a genuine conflict of interest between employer and employee about the question of salary.

In both the above cases it is in the interest of both parties to resolve the conflict – otherwise there is no sale in the first case and a strike in the second. In order to negotiate a solution it is necessary to

(1) listen to and understand the point of view and needs of the other party (don't waste time reiterating your own point of view) – try to be fair;
(2) look for trade-offs, i.e. is there something that I can concede to the other party that means more to them than it 'costs' me?; and
(3) focus on issues and facts and avoid personalizing the conflict.

These are the principles of positive negotiation which should produce a 'win–win' situation.

However, it is all too easy for an emotional desire to 'beat the blighter' to creep in and, once it does, it may well spread from one party to the other. At the other end of the spectrum many so-called 'personality clashes' have an element of conflict of interest, and are attributable to role, system or culture problems as much as individual cussedness.

Some conflicts do have their roots in the contestants' personalities; for example, introverts may resent flamboyant behaviour by extroverts, and two deputy heads with different management styles may find it difficult to work together. We find it helps some management teams to deal with such situations when they have jointly received training that incorporates the use of psychometric instruments such as the Myers–Briggs inventory, management style questionnaires – or even so simple an exercise as the Team Role Inventory cited on page 168. However, some people are strongly opposed to the use of any personality tests, despite their potential, in the right hands, for enhancing mutual understanding and professional respect. For this reason it is usually wiser, in the absence of a competent facilitator, to adopt more procedural approaches to the management of conflict.

THE DANGERS OF CONFLICT

Conflict becomes a dangerous and disruptive force whenever personal 'glory' is staked on the outcome. The further the conflict develops, the more 'glory' is staked, the more bitter the conflict becomes and the less easy it is to achieve a solution. Decision-taking is paralysed because neither party dares to make any concessions for fear (probably justified) that these will be seized upon by the other party as a victory and a bridgehead for further advances.

At such a point, we speak of a 'win–lose' situation since this is how the parties approach each issue. In reality the situation is often 'lose–lose' since the parties both do things which are against their own real advantage (as well as wasting their own time on the conflict). Real – or 'superordinate' – goals and interests are lost sight of in the heat of battle. Conflict may be overt, leading to a rehearsal of the same arguments at each meeting. More dangerously it is covert, and the parties do not actually talk to each other about the real issues but canvass support from those whom they believe to be influential. They will each also take actions which affect the other party, without informing him or her.

INTERGROUP COMPETITION

Competition, like conflict, can be of great value to an organization. However, it can easily be destructive. The process can be seen diagrammatically in Figure 7.1. Once intergroup competition develops into a 'win–lose' situation it is even more difficult to handle than between individuals. If any one member of a group departs from the 'party line' he or she may be perceived as a traitor and outcast.

Unfortunately, 'win–lose' conflict with another group is, as shown in Figure 7.1, a very effective means of achieving allegiance within a group. Napoleon and General Galtieri of Argentina both recognized this fact and used it, while the government of Margaret Thatcher, whatever may or may not have been its degree of fault, undoubtedly benefited at the polls in 1983 from the 'Falklands effect'. Subconsciously or consciously, managers who are unsure of themselves will use conflict to win support – often with disastrous consequences for the organization. The head, the local authority, the examining board or another department will be perceived as the 'enemy' who are always doing things wrong: 'Look what they've done now!'

ATTITUDES TO CONFLICT

There are basically four possible attitudes that can be adopted by the participants in any conflict and these are based on permutations of whether or not they believe that they can avoid confrontation, and whether or not they believe that they will be able to reach agreement. The combinations and their results can be represented in tabular form as in Figure 7.2.

The two central columns are self-explanatory. It is worth noting how many so-called 'communication' problems occur because there exists at the root a conflict of view which is not brought into the open. Instead, the parties each 'do their own thing' in the hope of 'getting away with it'. They may also devote a great deal of time to building up support for their point of view and talking *about* the person with whom they are in conflict rather than talking *to* him or her.

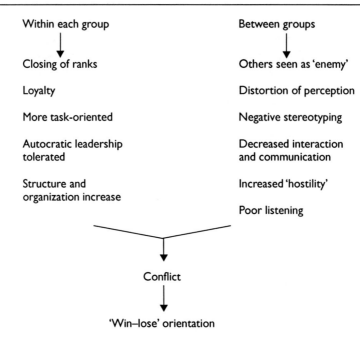

Within each group	Between groups
↓	↓
Closing of ranks	Others seen as 'enemy'
Loyalty	Distortion of perception
More task-oriented	Negative stereotyping
Autocratic leadership tolerated	Decreased interaction and communication
Structure and organization increase	Increased 'hostility'
	Poor listening

Conflict

↓

'Win–lose' orientation

Figure 7.1   Possible consequences of intergroup competition

In the first and fourth columns of Figure 7.2, behaviour will depend on how high or low are the *personal* stakes. These 'stakes' are not necessarily those which have the highest monetary value or are of the greatest importance to the organization, but tend rather to be measured in terms of the ego of the parties. How strongly have they expressed their opinion on this point and to how many people? How many battles have they fought for this principle? Personal stakes may be higher on issues such as car-parking facilities, book stores and dinner duties than they are on curriculum development or provision of new teaching facilities. Indeed, any astute local government official who seeks agreement to a major project will ensure that it is preceded on the council agenda by some highly controversial, but often low-cost, subject such as the provision of an extra facility for old-age pensioners or even an additional public toilet. After a heated debate on such a topic, a high-cost project may well pass 'on the nod'.

With conflicts in the first column (Confrontation Inevitable/Agreement Impossible) the logical approach is to refer the matter to arbitration, i.e. ask the boss to decide. This may well happen if the 'personal stakes' are of medium weight. However, where personal stakes are really high, it often happens that neither party will risk 'losing'. Furthermore, a boss who steps into such a conflict and passes judgement may completely alienate the party against whom he or she decides.

If the personal stakes are low, the decision may be left to 'fate', or the conflict may easily pass into one of the other columns.

	1	2	3	4	
Confrontation	Inevitable	Avoidable	Avoidable	Inevitable	Personal Stakes
Agreement	Impossible	Impossible	Possible	Possible	High
	Power battle	Frequent 'communication' problems and 'muddles' which are more or less frustrating and lead to increasing tensions and stress for all concerned	Fool's paradise	Problem-solving	←→
	Arbitration		Avoiding		
			Smoothing	Compromise	
			Postponement		
	'Fate'		Inaction	Give and take	Low

Figure 7.2 Attitudes to conflict

The attitude most conducive to resolving conflict is, of course, that suggested in column 4. If the stakes are low or medium, it may not be worth while for either party to spend time on in-depth problem-solving, and some quick compromises or give-and-take 'horse-trading' may be the answer. Where problems are a little deeper, however, or where 'horse-trading' and give-and-take are leading to inconsistency and confusion, a more thorough attempt to solve problems will pay off handsomely in terms both of the effectiveness of the organization and of reducing the stress on the protagonists.

As the contents of the columns in Figure 7.2 indicate, your attitude to conflict in general and/or any particular conflict will condition the approach that you adopt. If you would like to examine your own approach in greater depth, you may find the Conflict Orientation Questionnaire (Exercise 4) at the end of this chapter of help. You can either try to be honest in completing it about yourself or ask someone who knows you well to complete it for you. Responsibility charting may also help (p. 280).

PERSONAL APPLICATION

Consider a conflict which exists among two or more people whom you know. List

(1) the issues of interest; and
(2) the emotional or personality aspects of the conflict. Try to describe the attitude of each towards the conflict.

SOLVING PROBLEMS OF CONFLICT

The first point to make is the obvious one that no party to a conflict can solve the problem unilaterally. If the attitude of the other party is firmly locked into columns 1, 2 or 3 of Figure 7.2, the situation may prove impossible and the only resort may be to face the issues and seek arbitration. If a strong 'win–lose' orientation has been developed, resolution may be complicated by the fact that any problem-solving approach or concession may be interpreted either as a sign of weakness (to be exploited to maximum advantage!) or as a subtle 'ploy' to be treated with great caution and mistrust.

For these reasons conflict should be recognized and dealt with as early as possible. If you have a problem with someone, go immediately to talk to him or her, before acrimony builds up. If you think of the person you least want to meet and the thing that you least want to do, these are probably your first two priorities for the day!

If acrimony has built up, it may be necessary to choose your time well and to spend some time in making it clear that you really do want to solve the conflict. Some friend of both parties may be needed to act as a catalyst, to reassure both parties that intentions are sincere and to act as mediator or 'process consultant'. In conflicts between other members of staff, particularly those reporting to you, your job as a manager may well be to step in as the 'process consultant', to try to understand the point of view of each protagonist individually and to bring each one into a 'problem-solving' state of mind. Having set the stage for a meeting to solve the conflict, the following principles should guide the discussions:

(1) The parties will talk to each other as openly as possible about the real issues that concern them.
(2) They will state their aims, views and feelings openly but calmly, and try to avoid reiteration.
(3) They will try to put the conflict into the context of superordinate goals and of the interest of the total organization (a 'helicopter' view). They will look for common goals.
(4) They will focus on future action rather than on the events of the past.
(5) They will listen carefully to each other's point of view and seek to understand it. To ensure that their understanding of it is correct, they may rephrase the other's point of view. However, this must be a genuine attempt at restatement and not a parody of what was said.
(6) They will try to avoid moving on to the attack or defence.
(7) They will try to build on each other's ideas.
(8) They will trust each other's good faith and try to act in good faith (see the 'OK matrix' discussed in Chapter 8).
(9) They will plan some clear actions to follow the discussion specifying *who* will do *what* by *when*. (This is extremely important and may easily be forgotten in the euphoria of finding that the other party is not as unreasonable as had been anticipated!)
(10) They will set a date and time to review progress *and will keep to this at all costs*.

If a third party is acting as a 'process consultant' in such a meeting, his or her role should not be to comment on the issues (this is a dangerous trap) but simply to draw attention to any departure from these principles.

A number of useful structures can be used to help individuals or groups to overcome cultural reluctance to put conflict 'on the table'. These structures have the twin values of

(1) enabling strong feelings and prejudices to be expressed in a form which is less antagonistic than the spoken word. The feelings become factual (though possibly hurtful) data rather than barbed attacks; and
(2) asking for 'balance' in the data, i.e. what we like as well as what we dislike and what we do as well as what they do.

Two of these structures are set out at the end of this chapter, namely

(1) Role Revision Strategy (Exercise 5); and
(2) Image Exchange (Exercise 6).

HANDLING ORGANIZATIONAL CONFLICTS

Conflict and frustration will often centre on the way in which a school, college or department is being run, 'the way things happen here'. Such conflicts have a tendency to build up in any organization, and they can assume more and more importance. There is often no coherent opinion about how things *should* be done – just a generally negative attitude towards the way in which things *are* being done.

For the head or head of department, the situation is very frustrating, and the feeling grows that the staff are working not for you but against you. If you bend to the suggestions of one body of opinion, another group will be even less satisfied. You feel misunderstood by everyone and alone in trying to make the organization work. You may, rightly, feel the need to bring key staff together to examine the way in which the school or department operates and, it is hoped, to get commitment to an agreed form of amended practices. The trouble is that any such meeting can descend into chaos with all the old arguments and prejudices rehearsed.

Exercise 7 at the end of this chapter presents a structure which has been found helpful in channelling a review of school organizational practices. It may be amended to suit particular circumstances, but amendment should always be towards highlighting controversial issues, never towards avoiding them. The 'school review' uses a number of useful techniques:

(1) 'Gap' theory – asking people to state their ideal view and compare it with their actual perceptions. (The 'gap' between the two is what then has to be bridged.)
(2) Categorizing and quantifying views of what is wrong by focusing analysis round a structure of statements – always, of course, with the possibility of formulating a group statement which does not correspond exactly with any of the alternatives.
(3) Concretizing statements round 'for instances'. (These should be recorded in the 'notes' column within the exercise.)

The effect of these techniques is to take much of the heat out of the discussion and to enable deep-seated problems to be treated at a rational level. There is always a fear that individuals may be hurt by such a process, especially the head who feels responsible for the processes under review. For this reason it is important that a review meeting should be instigated from the top of the group, with a genuine desire to understand people's feelings. Provided this is done, members of the group can usually be relied on to have a high concern for feelings and, as the 'we' spirit develops, to be able to compensate for painful home truths by supportiveness or willingness to put things right. But it is important to prepare the group by agreeing that the meeting will be based on the positive principles set out above.

Finally, it is important not to involve too many levels – or too many people – in such a review. Two levels are ideal. As soon as three or more are involved, great care has to be taken not to lay all problems unfairly at the door of the intermediate level. In a meeting involving head, deputy head and heads of department, there is real risk that the deputy head will be blamed for communication failures, for 'failing to pass on the message'.

PREVENTING UNNECESSARY CONFLICT

Certain behaviours are liable to provoke an unnecessary degree of conflict. The social policies of the European Union – and many of the member states – speak of the difference between a 'harmony model' and a 'conflict model' of relationships. In the *conflict* model the parties

(1) are concerned only to protect their own interests. 'It is the task of management to manage in the interests of the employer and the job of the unions to look after the interests of their members', is a statement made both by some managers and by some trade unionists, and there is a risk that teachers who feel that their profession is under governmental attack (from right or left) may adopt similar attitudes; and
(2) involved in taking or implementing decisions will take up their positions, make their decision, possibly try to sell them to the other parties and, if necessary, fight.

In the *harmony* model, on the other hand, the aim is

(1) collective responsibility both for the interests of the school and for the individual interests of staff; and
(2) participative decision-taking in which the views of interested parties are sought out *before* coming to a decision (see Chapter 4). This allows differences of opinion to be handled before a position is taken up from which retreat means loss of face.

GUIDELINES FOR HANDLING CONFLICT

In order to minimize the destructive effects of conflict, the following principles should be observed:

(1) Maintain as much communication as possible with any party whose ideas, interests or attitudes appear to be in conflict with your own. Do not postpone discussing the problem in the hope that it will go away – it will usually get worse.
(2) Refrain from the temptation to talk *about* the other person behind his or her back. Do not try to build up an army of opinion on your side. Talk *with* the other person.
(3) If you see signs of interdepartmental conflict, try to establish projects, on either neutral or sensitive subjects, in which individuals from the various departments will work together. As a general principle, it is good to prevent the build-up of rigid departmental demarcation by having cross-departmental groups. Where there is competition for scarce resources –

computers, overhead projectors, rehearsal space, secretarial services or even money – it can be far more fruitful to ask a cross-departmental group of keen junior staff to meet to propose a policy to the head and heads of department than to proceed via the traditional route of inviting each department to submit its claim and thereby close ranks in battle order. Such joint projects are also an excellent personal-development activity.

(4) Try to avoid all the phenomena of the 'win–lose' orientation, and above all try to see all sides of a dispute, remembering that most staff will only behave negatively if they believe they are under threat or attack.

(5) Try to avoid setting up conflict situations through the 'reward' structure and, if they are already in the structure, change them. If two teachers see themselves as competing for your favour, a lot of their effort may be directed into 'political' activity and they may each become high consumers of your time in 'showing off' rather than getting on quietly with the job. Ensure that you recognize results and not flattery or 'show'.

CONFLICT-MANAGEMENT SKILLS

If we are to be effective managers of conflicts to which we are a party, and of conflicts between other members of staff, we need to develop certain attitudes and skills. The only way to develop these is by self-control and practice.

First, we need the ability to confront, to be able to say 'No' when a difference of opinion emerges. We should show by our attitude that we are open to reason, logical discussion and problem-solving. Second, we must be able to present our ideas and feelings clearly, concisely, calmly and honestly. Third, we need to develop listening skills, which include the ability to show someone that we understand what has been said by 'playing it back'. We also need to develop the habit of asking questions rather than making statements, remembering that successful salespeople (of products or ideas) are those who ask the most questions. Fourth, we need skill in evaluating all aspects of the problem, understanding the pressure on the other party, 'helicoptering' above the limited perspective which we might normally adopt. Finally, we need to be able to articulate the common goals which should help both parties to rise above their differences about methods to look to future achievement rather than past frictions.

It is in managing conflict that 'emotional intelligence' really comes into its own – although it is also relevant in many other management situations. The concept was popularized in Daniel Goleman's best-seller (Goleman, 1996; see also Goleman, 1998) and it is particularly useful in countering the paramountcy of the intellect, which often typifies educational institutions. Emotional intelligence is claimed to be twice as important as IQ plus technical skills for outstanding performance.

Emotional intelligence is defined as 'the capacity for recognizing our own feelings and those of others for motivating ourselves and managing emotions well in ourselves and our relationships'. Thus it includes self-control, anger management, zeal, persistence and, above all, empathy. Such skills can be learnt, and this can help to prevent unnecessary conflict, e.g. when giving criticism, dealing with aggressive children or influencing moods. Almost any sort of relationship (including marriage) can be improved by the application of emotional intelligence. You can assess your own by visiting the following website: www.EISGlobal.com.

PERSONAL APPLICATION

A useful exercise is to think about some conflict in which you are involved and to try very deliberately to understand the position of your adversary or adversaries. Why are they behaving as they are? What are the pressures on them? What do they wish to achieve? What common goal is there? What possibilities are there for accord? Often it can be helpful to discuss your perceptions with a colleague. Much learning and many solutions have been achieved in this way.

DISCUSSION TOPIC

What does the group find to be the major causes of conflict? What are the implications for working and social relationships?

FURTHER READING

Fisher, R. and Brown, S. (1989) *Getting Together*, Random House Business Books, London.
Fisher, R. and Ury, W. (1997) *Getting to Yes*, Arrow, London.
Katz, N.H. and Lawyer, J.W. (1994) *Preventing and Managing Conflict in Schools*, Corwin Press, Thousand Oaks, Calif.
McBride, P. and Maitland, S. (2002) *The EI Advantage*, McGraw-Hill, Maidenhead.
Sloan, A.P. (1986) *My Years with General Motors*, Sidgwick & Jackson, London.

EXERCISE 4: Conflict Orientation Questionnaire

Score each of the following questions (and/or ask someone who knows you well to score them for you) on a scale of 4 (very often) to 1 (hardly ever). You may find that your answers would vary according to the person or situation: in this case you should initially try to score your conflict behaviour overall, and later you may find it useful to redo the test for each separate conflict.

When in conflict do you:

(1) Make your views and requirements very clear
from the outset?   4 3 2 1
(2) Start by asking the other party what you have
done wrong?   4 3 2 1
(3) Avoid meeting the other party?   4 3 2 1
(4) Tell other people about your problem?   4 3 2 1
(5) Seek the support of other people?   4 3 2 1

(6)	Try to split the difference?	4 3 2 1
(7)	Apologize for having to raise the issue?	4 3 2 1
(8)	Listen carefully to what is said by the other party?	4 3 2 1
(9)	Become aggressive?	4 3 2 1
(10)	Keep calm?	4 3 2 1
(11)	Explore the other party's point of view?	4 3 2 1
(12)	Try to placate the other party?	4 3 2 1
(13)	Go for a quick 'deal'?	4 3 2 1
(14)	Speak more than the other party?	4 3 2 1
(15)	Focus on a series of possible solutions?	4 3 2 1
(16)	Look for a fair solution?	4 3 2 1
(17)	Let the other party have his or her own way?	4 3 2 1
(18)	Play down the importance of the conflict?	4 3 2 1
(19)	Act as if there is no problem?	4 3 2 1
(20)	Restate common interests?	4 3 2 1
(21)	Try to get your own way?	4 3 2 1
(22)	Apologize readily?	4 3 2 1
(23)	Shift responsibility from yourself?	4 3 2 1
(24)	Try to find a compromise?	4 3 2 1
(25)	Give way on some issues in return for others?	4 3 2 1

Scoring the questionnaire

When you have completed the questionnaire, transfer each of your scores to the appropriate column below:

Avoiding Question Score	Smoothing Question Score	Fighting Question Score	Compromising Question Score	Problem-solving Question Score
3	2	1	6	8
4	7	5	13	10
17	12	9	16	11
19	18	14	24	15
23	22	21	25	20
Total	Total	Total	Total	Total

Interpreting your score

You now have a score for five different behaviours or orientations which are among those listed in Figure 7.2. They are set out below and correspond to the management style diagram in Figure 2.2.

As with management style, and as we have indicated in this chapter, we should have an underlying high concern for both relationships and results (problem-solving). Have I really 'won' if I have sown the seeds of vengeance in my opponent? Has a conflict that I have smoothed over or avoided really gone away? Do I feel satisfied with the outcome?

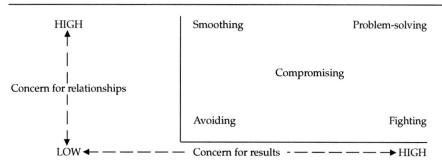

However, there are occasions on which it may be appropriate to adopt different *behaviours* and some guidelines on these occasions are set out below.

Avoiding

This involves side-stepping conflict, postponing confrontation, hoping the problem will go away or pretending it does not exist. It usually imposes stress on all concerned, causes communication problems and means that decisions are made by default. However, it has a positive use where

(1) the issue is a 'storm in a teacup' and will pass away of its own accord;
(2) you have no power to achieve a solution, or the potential damage of confrontation outweighs the benefits of the solution;
(3) time is needed for cooling off or to gather information; and
(4) others are better equipped to solve the problem than you are and you expect that they will step in.

Fighting

This may mean standing up for what you believe to be right or simply trying to score a personal victory. It involves bringing emotional, intellectual, hierarchical or any other form of power to bear in order to get your own way and implies a lack of respect for other people's interests. It often breeds resentment, 'back-stabbing' and deviousness or, if your opponent is of equal status, a 'shouting match'. It can, however, be used to good effect where

(1) there is an emergency calling for quick, decisive action;
(2) unpopular actions have to be enforced; and
(3) you know that you are right and the other party is not prepared to listen to reason or will take advantage of any attempt to compromise or problem-solve.

Smoothing

This approach is unassertive and co-operative. It puts the interests of others first. Overuse of this approach can cause other people to lose respect for you and your opinions, to ride roughshod over you, and discipline may become lax. However, the approach is appropriate where

(1) you realize that you are in the wrong;
(2) others are reticent to put forward their ideas and you wish to show that you respect their views and wish to hear them; and
(3) the issue is very important to the other person and you wish to build up credit.

Compromising
Those who compromise seek expedient, quick solutions that satisfy both parties. Focus is often less on the quality of the solution or on finding a creative solution than on finding middle ground. A compromise culture leads to 'wheeling and dealing' that may be at the expense of principles and values. However, compromise can be used where

(1) two opponents of equal power are committed to mutually exclusive goals;
(2) the issues are moderately important but there is no time to go into problem-solving mode. Often compromise can be used as a temporary expedient; and
(3) the conflict centres on a false dichotomy, an example of which is given on page 16; can a polarized relationship be transformed into an orthogonal relationship?

Problem-solving
This involves working with the other party or parties to try to find a solution which goes as far as is possible towards mutual satisfaction. It involves thoroughly exploring each other's interests and concerns and looking for creative alternative courses of action. The difficulty is that this takes time and energy and may be an excuse for postponing decisions which need to be taken. Problem-solving should be used when

(1) issues are too important to be compromised;
(2) long-standing conflict needs to be resolved;
(3) high commitment and understanding are important; and
(4) the quality of the decision is important and all possible insights, perspectives and ideas need to be taken into account so as to produce and test creative solutions.

EXERCISE 5: Role Revision Strategy

This technique is usually used with individuals and is described for such, but it can readily be adapted for intergroup application. There are seven steps which may be grouped as follows:

Steps

$\left. \begin{array}{c} 1 \\ 2 \end{array} \right\}$ problem identification

3 ⎫
4 ⎬ problem communication

5 ⎫
6 ⎬ negotiating resolutions
7 ⎭

Step 1

The facilitator asks each participant to produce a list of the things he or she would like the other person(s) to

(1) do less of;
(2) do more of; and
(3) continue doing as now.

These things should be specific actions or behaviours. The list should include everything salient to the situation; nothing important should be suppressed.

Step 2

The participants then mark their own list to indicate how strong is their desire for change in each item listed, in order to facilitate improved collaboration.

Step 3

The participants read each other's lists and through discussion seek to clarify the changes that the other person(s) are demanding. The facilitator may well say: 'Can you give a specific example of when "X" has happened in the past, and you don't want it to happen in the future?'

Step 4

Each participant thinks for about two minutes about what the other participant(s) are demanding, and puts a '+' against the things he or she thinks he or she can do something about; also a '–' against things he or she does not agree with, or will not change without a quid pro quo.

This completes the first round of the role revision strategy. It is based on the assumption that the status quo is held steady by forces (whatever people are now doing, they have reason for it) which must change if behaviour is to change. One of these forces is likely to be misapprehension of what the other people want. There are others, however. To achieve change, there must be a change in the driving or restraining forces (see force-field analysis in Chapter 17), and that change must be perceived or experienced by the individual. A change strategy is needed to bring this about.

It is unrealistic to expect one participant to change his or her behaviour unless the other participants do *something different* – like giving help, or putting pressure on. One cannot assume that people of goodwill will change their behaviour merely as a result of a discussion. So we have to ask: 'What am I prepared to do to influence others to change their behaviour?' The second round of the strategy is, therefore, to obtain answers to this question.

Step 5

The facilitator may explain the foregoing, and will ask the participants to identify the areas where they think they can make progress. It is best not to tackle the tougher things first, unless there is a high degree of trust, but to go for something in the middle, success in dealing with which will lay the groundwork for dealing with the bigger issues.

Step 6

The facilitator asks the participants to talk about what could be done in the area selected, and constructs a chart under two headings:

Desires   *Difficulties*

The facilitator encourages the participants to offer help in overcoming the difficulties that emerge.

Step 7

When pseudo-agreement has been reached, the facilitator gets the participants to specify exactly who is going to do what by when. There is likely to be a further meeting to review progress, and this should be set up. Also there needs to be agreement on the first step to be taken to deal with those issues which have not yet been processed to quid pro quo.

Thus the process is iterative, and success in the first round encourages the participants to tackle the more difficult issues.

EXERCISE 6: Image Exchange

This technique is normally used with groups and is described as such, but it can also be applied to an interpersonal situation.

Step 1

The facilitator explains the phenomenon of stereotyping in such a way as to 'blame' it not on the shortcomings of the individuals or the groups, but on the organization structure; stereotyping is the natural outcome of a situation in which any two groups that have to relate are deprived (for example, through overwork) of social contact. He or she might give examples of a humorous nature because by setting a mood of lightheartedness he or she can often dispel apprehensions. Indeed, doing this exercise sometimes gives rise to much hilarity, which is an effective solvent for bitterness.

Step 2

Each group goes to a separate room, equipped with flipcharts, to produce two lists, on separate flipcharts:

(1) A list that characterizes (even caricatures) what they think and feel about the other group – their outlooks, their aims, their *modus operandi*, etc. Candour is to be encouraged.
(2) A list of what they predict the other group will be writing about them, trying to anticipate what the other group dislikes about them.

A variation on the procedure is to produce a third list, of how they would *like* to be seen by the other group. If there is a cartoonist in the group, it is often helpful (and entertaining) to illustrate the lists.

Step 3

The two groups come together, the flipcharts are displayed, and each group in turn reads out and clarifies what it has written about the other group in the first list. No discussion is allowed but questions of clarification may be put. Then each group in turn reads out and explains their second list similarly.

Step 4

The groups return to their rooms, each with all the lists describing their own group, and they discuss which items are based on incorrect perceptions or failures to communicate.

Some items will have a rational explanation which can probably be conveyed to the other group in the expectation that they will exclaim 'Ah, so *that's* why you always keep doing so-and-so!' – or some such remark. It is probable, however, that there will be other items that cannot quite so easily be explained away, and constitute a genuine source of friction or a problem that needs to be resolved – such as a chronic shortage of resources to do what the other group needs. These items are listed, and placed in order of priority.

Step 5

The groups reconvene, share their lists, dispose of the 'easy' items (it is hoped), and then construct from the more difficult items a single list of problems to be resolved, in an agreed order of priority. They then draw up a plan for dealing with those problems that they agree to tackle. This plan should spell out who does what by when.

Step 6

Still meeting together, the two groups agree on a process for monitoring progress towards solving the problems, for example, regular exchange of written reports, dates for follow-up meetings to review progress, and any meeting to be held after several months have elapsed to return to the particularly difficult problems on which agreement to work on could not be obtained.

The exercise proves more valuable if carried out in a congenial setting where it can be followed by informal social intercourse between members of the two groups – for example, in the bar of a residential centre. In such a setting, the 'ogres' become more like us, taking on a human face, and this lends credence to the facilitator's suggestion in Step 1, that the source of intergroup problems is usually structural.

A similar exercise can be carried out when three or more groups are involved, but if this gives rise to unwieldy numbers, it can be combined with a 'fish-bowl' approach, in which the key representatives (for example, managers) carry out Steps 3, 5 and 6, with an outer circle of the remaining participants looking on. Subgroups of members drawn from each of the main groups can meet separately at the problem-solving stage, following Step 6 to work on the problem(s) allocated to them.

EXERCISE 7: School Review

Introduction

The aims
For a school review these are to

(1) examine frankly the way in which the school and its staff currently operate;
(2) diagnose problems and opportunities for improvement;
(3) set objectives for organizational improvement in the light of the diagnosis; and
(4) (starting from the second review) examine progress towards the achievement of the organizational objectives set at the last review.

Organizing the review
In the top team (i.e. the head, the deputy head and the heads of department) responsibility for organizing review sessions lies with the head. In other groups the responsibility is that of the senior member of the group, though any other member should feel free to 'trigger' the process.

The time needed for the meeting will vary according to the size of the group, but usually six hours should be set aside for even the smallest group. It is very important that staff arrange not to be disturbed during the meeting.

The questionnaires below should be handed out by the head or senior group member before the meeting, and individuals should be asked to complete the checklist, the group development assessment and the intergroup problems questionnaire and to bring them to the meeting. There should be no consultation with other members of the group.

Checklist

Under each of the headings below are listed five alternative ways in which a work group may operate. All or most of the statements have probably been true of your own work group to some degree at some time.

Under each heading rank the statements in order (1 = 'best', 5 = 'worst') according to how well they describe the situation

(1) in your own work group (i.e. the group to be reviewed at the meeting); and
(2) which should ideally obtain in your work group.

	Actual ranking	*Ideal ranking*	*Notes*

1. *Decision-taking:* Decisions which affect the group as a whole are
   (a) taken by the head/department head;
   (b) allowed to drift;
   (c) thoroughly thrashed out in the group under the head/departmental head leadership;
   (d) left to members of the group. The head/departmental head 'falls into line'; and
   (e) usually based on compromise or established precedent.

2. *Communication*
   (a) The work of the group is hampered or effort wasted through serious lack of communication.
   (b) Too much time is spent in exchanging irrelevant information. There is too much 'gossip' and not enough action.
   (c) Most communication is 'vertical', e.g. between the head/departmental head and individual subordinates.
   (d) Most communication is 'horizontal'. Subordinates exchange information and ideas but there is an absence of upward and downward interchange.
   (e) There is a steady exchange of relevant ideas, information and problems among all members of the work group.

*Actual   Ideal
ranking   ranking   Notes*

3. *New ideas*
   (a) The group's main aim is to maintain
       the 'status quo'. Crises are dealt with as
       they arise.
   (b) The group constantly takes up new ideas,
       but it fails to carry them through.
   (c) Individuals who come up with new ideas
       or show initiative are 'left to get on with it'.
   (d) All members of the group are
       constantly on the lookout for possible
       improvements and long-term solutions
       to problems. After careful evaluation these
       are systematically implemented with the
       active co-operation of the whole group.
   (e) Initiative or impetus comes from above or
       outside the group. The group responds.

4. *Relationships with other groups*
   (a) The group resents intrusions, advice
       or criticism from the outside. Group
       members staunchly defend group ideas,
       action and policies.
   (b) There is a free exchange of information,
       ideas and help with those outside the
       group and with other groups.
       Competition with other groups is
       never detrimental to the effectiveness of
       the total organization. Responsibility for
       action is accepted by all.
   (c) Some members of the group are apt to
       dissociate themselves from group actions
       when dealing with others outside the group.
   (d) Efficiency is hampered by destructive
       competitiveness and lack of co-operation
       between this group and certain others.
   (e) The status of the work group is more
       important than the well-being of the
       organization.

5. *Review*
   (a) The group seldom examines the way
       in which it has operated. Patterns of
       work are either established or establish
       themselves.
   (b) Some group members discuss among
       themselves shortcomings in the group's

operations and relationships with other
groups but are afraid of hurting feelings
or causing upheaval by bringing
these shortcomings into the open.

(c) There is a 'shake-up' from time to time,
especially when there has been a
clear case of inefficiency.

(d) The workings of the group are
examined frequently and frankly; all
members seek ways of improving efficiency.
The group learns from experience.

(e) The group usually manages to blame
some other department for any failures.
It is content that it has played its
own part satisfactorily.

6. *Objectives*

(a) Group objectives and each person's role
are regularly examined and realistic
targets are set to which all feel
committed. Objectives are updated as
circumstances change.

(b) While individuals are concerned for
their own objectives, there is little
concern for group objectives. Objectives
encourage competition rather than
co-operation.

(c) Objectives either are not set, are ignored
or are so easily attainable as to have no
real value in improving performance or
targeting effort.

(d) As reports and salary increases depend
largely on achievement of fixed, annual
objectives, these are pursued irrespective
of changing conditions or long-term
considerations.

(e) Effort and time are devoted to trivialities
which contribute little to the fulfilment
of the team's most vital functions.

7. *Planning*

(a) Many plans are made but few are
executed.

(b) After careful consideration of
circumstances, plans are made to
which the group feels committed

Actual | *Ideal*
ranking | *ranking* | *Notes*

and which enable work and development
to proceed in a timely and
systematic fashion.
(c) Plans are imposed and must be strictly
adhered to.
(d) Panics are frequent through lack of
adequate planning.
(e) Work follows an established pattern.

8. *Commitment*
(a) All members of the group feel
personally committed to achieving
the highest possible standard of
performance.
(b) There is more group loyalty than job
commitment.
(c) People do only as much as is required.
(d) The head/departmental head drives the
group hard.
(e) Members of the group are anxious to
avoid any criticisms of their operation.

9. *Responsibility*
(a) Responsibilities are clearly defined,
are logical and are accompanied
by the appropriate authority to take
decisions.
(b) Many decisions which should be
taken by an individual are referred
to a group or to a higher level than
necessary.
(c) Too many decisions which should
be taken as a group are taken by
individuals without adequate
consultation.
(d) Responsibility and authority are far
from clear.
(e) Responsibilities have become
established in a pattern which is not
the most effective.

10. *Use of resources*
(a) Financial and other resources are
allocated to group members in
accordance with a well established
pattern. They deploy these resources
as they think fit.

(b) In some areas money has to be 'used
     up' while in others it is sadly lacking.
(c) Resource allocation is too flexible and
     money is made available to those areas
     in which the group agrees that it can be
     of most benefit to the total system.
(d) Resource allocation is a matter of great
     controversy. Individuals each bid for as
     much as can be got irrespective of the
     needs of others.
(e) Many ventures are undertaken without
     full consideration of the financial
     implications.

Group development assessment

(1) List what you believe to be at present the group's three main
     organizational problems or opportunities for improvement.
(2) If the group has had a previous review, list
     (a) the organizational objectives then set for the group; and
     (b) your own personal and organizational objectives.
(3) To what extent do you consider that the above objectives have been
     attained by
     (a) the group?
     (b) you personally?

Intergroup problems questionnaire

(1) With what other groups does this group have to work most closely?
(2) What problems prevent more effective co-operation between this group
     and any of the above groups?
(3) Which three of these problems most impair effectiveness?
(4) How might the above three problems be solved?

8

Managing Yourself

THE MANAGER AS A RESOURCE

So far we have emphasized the fact that the manager is an organizer, a director, a controller of resources. Nevertheless, even in fulfilling these functions we are ourselves resources of the organization, and our managerial function extends to the control of our own time, skills and attitudes, to coping with stress, to the direction of our own efforts and to the development of our competence.

We have indicated already many of the ways in which we need to control our managerial behaviour in order to be effective in, for example, motivating others, taking decisions, participating in meetings and handling conflicts. This chapter is intended to focus on some key principles and to bring in some guidelines and techniques which have not been discussed elsewhere.

THE USE AND ABUSE OF TIME

It is very easy to be very busy doing the wrong thing. Those colleagues who are perpetually racing against time are seldom the most effective, and it should be recognized that just 'thinking' is one of the most positive uses of time. It is then that we are able to 'helicopter' above the hurly-burly of the school and do our managerial job of planning, organizing and controlling to make the best use of the resources available to us to achieve the desired result. Yet some teachers feel guilty if they are not seen to be bustling here and there, always doing something 'urgent'. Often the 'urgency' has arisen because they have failed to think ahead or act earlier, and they find themselves on the treadmill of crisis management. Managers will often find themselves doing things which they could – and should – have delegated if they had given the matter their attention earlier – but then they were too busy with the last crisis.

A great deal of effort can be expended to no avail. Geoffrey Morris was called in some years ago as a consultant to the head of a large comprehensive school, in which crisis management had developed to the point at which everyone was calling meetings at short notice, with the result that less than 50 per cent of the involved parties could attend because they were at other meetings. Further meetings, therefore, had to be called with many similar results, and the amount of wasted time and energy was almost unbelievable. Frustration and stress were apparent at every level. In such a situation it is very hard to get off the crisis treadmill, because no one has time to think about solving the real problems.

In this situation, despite the 'urgency' of the crisis, we had to lay down a programme of discussion, training and eventually 'school review' (Exercise 7, p. 116) *well in advance* (a novelty in that school), and insist that it had absolute priority over commitments which might subsequently arise. Three months later the effect of the programme on the running and atmosphere of the school was dramatic. The time taken actually to sort things out was about 8 hours per departmental or pastoral manager, plus 12 hours each of the time of both the head and the deputy head, spread over six weeks.

Much of the success of the programme could be attributed to group work to establish new guidelines for managing the school. However, it was also essential that each manager should learn to manage his or her own time.

ESTABLISHING PRIORITIES

In determining how we use our time, we should be clear about our priorities and relate our activities to these. We should recognize that there are different kinds of priority, and the different categories have to be treated differently. The critical distinction is between what is urgent and what is important. It may well be that in time sequence we have to deal with the urgent before the important, but we must not be lured into the trap of being caught up in the urgent to the exclusion of the important. Are all the 'urgent' matters really so? Should I respond to every request to see me by allocating the next available slot of free time, or should I deliberately allocate a period of time to the important and keep that thinking, organizing or writing time as carefully as I would an appointment with Mr X? Do I myself have to deal with the things that are presented to me as urgent (or important for that matter) or can I delegate some of them, perhaps thereby motivating and developing one of my staff?

Within the 'important' category we need to think in terms of 'long term' and 'short term', with all the intermediate possibilities. If a priority is long term, we need to review the shorter-term implications and lay down the intermediate steps. These then need 'do-by' dates and allocation of time.

CRITERIA FOR EFFECTIVENESS

A useful background to priorities is to ask yourself what your job is really about. In Chapter 6 we wrote of the importance of establishing with staff the criteria against which the performance of each one is judged. Even if there is no machinery for doing this with your own supervisor, the exercise is worth carrying out for your own guidance and it is well worth going beyond the level of the *actual* criteria by also asking what

(1) *ought* to be the criteria against which you are judged in the interests of the organization?

(2) personal criteria do you additionally apply in judging your performance? (For example, are you managing to achieve goals which may be related to your own interests, rather than to those of the organization?)

A format for carrying out such an analysis is in Exercise 8 at the end of this chapter.

TIME-MANAGEMENT TECHNIQUES

If we have used a process such as the above to establish our priorities or if we just know them instinctively, the critical factor in management success is, of course, to control our use of time in relation to our priorities. A number of well tried techniques are available to help us to do this. Two of these relate to an analysis of the recent past, namely

(1) use-of-time analysis (Exercise 9 at the end of this chapter), which offers a rough-and-ready way of analysing your impression of how your time is being spent; and

(2) time log (Exercise 10 at the end of this chapter), which enables a detailed analysis of the use of time over a relatively short period.

Both these documents are intended for occasional use and enable us to learn from what has happened and, repeated at a later date, to assess improvement. In each case the objective is, of course, to use 'gap' theory by comparing our actual use of time with the way in which we ought to use it, in line with our real priorities. Having learned from the past, the important thing is the continuous control of the present and future, and for this we need to build into our daily routine some basic administrative disciplines, i.e.

(1) an action diary;
(2) a daily action sheet; and
(3) project planning.

These disciplines are neither elaborate nor original, and most managers and headteachers come to use them sooner or later without any need for prompting from writers on management.

The action diary

This is a development of the appointments diary and the discipline consists simply in having the diary (preferably of the 'desk' variety) always in one's briefcase (possibly with a small emergency diary also in one's pocket or handbag) and writing down as they occur not only future appointments but also dates by which things have to be done. Periodically, at least weekly, the diary should be reviewed and slots of time allocated for items such as 'prepare examination papers', 'plan overseas visit', 'practise with computer' or even 'administration and organization'.

The daily action sheet

This is an equally fundamental discipline. It can be a separate notebook or can be incorporated into a suitably large action diary. Here the discipline consists in starting each day by

(1) writing a list of all the things that should be done that day;
(2) reviewing the previous day's list and carrying forward anything not done;
(3) numbering the items in order of time priority (i.e. the order in which you hope to tackle them); and
(4) starring (or whatever other system you like to use) to indicate importance.

Project planning

This is the final basic discipline which consists in thinking through, for a project involving a series of action points or check points, what has to be done by when and

(1) recording the total project plan on a sheet of paper or in a file;
(2) publishing whatever parts of the plan others may need to know;
(3) recording 'do-by' dates in the action diary; and
(4) recording slots of time in the action diary for doing the actions.

MANAGING STRESS

Failure to manage our time will induce stress. As the educational environment has become more turbulent and where pupil misbehaviour has grown, so stress has become more widespread in the teaching profession. Not only does it impair the quality of life but it can also detract from performance; for both reasons, it needs managing.

There are three issues to examine: causes, symptoms and remedies. But first we need to understand that *some* stress is a valuable element in any job. It provides challenge and motivation, helps to raise performance and is an ingredient of job satisfaction. Lack of stimulation such as stress provides can lead to boredom, which paradoxically is itself stressful. Moreover, internal stress is a natural, animal response, connected with survival. In the face of external challenge, the body secretes adrenalin, which boosts the performance of the heart, muscles and brain and prepares the animal for 'fight or flight'. But if we do nothing physical after the adrenalin flows, we remain tensed up.

It is excessive, prolonged, unmanaged stress that causes problems, especially with 'Type A' personalities (pushy, active). Some problems can be severe, such as ulcers, heart attacks, strokes, anxiety-depressive illnesses and even suicide. But these are largely preventable. Unfortunately our national culture is an obstacle to prevention: males particularly are conditioned not to expose their feelings or to display emotion, so stress tends to be a taboo subject for discussion. Admitting to it is felt to be tantamount to a confession of weakness or incompetence.

Causes

The causes of stress have a cumulative effect. Family crises such as divorce or bereavement pile on top of work pressures, of which the main factors in schools are

(1) pupil misbehaviour;
(2) educational changes;
(3) poor working conditions;
(4) time pressures;
(5) role conflict, confusion or overload; and
(6) a school ethos that denies information and support.

Our own attitudes can exacerbate stress: we may be perfectionists who set impossibly high standards; we may worry too much about what others think of us; we may bottle up emotion; we may not be assertive enough to say 'no' to unreasonable demands.

Symptoms

People react in different ways to excessive stress; symptoms can be behavioural, emotional, mental or physical. Surveys among teachers identify the main symptoms as feelings of exhaustion, reduction of contacts outside school, frustration at lack of achievement, apathy, irritability, displaced aggression and a wish to leave teaching. Others are listed in Figure 8.1. Each symptom may have other causes, but if you find you have several, they could be due to stress. Experience will tell you which you usually evince and help you recognize the onset of stress. Self-diagnosis is important, so that you know when to deal with the condition. Some of the symptoms are observable and may help you to discern when a colleague needs support.

Remedies

Organizations can help to deal with stress by adopting preventative measures. Generally, industry has the edge over schools in this respect. Large firms employ occupational health specialists. They have better selection processes, which help to ensure a better fit between person and job. They practise systematic appraisal, which helps to nip incipient work-related problems in the bud. They invest more money in training so as to develop confidence In the job. There is much more teamwork, which provides group support. Heads can take similar measures in their schools. They can also find out how their own management style and the school's ethos lead to unnecessary stress among the staff, and modify them accordingly. They can review teachers' roles to minimize confusion, conflict and overload.

Behavioural	*Physical*
Overeating	Headaches
Drinking too much alcohol	Upset stomach
Compulsive smoking	Dizziness
Neglect of personal appearance	Sweaty and/or trembling hands
Insomnia	Blurred vision
Restlessness – fidgeting	Skin rashes
Lethargy	Palpitations
Change in sex drive	Dry mouth
Unusual clumsiness	High blood pressure
Accident proneness	Backache
Letting things slide	Neck pains
Less communicative	Nausea
Emotional	*Mental*
Depression	Loss of concentration
Tenseness	Increased forgetfulness
Irritability	Increased mistakes
Remorse	Increased day-dreaming
Thoughts of suicide	Poor judgement
Defensiveness	Less rational thinking
Crying	Indecisiveness
Aggressive behaviour	
Anxiety	

Figure 8.1   Some symptoms of stress

At the personal level those experiencing stress have several options open to them. Different people find help in different coping strategies, so you may have to experiment. Some things you can do by yourself are

(1) managing your time better (see above);
(2) identifying the people or tasks that steal your time and saying 'no' more often;
(3) 'brain-dumping' on to paper all the things that are worrying you, before you go to bed;
(4) deep breathing and other relaxation exercises (you can buy tapes for this purpose); and
(5) carving out time to pursue your favourite pastime or sport after work.

Try to view yourself objectively within your environment; reason with yourself and realize that the seat of the problem may lie in the environment rather than in you, in which case self-reproach is misplaced.

Another approach is to share your concerns with a member of your family or trusted circle of friends. Let them listen and then help you to tease out the problem and come to terms with it. Agree with them the specific actions you will take, by when, to manage the stress, and arrange to meet again to review progress. Make sure that they understand the confidential nature of the discussion. The chances are that the person you choose to talk things over with will have experienced stress him or herself, so you can probably count on a sympathetic understanding. However, you may do even better to meet others in the same boat; sometimes you will find a stress workshop being run locally by a trained counsellor. Such support systems can be of real help in generating the will to take effective action, especially at a time when your decision-making capacity is impaired.

ASSERTIVENESS

We have already mentioned that one of the techniques for reducing stress is to learn to say 'no' to unreasonable demands. This is one of the principles of assertiveness training, which has primarily been introduced to help women to claim due recognition for their ideas and rights, but which can be of value generally in clarifying communication and preventing the build-up of commitments which cannot be met – hence stress on all parties.

'Assertiveness' in this particular sense can be summarized as 'openness, honesty and conciseness' and means

- letting people know how you feel;
- stating your viewpoint and, if necessary, restating it until you are sure that it has been listened to;
- not hesitating to tell people what you can and cannot achieve and what will be the consequence of their pushing a demand;
- clearly stating your requirements of others; and
- avoiding unnecessary padding which may soften or mask the impact of the message you wish to convey.

Being assertive must be distinguished from being aggressive. The latter usually involves some degree of emotion and a positive desire to impose one's will on the other party or to dominate. The 'assertive' person, on the other hand, should

- keep calm and keep the emotions under control;
- make factual, objective statements (this also applies to statements about one's feelings); and
- respect the interests and feelings of the other party and seek fair solutions in which neither party uses undue pressure to subjugate or dominate the other.

The simple techniques of 'assertiveness' are surprisingly powerful. The only danger is that those who practise them may overcompensate for their previous submissiveness and that, despite all warnings, the dominated may become dominators or even 'aggressors'.

DEVELOPING YOUR OWN COMPETENCE

Great strides have been made over the past 10–20 years in establishing systematic approaches to the assessment, enhancement and accreditation of competence. For heads, the lead agency was the Teacher Training Agency (TTA), with its three national training programmes, the National Professional Qualification for Headship (NPQH), to be mandatory by 2004, the Headteacher Induction Programme (HIP) and the Leadership Programme for Serving Headteachers (LPSH), for aspiring, newly appointed and experienced heads respectively. Since 2002 the National College for School Leadership (www.ncsl.org.uk) has taken over responsibility. These programmes are based partly on those used to improve the output performance of senior managers in commerce, industry and the public services, modified to take account of research on fifty high-performing headteachers (Parsons, *et al.*, 2000).

Outside education, the lead agency in the UK was originally the Management Charter Initiative (MCI), but is now the Management Standards Centre (www.management-standards.org). These standards of competence form the basis of National Vocational Qualifications in Management (and from 2004, Leadership). They draw on best practice across the developed world. One of us (Everard) has been involved in the updating of these standards and recommends that education managers take note of them when they are launched in spring 2004. In draft, several units closely match aspects of the head's role. An inkling of the functions to be covered can be gained from Figure 1, (p. xii).

There are other sets of competence standards which have been used for headteachers. Jirasinghe and Lyons (1996) have reviewed and critiqued these; they have developed a new set using a psychometric test (OPQ) and based a self-evaluation and self-development questionnaire on them. They advocate the use of techniques widely adopted in non-educational employment sectors, based on job analysis. Their work is underpinned by an extensive research project and a theoretical framework.

It is government policy that standards (or benchmarks) of competence should exist for every occupation and a National Qualifications Framework is being developed to accredit all those who have attained the standards relevant to their job. Although such an approach has its critics, the grounds for criticism often stem from the inflexible way in which the model is implemented, rather than from the underlying concept of standard-setting itself.

We believe that standards are here to stay and not a passing fad. From time immemorial, sportsmen and women have used standards to improve their performance, by competing with their previous best. Standards are equally useful to managers as benchmarks of their performance. It is worth encouraging managers and leaders in schools to use them as part of their professionalism, to take responsibility for systematic self-development. The steps in the development process are

(1) recognition of the various elements or units of competence;
(2) understanding their nature and how they relate to managerial and leadership effectiveness;
(3) self-assessment or other feedback (such as appraisal) on the level of competence;
(4) experimentation with reflectively applying the competence, or demonstrating it at a higher level of effectiveness, with systematic feedback;
(5) continuing conscious, reflective practice in using the competence; and
(6) applying it, along with other relevant competences, as an integral whole in a range of work situations.

While training courses are helpful in taking groups of individuals through steps 1–5, the process can also be followed on the job, especially if facilitated by a trusted colleague, adviser, coach, mentor or consultant.

Competence is a combination of knowledge and skill plus the ability and will to apply them to particular situations. It thus includes motives, traits, attitudes, values and aspects of self-image and role. Competence is related to performance in regard to both the functions and demands of the particular management job and the requirements and constraints of the organizational setting (e.g. LEA policy). In developing competence, therefore, there has to be some definition of what constitutes effective performance (effectiveness criteria – see above and Chapter 6).

The functions that managers are required to perform call for a variety of competences which are largely generic, in that they are needed in all kinds of settings. These have been classified in various ways; one of us (Everard, 1986) used Burgoyne's taxonomy (Burgoyne, 1976) to group the qualities that senior teachers associate with managerial competence.

However, it is insufficient to analyse competence, which is a holistic concept, into its elements; there is also a need for an overarching 'integrative competence', which enables a manager to assemble and orchestrate the necessary elements in dealing with particular situations.

Competences can be improved by systematic development and training; none is so innate that it cannot be influenced, although people's aptitudes for acquiring particular competences differ widely.

Boydell and Leary (1994) have categorized the development of competence under three types and seven modes of learning (italicized below), all of which relate to the characteristics of a 'learning organization', namely, that it does

(1) things well (implementation);
(2) things better (improvement); and
(3) better things (integration).

To 'do things well', managers must learn to *adhere* to rules, to *adapt* and modify rules to suit particular situations, and to *relate* these rules and procedures to some kind of rationale that gives them meaning. Learning to improve involves reflecting on one's *experience*, analysing it and *experimenting* systematically in order to 'do things better'. 'Doing better things' involves *connecting*, seeking patterns, empathizing with others, and this is followed by the seventh mode of learning – *dedicating* oneself to one's purpose in life, in the sense of doing something in and for the external world.

MANAGING YOUR LEARNING

Competence is developed by repeatedly going round an experiential learning cycle. The most effective learning occurs when all four stages of the cycle are fully used (concrete experience, reflective observation, abstract conceptualization, active experimentation). However, people have different preferences for the four stages; they are said to have different 'learning styles' (Kolb, 1984). Honey and Mumford (1989) call these styles Activist, Reflector, Theorist and Pragmatist, and have developed a useful questionnaire for determining one's learning style profile. They have kindly allowed us to reproduce the style descriptions (Figure 8.2), but if you want the best-selling questionnaire you must purchase at least ten copies or you can buy one inexpensively on-line (www.peterhoney.com). It helps you to interpret your scores, use your learning strengths and improve your learning style. Alternatively, write to Dr Peter Honey, 10 Linden Avenue, Maidenhead, SL6 6HB.

In interpreting your profile from the questionnaire, you need to compare your results with the norms for your occupational group. Kelly (1995) gives a set of norms for headteachers ($n = 149$), but is finding an upward trend in the activist score over time. Seymour and West-Burnham (1989/90) give a set for middle/senior education managers, predominantly deputy heads and heads of department, and Butcher (1995) has found a difference between primary and secondary heads, as follows:

	Activist	Reflector	Theorist	Pragmatist
Heads (Kelly)	9.0	12.6	10.5	11.5
Middle/senior (Seymour)	8.3	13.9	12.7	13.1
Secondary (Butcher)	8.9	13.9	12.9	12.8
Primary (Butcher)	10.6	9.0	10.0	10.6

Honey's manual contains norms for other occupations, including industrial and commercial managers.

Although your score can be used to select management training courses that suit your learning style, remember that practice in a less preferred mode

Activist

Strengths
- Flexible and open-minded.
- Happy to have a go.
- Happy to be exposed to new situations.
- Optimistic about anything new and therefore unlikely to resist change.

Weaknesses
- Tendency to take the immediately obvious action without thinking.
- Often take unnecessary risks.
- Tendency to do too much themselves and hog the limelight.
- Rush into action without sufficient preparation.
- Get bored with implementation/consolidation.

Reflector

Strengths
- Careful.
- Thorough and methodical.
- Thoughtful.
- Good at listening to others and assimilating information.
- Rarely jump to conclusions.

Weaknesses
- Tendency to hold back from direct participation.
- Slow to make up their minds and reach a decision.
- Tendency to be too cautious and not take enough risks.
- Not assertive – they aren't particularly forthcoming and have no 'small talk'.

Theorist

Strengths
- Logical 'vertical' thinkers.
- Rational and objective.
- Good at asking probing questions.
- Disciplined approach.

Weaknesses
- Restricted in lateral thinking.
- Low tolerance for uncertainty, disorder and ambiguity.
- Intolerant of anything subjective or intuitive.
- Full of 'shoulds, oughts and musts'.

Pragmatist

Strengths
- Keen to test things out in practice.
- Practical, down to earth, realistic.
- Businesslike – get straight to the point.
- Technique oriented.

Weaknesses
- Tendency to reject anything without an obvious application.
- Not very interested in theory or basic principles.
- Tendency to seize on the first expedient solution to a problem.
- Impatient with waffle.
- On balance, task oriented, not people oriented.

Figure 8.2 Learning styles – general descriptions © Honey and Mumford

helps you to enlarge your repertoire and thus to take better advantage of different sorts of learning opportunity; also, that competence develops as you follow every stage of the learning cycle.

The learning styles questionnaire is an example of a self-perception tool that we recommend for getting to know yourself better; accurate self-perception is a key management competence and vital to self-development. Peter Honey has developed forty of these, which are generic to all learners and managers. Other do-it-yourself tools will be found in Pedler's books (see further reading). We also recommend the Myers–Briggs test as particularly suitable for teachers, but this requires a psychologist to administer, as do the 16PF, OPQ and Firo B, which are also used.

MANAGING OUR ATTITUDES AND BEHAVIOUR

In the preceding chapters we have seen that 'natural' reactions to situations are not always the best. We can, in fact, easily become 'hooked' into behavioural patterns which are counterproductive, such as developing intergroup conflict in order to cover up our own feelings of insecurity or threat. We may be unduly ready to perceive an attack and respond defensively when suggestions are offered.

We have already looked at models, checklists and guidelines which may help us to check on our behaviour in one-to-one or group situations, and to adopt constructive approaches. Other helpful models exist, and we would recommend, as a perceptive insight into behaviour (though not to be taken too seriously), insight into behaviour, the theories of transactional analysis (Berne, 1968), which start from the premiss that behavioural patterns can be classified as those of the Parent, the Adult or the Child with classic attitudes of

(1) *Parent* – telling, guiding, asserting, dominating, criticizing;
(2) *Adult* – reasoning, listening, suggesting;
(3) *Child* – feeling, creating/destroying, accepting/resisting, enquiring.

It is surprising how often we can catch ourselves, especially as teachers, treating our colleagues or social contacts as 'children' by adopting 'know-all' or 'patronizing' attitudes. How often are we instantly recognized as teachers?

In a book of this scope it is impossible to do justice to this or other helpful theories. However, one of us (Morris) has found the following adaptation of another of the transactional analysis concepts particularly useful in helping managers to understand and control their own behaviour (Harris, 1995). It is a useful model in dealing with conflict, since it enables us to recognize the psychological realities that may underlie the reactions of ourselves and/or others.

The OK matrix

The OK matrix (Figure 8.3) illustrates four basic ways in which we may feel about ourselves and other people. However self-confident we are, there are bound to be times when each of us will not feel 'OK', i.e. sure of ourselves. For example, no one feels completely 'OK' on his or her first day in a new job. The adolescent does not basically feel 'OK' in an adult world. Some people consistently feel less 'OK' than others and are then said to have an inferiority complex.

At times when we do not feel 'OK' most of us will try to prove ourselves in a variety of ways. If these ways fit into the value system of the organization to which we belong, the effect will be perceived as positive – teenagers may strive for distinction in the examination room or on the sports field; salespeople will seek to achieve their targets and possibly to be the best; managers will seek to demonstrate their effectiveness to their superiors.

However, if these methods do not succeed, individuals may, in their under-confidence, adopt less constructive approaches. Teenagers may seek the approbation of their fellows by being disruptive; salespeople may blame the market, the system, the targets; managers may feel that they must suppress the initiatives of their subordinate which they perceive as a threat. Ironically, people with inferiority complexes do not behave modestly but, on the contrary, often behave in an aggressive, patronizing, arrogant way in an attempt to prove themselves. Finally, there is the possibility of withdrawing into one's shell and opting out.

Such patterns of behaviour can be disturbing enough when directed towards someone else whom we see as 'OK'. However, they have the potential to become really vicious when someone, who does not him or herself feel 'OK', takes the opportunity to prove him or herself at the expense of someone whom he or she perceives to be also 'not OK'. This is the behaviour of the bully. It is also the behaviour of the manager who tries to shift blame on to, or take advantage of, a weaker colleague.

In the top right-hand corner of the matrix we have the situation where I may feel 'OK' but may find someone else 'not OK'. This means that I do not trust the other person or have confidence in his or her ability. Such an attitude may be justified. However, there is the risk in a conflict situation that I am

	You're OK	You're not OK
I'm OK	We can work together effectively	I don't trust you
I'm not OK	I must prove that I'm worth something or opt out	I may be able to prove myself at your expense

Figure 8.3 The OK matrix, from Harris (1995), reprinted by permission of Jonathan Cape Ltd

stereotyping the other person negatively – inclined to attribute the wrong motives to his or her actions. I may well be right, particularly if we have both become locked into a vicious circle where neither trusts the other and where the actions of both will therefore be loaded.

The important thing to bear in mind is that most negative behaviour occurs because people feel unsure or threatened – perhaps not by us but by others or by circumstances.

Finally, it must be remembered that how a person perceives him or herself and others in terms of the OK matrix depends to a large extent on that person. If we treat others as though they are 'not OK' in our eyes they will seldom prove the contrary.

As far as possible the aim should be to feel 'OK' in ourselves and try to accept others in a positive way. This is the basis for a sound working relationship or friendship. In attempting to resolve conflict, the parties must make a real effort to move towards the 'I'm OK/You're OK' corner, though it will never be easy! (Harris, 1995).

EQUAL OPPORTUNITIES

An increasingly important aspect of managing our attitudes and behaviour relates to equal opportunities; we may even fall foul of the law if we neglect our responsibilities towards minorities and towards the opposite sex. It certainly erodes our effectiveness as managers if we are insensitive to other people's feelings, and there is no doubt that women and ethnic minorities sometimes feel that they are the victims of oppression by men and by white Anglo-Saxons respectively. Sexism and racism are usually present in schools whether we like to admit it or not. Statistics show, for example, that women are under-represented in more senior management posts. Many business organizations and public authorities are taking positive action to ensure that such inequalities are addressed. Educational institutions have been in the van of this movement, sometimes to the point that 'political correctness' and zealotry have become counterproductive.

The least that effective managers should do is to train themselves to avoid language traps (yes, we've had to learn too!). Gender-specific terms are not always interpreted as generic, even when the context might suggest the contrary. Unfortunately some well established management terms fall into this category: 'man the office', 'manpower', 'chairman'. Women can also upset men by talking about 'bringing feminine values to management', as though the values to which they refer were exclusively gender-specific. Many managers are so unaware of giving offence to minority groups that they would do well to legitimize a feedback system to let them know when they have inadvertently transgressed; but beware of 'witch-hunts'.

The positive manager	*The negative manager*
Acts	Is a victim
Accepts responsibility	Blames others
Is objective	Is subjective
Listens and responds	Rejects suggestions
Proposes solutions	Criticizes
Delegates	Is incapable of delegation
Sees opportunities	Sees threats
Has breadth of vision	Is preoccupied with detail
Faces up to problems	Conceals problems
Confronts the source of problems	Talks about the source of problems
Learns	Is taught
Has foresight	Has hindsight

Figure 8.4   Positive and negative management

POSITIVE AND NEGATIVE MANAGEMENT

Finally, we suggest that the behavioural checklist in Figure 8.4 may serve to crystallize the key behavioural issues for the manager.

PERSONAL APPLICATION

Consider any two colleagues and mark each of them against the checklist in Figure 8.4 by ticking for each line which of the two alternative behaviours predominates. Do the same for yourself and consider how you should change your behaviour.

DISCUSSION TOPIC

'Recent changes have made many teachers feel threatened or "not OK". They are reacting predictably to this.' Do we agree, and if so what can school managers do to alleviate the situation?

FURTHER READING

Brown, M. and Ralph, S. (1994) *Managing Stress in Schools*, Northcote House, Plymouth.
Cooper, C.L. and Payne, R.L. (eds) (1994) *Causes, Coping and Consequences of Stress at Work*, Wiley, London.
Esp, D. (1993) *Competences for School Managers*, Kogan Page, London.
Foster, M. (2000) *Get Everything Done and Still Have Time to Play*, Help Yourself, London.
Honey, P. and Mumford, A. (1989) *Manual of Learning Styles*, Honey, Maidenhead.
Mill, C. (2000) *Managing for the First Time*, Chartered Institute of Personnel and Development, London.
Pedler, M. and Boydell, T. (1999) *Managing Yourself*, Lemos and Crane, London.

Pedler, M., Burgoyne, J. and Boydell, T. (2001) *A Manager's Guide to Self-Development* (4th edn), McGraw-Hill, Maidenhead.

Rogers, B. (1995) *Managing Teacher Stress,* Financial Times Prentice Hall, London.

Ward, P. and Nattrass, M.S. (1990) *Managing Occupational Stress: A Guide for Managers and Teachers in the Schools Sector,* Health and Safety Executive, London.

EXERCISE 8: *Criteria for Effectiveness – Establishing Priorities*

List criteria detailed, and then rank them in order of importance to you:

(1) The main criteria against which you believe that your performance is judged by your immediate superior and by others who can affect your career.
(2) *Additional* criteria against which you feel that your performance ought to be judged in the interests of the school or college.
(3) *Further* criteria against which you personally judge your success or failure.

EXERCISE 9: *Use of Time Analysis*

This exercise is fully intended to help you think about how you spend your time currently, and how you would like to spend your working day, with a view to developing some concrete action plans directed towards improving your overall effectiveness.

(1) Using the activity categories shown on the analysis sheet and *any others you feel are applicable,* estimate the amount of your time you have spent on each activity during the past three months, expressed as a percentage of your total working time. Use the first column ('Actual') for recording your estimates.
(2) Use the second column ('Ideal') to fill in the time allocations as percentages which you feel you would like to be able to record for a future period.
(3) Which five (approximately) activities show the greatest discrepancy between 'actual' and 'ideal' in terms of time commitment? Enter these below.
(4) Which major obstacle (if any) do you see preventing you from achieving the sort of time allocation which you think would be ideal for you in your job?
(5) What concrete steps can *you* take in order to come closer to your ideal in terms of spending time on the job? Be specific.
(6) What can others (who?) do to help you or indeed make it possible for you to achieve this ideal? Be specific.

Analysis sheet

		Actual	*Ideal*

(a) *Teaching*   (overall)
   • lesson preparation
   • practical teaching
   • marking

(b) *Administration*   (overall)
   • staff management
   • tidying up, sorting out, 'getting organized'
   • reports
   • general administration

(c) *Miscellaneous*   (overall)
   • meetings (if not covered above)
   • reading, studying, thinking
   • parent/teacher co-operation
   • 'out-of-school' activities (including clubs,
     societies, one-day and extended visits – UK
     and abroad)

(d) *Specialized activities (please list)*

EXERCISE 10: Time Log

Day ....

Date ....

Describe *what* happens in detail – the subject of meetings, telephone calls, letters, reading, conversations. Note the *duration* of each happening. Note the *name and position of other people involved*. Include even casual encounters.

Time	What happened?	Duration	People involved	Comments
8.00 8.30				
8.30 9.00				
9.00 9.30				
9.30 10.00				
10.00 10.30				
10.30 11.00				
11.00 11.30				
11.30 12.00				

Time	What happened?	Duration	People involved	Comments
12.00 12.30				
12.30 1.00				
1.00 1.30				
1.30 2.00				
2.00 2.30				
2.30 3.00				
3.00 3.30				
3.30 4.00				
4.00 4.30				
4.30 5.00				
5.00 5.30				

PART II
MANAGING THE ORGANIZATION

9

Organizations

THE ORGANIZATIONAL DIMENSION

Most of Part I was addressed to the ways in which managers deal with people as individuals. However, managers also have to operate at points further along the organizational dimension (Figure 9.1) and this is tackled in Part II. We shall first look at some of the characteristics of organizations and their implications for managers; then, in Chapter 10, at groups. Forming groups of individuals, building them into effective working units or teams, and getting these teams to work together effectively in pursuing the organization's purpose and goals, are at the heart of organization management. Teams, or whatever word is used to describe these groupings of collaborating individuals, are the building blocks of organizations, and managers (as we have seen) are the glue that holds them together. But first we look at organizations as a whole.

ORGANIZATIONAL GOALS

We believe that all organizations, including educational ones, should be actively managed against goals; in other words, not only should there be a clear sense of the direction in which the organization is being steered but also markers whereby we can assess progress. The words that we use to describe concepts of direction and progress vary from the broad to the more specific. At the specific end, we have words like 'goals', 'objectives', 'targets' and 'success criteria', which more or less define endpoints or milestones. 'Aims' are broader in concept, and subsuming the rest, we can talk of a 'central purpose', a 'reason for being' or a 'core mission' for the organization. A sense of purpose is like gravity – a continuous force that moves the organization in a particular direction. There is no agreed generic word that describes these concepts collectively, but we usually speak of 'opening' and 'closing' an objective when we want to indicate a movement towards, respectively, breadth or specificity.

Organizational aims (used here in a generic sense) nurture and steer creative tension and release and harness energy; they keep the organization on the move, heading in a certain direction. Some heads we interviewed conceive it as one of their most important tasks to keep their schools moving. 'My recurring nightmare is stagnation and not moving forward', said one.

Interestingly, this same idea of inducing movement was picked up as a key activity of executives of successful companies by Peters and Waterman in *In Search of Excellence* (1995, p. 119). For instance, they quote a Cadbury's executive as saying 'Ready. Fire. Aim'. And (p. 107):

> organizations are to be sailed rather than driven ... the effectiveness of leadership often depends on being able to time interventions so that the force of natural organizational processes amplifies the interventions rather than dampens them ... organizational design is more like building a snow fence to deflect drifting snow than like building a snowman.

Similarly, John Harvey-Jones, a former chairman of ICI, said in a nautical metaphor: 'I know this sounds terrible, but I'm more interested in speed than direction. Once you get moving, you can sort of veer and tack. But the important thing is, you're moving' (Huxley, 1984).

So the message to organization managers is: get moving! Don't drive it; steer it. Use the force of the wind and snowstorm, not just letting them buffet you around like a cork, but to help you *aim* in roughly the right direction. Once you have got it on the right course and everyone knows in what direction you are trying to head, you can start to close down the broad objectives and set more specific markers of progress, such as targets. For example, if you want to stimulate new thinking on curriculum development, you could assemble a small informal group of, perhaps, staff, pupils and parents who are constructively dissatisfied with the present curriculum, and give them the general aim of helping you to decide what most needs change. You may not agree with all they say, but you will probably like at least one suggestion which you might give to, say, the English department to shape into a concrete proposal by the end of the Easter term. After discussion, you might agree a target date for incorporating the change into next year's curriculum.

The same approach is needed for the constituent parts of the organization

Individual——▸ Group ———▸ Organization ———▸ Network of ——▸ Government
Organizations

deputy	classes	schools	LEA	DfES
teacher	sets	community colleges	NAHT	SEED
pupil	depts	sixth form colleges	SHA	etc.
caretaker	years	etc.	Headmasters'	
secretary	houses		Conference	
technician	committees		etc.	
etc.	working parties			
	etc.			

Figure 9.1   The organizational dimension

– the departments, the teams, the committees. Their aims should be kept aligned with those of the school. The setting of organizational and departmental aims should normally involve the people in them, together with other stakeholders (see next section), but it is ultimately for the manager to decide what these should be. This is laid down as the first professional duty of headteachers under their conditions of employment (DfES, 2002): 'formulating the overall aims and objectives of the school'. Peters and Waterman (1995, p. 85) state: 'The in-building of purpose is a challenge to creativity because it involves transforming men and groups from neutral, technical units into participants who have a particular stamp, sensitivity and commitment.'

Organizations usually have more than one objective: it is a fallacy, for example, to suppose that business organizations only exist to make the maximum profit. Study of the published objectives of such companies as Shell, Astrazeneca and Securicor show that they pursue social as well as economic objectives, which it is the task of management to keep in balance. Similarly, those schools that make their aims explicit often find that they are having to harmonize different though compatible aims.

STAKEHOLDERS

Take, for example, the set of aims of a comprehensive school, reproduced in Figure 9.2. Not only does the school aim to serve the needs of the individual pupil but it also seeks to respond to the legitimate demands of employers, colleges, universities, examining bodies and society as a whole. There are different 'stakeholders' in all organizations: businesses need to serve customers, offer a market to suppliers, reward shareholders, look after employees and be good corporate citizens in society; likewise schools have as stakeholders pupils, parents, LEAs, governors, teachers, feeder schools, higher education, employers and the local community.

The management's task is to look after the interests of all the stakeholders and keep some sort of balance between them. An industrial manager is no more the paid lackey of the shareholders (or expected by them to be so) than a headteacher is of the LEA or DfES. Both have a right and duty to resist demands that seriously upset the balance and health of the organization. Not all organizational aims are perfectly aligned, and the manager has to resolve conflicts of interest, some of which are more apparent than real. It is a help when the different stakeholders recognize and respect each other's legitimate aims for the organization, and can see that its best interests are served when any conflict is resolved by consensus: hence the importance of the last objective in the list in Figure 9.2.

Another objective in the list mentions the concept of 'reciprocal responsibility'. Organizations have to strike deals with their stakeholders whereby, in return for certain advantages flowing one way, other advantages will flow the other way. The head may well have to supervise unwritten contracts of this kind.

Aims are ideals and they are like stars in that though we may not reach them, we use them to guide us. If we do not know where we are going, it is likely that we will end up somewhere else!

- To recognize the individual's talents of all kinds and degrees and to develop this intellectual, physical and creative capacity.
- To ensure that the curriculum serves the individual's needs.
- To develop a curriculum which is flexible enough to respond to the sensible needs of students at different ages and stages.
- To recognize the legitimate demands of employers, colleges, universities, and examining bodies.
- To recognize the legitimate demands of society as a whole with respect to adequate numeracy, literacy and other fundamental skills relating to the processes of communication; oral, written and visual.
- To enable students to acquire the required education relating to the necessity to earn a living and, when appropriate, to enter into skilled occupations and professions.
- To seek to measure the extent to which an individual is being successful in making the maximum use of natural gifts and opportunities.
- To be rigorously selective in the material presented to students, bearing in mind the above aims and having particular regard to the following aims:

  - The instilling of an attitude to learning that shows it to be a life-long process.
  - The stimulation of intellectual curiosity.
  - The direction and exercising of the emotions.
  - The encouragement of discrimination.
  - The development of the art of learning.
  - The fostering of a capacity to tackle unfamiliar problems.
  - The emphasizing of the need to differentiate between truth and lies and between fact and feeling with the associated understanding of the nature of evidence.
  - The growth of understanding of the nature and importance of knowledge plus the involvement with the processes and resources of learning.

- To recognize and accept differences in natural endowment and environment and to hold every individual in esteem as of right.
- To accept responsibility for identifying the physical, aesthetic, creative, emotional and social needs of each individual student as a necessary starting point to satisfy these needs.
- To maintain the school as a caring community emphasizing the central importance of good human relationships based upon sensitivity, tolerance, good will and a sense of humour.
- To promote the understanding of the fact that the individual and the community have a reciprocal responsibility and that individual needs must at times be secondary to the greater need of a large group; that collaboration and co-operation are a two-way activity.
- To foster habits of responsibility, self-discipline, initiative, endeavour and individual judgment.
- To obtain a positive response to the needs of a changing society whilst emphasizing established fundamental values and standards.
- To promote the idea that the school is the servant of the community in both local and national terms and to accept the responsibilities which flow from this understanding.
- To secure the active involvement of all people concerned with the school's welfare, staff, students, governors, parents and the authority, in the continuous reassessment of the aims and objectives of the school.

Figure 9.2 Aims of a comprehensive school

List the stakeholders in your school. What aims does each stakeholder have for the school? Is there any conflict, actual or potential? Is there an 'umbrella' statement of purpose that subsumes all these aims? Do all the stakeholders subscribe to this? How well are these aims articulated and used in directing the affairs of the school? What more can you do to generate a sense of common purpose and commitment to agreed aims or ends?

ENVIRONMENT

Much criticism is levelled at schools for being out of touch with the world outside them. Some of it may be justified in the sense that few teachers have had an opportunity of working anywhere other than in an educational establishment: those who have held a responsible post in industry or in the public service outside education develop a useful frame of reference by which to judge what goes on in school.

Those who manage organizations should remember that they are part of a bigger system; they are interdependent with the rest of society, which they serve as society serves them. To ensure that they keep track of what is going on around them, successful organization managers make a point of having a wide circle of contacts and of staying interested in developments outside their immediate sphere. Blinkered managers are unlikely to pick up from the flow of events what may hit them tomorrow. They fail to anticipate what new demands may be made on them, and are caught unprepared. Managers have to take into account prevailing currents of opinion, to track the changing stance of the DfES, for example, and to aim not at where the environment is now, but at where it will be when they are able to respond. It is not easy to distinguish a fundamental shift from an ephemeral straying off course; but we have to try.

One way of picturing an organization such as a school in the context of its environment is shown in Figure 9.3. Rather like a living organism, it pursues its central purpose, denoted by the big arrow, within an environment with which it makes continuous transactions. It takes in various inputs (in the case of organisms, food and energy; for schools, younger pupils, funds, learning materials, etc.) and it gives out various outputs – older, educated pupils, service to the community, a livelihood for teachers and their families, etc. The organism or organization is designed to achieve the efficient transformation of all the inputs into the desired outputs – 'efficient' signifying that the transformation takes place with the minimum expenditure of internal energy (using an electrical metaphor, the battery has low internal resistance).

Such a model does not always appeal to schools as it suggests that they are a kind of sausage machine. No model tells the whole story, yet there is a sense in which schools exist to 'school' or socialize children and to equip them as future mature members of society.

The model also depicts the other important properties of organizations:

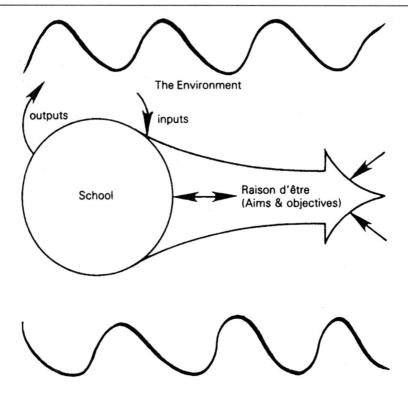

Figure 9.3   A school in its environment

the existence of a basic aim to provide a sense of purpose and direction, and the effect of the interactions with the environment which arise from pursuing this aim. The arrows on the right of Figure 9.3 show that the turbulent environment may tend to thwart the fulfilment of the school's central purpose; the double-headed arrow in the middle indicates that there is some feedback mechanism to enable the organization to know how well it is faring in pursuit of its aims, so that the helm can be set accordingly.

Many long-serving heads we have talked to have remarked how much over the past two or three decades the nature of their jobs has changed to one of 'boundary management' (Chapter 14): that is, they spend much more of their time managing transactions between their school and its environment. They are being forced to keep a weather eye on what is happening around them, so that they can successfully pilot their schools through the ruffled waters that lie ahead. Garratt (1987) depicts the dual role of top people in organizations in a double-loop model (Figure 9.4, adapted) and enjoins them to spend more time 'looking upwards and outwards', delegating more of the operational management to subordinates. This is a key part of organization

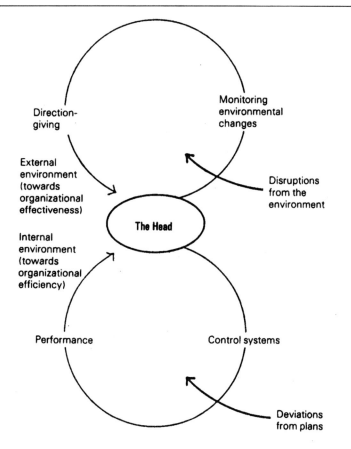

Figure 9.4   The learning organization model (after Garratt, 1987)

management. In Part III we shall explore further what this involves, and how
to influence the environment's demands.

MODELS OF ORGANIZATIONS

The way in which managers conceptualize organizations influences the way
they manage them, so it is worth exploring some of the main models that are
used in relation to organizations, in addition to the simple one described in
the last section. Managers familiar with the various models or schools of
thought about organizations are better able to select an appropriate one to
deal with the particular situation they need to manage.

There is no one 'right' model of so complex an entity as an organization:
different models are different approximations to the truth. On management
courses we have found that people are helped by having a map of the various
models or schools of thought which have had an important influence. Such a
map appears in Figure 9.5.

The classical model

This model emphasizes characteristics such as rationality, high job specialization, centralization, a command system, a tight hierarchy, strong vertical communication, tight control, rigid procedures and an autocratic approach. Though it bears some resemblance to certain bad companies and schools, it is the antithesis of the way in which the best companies are organized: 'The rational model causes us to denigrate the importance of values ... The top performer's ability to extract extraordinary contributions from very large numbers of people turns on the ability to create a sense of highly valued purpose' (Peters and Waterman, 1995, p. 51).

The humanistic model

This model is characterized by respect for the individual and other human values, job breadth, consultation, consensus, decentralization, loose project organization, flexible procedures, multidirectional communication, management by objectives and a participative approach. It comes closer to describing how the best companies are organized and it is a good deal more attractive to schools. However, without care, it tends to lead people to undervalue the achievement of the tasks of the organization and thereby to detract from the organization's effectiveness in achieving its aims. It can also give managers a sense of impotence and loss of control.

Nevertheless, a humanistic model has played a key part in the development of thought about organizations, counteracting the rational thinking of the classical school. Incidentally, the term 'rational' is usually misused in the literature on organizations: it actually means sensible, logical and reasonable. However, it has come to have a narrow meaning which excludes the messy, human stuff. Yet there is a great deal of rationality in the humanistic model: it takes human behaviour into full account, by postulating that human beings act rationally towards situations *as they perceive them*. The trick is to find out how they perceive them, at the level of emotions as well as intellect; then you can predict how they will respond.

The systems model

This model has been popular in industry for the last few decades and is particularly useful to organizations having to adapt rapidly to change. Although one of the conceptual roots of the model, control engineering, is alien to schools, the other root is more acceptable: it comes from a study of how living organisms work and survive, and especially of the properties of the central nervous system of the human organism. By comparing organizations to organisms that adapt and survive in a changing environment, this approach brings out a number of factors important to schools today.

Descriptions	Classical Mechanistic Bureaucratic	Behavioural Organic Human relations	Systems Cybernetics Socio-technical	Decisions	Technological or contingency
Dominant management style	Theory X	Theory Y	Situational	Authoritarian	Situational
Organizational structure	Formal Rigid Long-lived	Informal Flexible Transient	Interlocking	Stratified	Variable
Emphasis on	Specialization Rationality	Interpersonal relations	Information flows Groups	Decision bands Authority	Environmental Process technology
Sources of ideas	Army Mass-production	Psychologists Sociologists	Instrumentation Control theory Nervous system	Business enterprises	Investigational field-work
Predominant nationality	British French American	American (NTL)	British (Tavistock)	British American	British American
Period of main development	1900–40	1950–70	1950–72	1960	1950–55
Some key names	Urwick Fayol Taylor	Beckhard Argyris Likert Blake McGregor	Rice Emery Trist Beer Juran Crosby Deming	March Cyert Paterson Kepner-Tregoe	Woodward Burns and Stalker Lawrence and Lorsch Reddin Perrow

Figure 9.5 Classification of schools of thought on organization

Stafford Beer, in his *Brain of the Firm* (1981), has taken the metaphor of the living organism a stage further. He has used knowledge of human physiology to develop a theory that has been applied to industrial organizations, governments and a church. It states that there are five tiers of subsystems in the human central nervous system, which have their counterparts in all organizations. The successful survival and development of the human race are evidence of the effectiveness of such a system. The assumption is made that organizations can be made more effective by comparing them to the central nervous system, diagnosing in what respects they fall short and strengthening the subsystem that seems weakly developed.

Three of the tiers (systems 5, 3 and 1) are easily recognizable (Figure 9.6). They are associated with the functions of policy-making, managing the execution of policy and, finally, the actual 'doing' operation. In practice, the 'doing' can be complex – teachers share pupils, plant and equipment, crises arise, etc., so there is a cloud of buzzing communication across the 'doing' groups: a bit of give and take, borrowing and lending, reciprocal adjustment, ironing out problems. On the whole this tends to be fairly informal, but it is nevertheless vital to the smooth operation of the school. Its equivalent in the human body is the subconscious co-ordination of movement; when the system fails, this smooth co-ordination is lost.

This system (2 in Figure 9.6), which liaises, harmonizes, smooths and provides lateral information exchange to avoid imbalance or rocking of the boat, differs in kind from any of the three main tiers: it has no authority to *tell* anyone to do anything. It can, however, feed information upwards to suggest that plans are impractical and need to be changed.

Someone operating as just plain 'doing' often cannot see the need for liaison, or policy, both of which are apt to seem unnecessarily constraining because he or she cannot see the whole picture. We are all familiar with the apparently crass acts of management, yet from the management vantage point it all seems so obviously sensible. So it is important for organization managers to develop in staff some understanding of how organizations work.

Systems 5, 3, 2 and 1 are largely concerned with getting things done *now* within the organization. The model needs another function (system 4) which looks into the outer world and into the future: we need to know the future trends in pedagogy, educational technology, demography, legislation and so on. This is not to say that every department needs its own research institute; but somebody, somewhere, needs to spend some 'panic-free time' thinking about the future. Like the liaison function, it has no authority, except that of expert knowledge. It influences policy by making proposals for future action. It does the 'staff work' for the policy group. It must be in touch with what is happening inside as well as outside the organization; indeed, its need for information is just as vital as its need for panic-free time.

The counterpart of this system in the human body is the five senses which scan the environment continuously and send messages to the other systems about future danger or opportunities, either at conscious 'policy' level or at the unconscious 'execution' level, as when we remove a finger from a hot stove.

Another aspect of the sensing system is the scanning of the internal environment. We need a system that tells us when we have an abscess in our

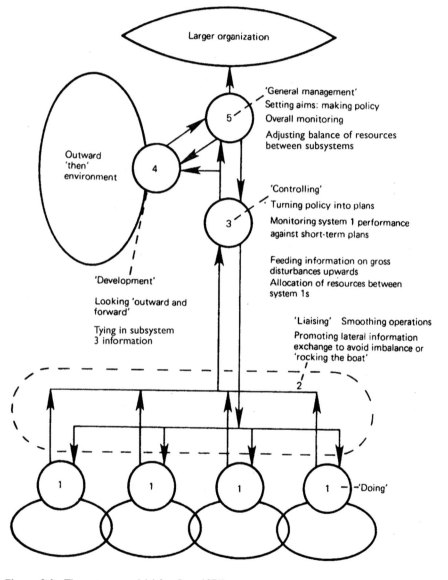

Figure 9.6 The systems model (after Beer, 1971)

gums, by giving us toothache. Organizations likewise need to know where they hurt. Normally such information comes up through other systems, if the communication channels are flowing freely, but sometimes it is necessary to 'poke a thermometer' or other instrument (an attitude survey, perhaps?) into the organization from the outside, to sense how it feels in relation to its environment and its 'normal state'.

In the model, system 5 – the policy-makers – are shown linked to a larger organization. The head of a local authority school needs to talk to the LEA, for example, on school policy. System 5 also has the key function of keeping the balance between systems 3 and 4. It cannot allow the neglect of scanning activities by overloading the same people with operational activities.

The theory suggests that all five systems must be present if an organization is to work. Their form and relative strength will depend on what the organization is trying to do, on its management style and on its environment. A one-teacher primary school does not need five people, but to be successful the one teacher must spend time in all five functions. At the other end of the scale of complexity, for example in a large comprehensive school on a divided site, the pattern of Figure 9.6 will be repeated many times. Thus each subsystem 1 (e.g. the maths department) will itself contain five subsystems, its subsystem 5 communicating with the larger organization, i.e. the school's senior management.

Individuals in such a complex organization may find themselves with a role in more than one subsystem in different parts of the organization; for example, a head with teaching duties may operate in a department's subsystem 1, and a head of year appointed to a policy-making working party will be operating in the school's subsystem 5. It is important to distinguish between these roles and to know in what capacity one is operating at any given time.

The model can be used in three main ways. These are to

(1) examine the health or viability of an existing organization;
(2) evaluate proposals for new organization structures; and
(3) clarify the purpose of committees or of roles.

It is not intended as a blueprint for an organization: it is more like a template to test an organization for fit.

PERSONAL APPLICATION

Apply the model to your school or department. Identify the subsystems in the organization: of what do they consist? Pay special attention to subsystem 4, because it is often found to be underdeveloped. Also assess whether vertical communication links operate as well upwards as downwards. Do you need to improve internal sensing? Are any 'organizational pathologies' apparent in your school? Which subsystems most need to be brought into a state of health?

The decision model

This model, which depicts organizations as an assembly of elements for taking decisions of varying levels of importance, has had its exponents in a number of firms, such as the Glacier Metal Company. It is not thought to offer much to schools, except that it does throw light on the different purposes of meetings and conferences. These are dealt with in Part I of this book.

The contingency model

The central idea in the contingency theory is that organizations are, and should be, different both from one another and from part to part. The appropriate structure, management style, etc., are contingent upon what the organization (or part of it) is there to do. There is no perfect organizational structure: the choice of structure depends on which set of problems you prefer to live with. For example, take the 'generalist–specialist' argument: is it better to let people specialize deeply in their subject so that they achieve mastery over it, or should one encourage the 'jack of all trades' who can turn his or her hand to anything? The compartmentalization of secondary schools by subject discipline may have contributed to academic excellence, but how effective is it in developing the whole person?

Contingency theory accepts that, left to themselves, organizations, departments and individuals tend towards specialization, carving out a more and more distinctive niche for themselves. In other words, the units tend to get more and more *differentiated* from one another, as the expertise builds up and becomes increasingly specialized. If this process continues, each unit begins to regard its own excellence as an end in itself, divorced from the interests of the organization, forgetting that the unit was set up in the first place to help the whole organization pursue common aims. People then complain that the organization is becoming fragmented, that departments are drifting apart, that empire-building is taking place, that overall objectives are obscured, that there is too much upward delegation and that they are becoming frustrated. The head of the organization feels that he or she is dealing with a set of medieval barons in charge of their various departments.

Integration is probably a key issue in many secondary schools, because of the high commitment of most teachers towards their subject disciplines. It also becomes more important under conditions of resource constraint, as a means of making the whole more than the sum of the parts. Somehow departments and staff have to enhance one another's contributions to the achievement of the main purpose of the school.

Effective integration calls for careful attention to relationships, a high degree of mutual trust, candour and respect, and an insight into organizational behaviour and complexities. Conflict has to be confronted and managed constructively: i.e. instead of being avoided altogether, smoothed over or resolved by the exercise of crude power, it is treated as a matter susceptible to a systematic problem-solving approach (Chapter 7). If this fails, there are other devices that can be used to secure a constructive resolution:

(1) Each unit or individual can report to a manager (e.g. a deputy head) who is made accountable for 'synergizing' the two roles (bringing them together so that the sum is greater than the parts).
(2) A third unit or individual (e.g. a head of year), seen by the other two as understanding their roles and as standing midway between them, is interposed to act as intermediary.
(3) Some kind of training or 'image exchange' can be undertaken to help each unit understand more accurately why the other unit behaves as it does (see Exercise 6, p. 114).
(4) Interdepartmental groups or task forces, with members selected from the two departments, can be formed on a temporary or permanent basis to resolve issues between the two departments.

However, rather than rely solely on formal mechanisms for cross-linking departments, the best organizations encourage an informal approach. Peters and Waterman (1995, p. 117) comment on this as follows: 'All of them [previous commentators on excellence] fall far, far short of depicting the richness, the variety of linkages that we observed in the excellent companies.'

PERSONAL APPLICATION

What problems arise in your school which can be attributed to high differentiation and low integration? How effective are the integrating mechanisms and lateral processes? What methods are used to get departments to work synergistically? What else needs to be done?

ELEMENTS OF ORGANIZATIONS

There is a temptation to think of organizations solely in structural terms – as in an organization chart. However, organizations can be said to consist of four interdependent elements, of which structure is only one (Figure 9.7). The elements are as follows:

Technology.   The 'technology' of an organization is its processes – in the case of a school, the process of education and the plant (classrooms, workshops, gymnasia, whiteboards, etc.) that goes with it.

Structure.   An organization's structure embraces the organization chart, the committees, the departments, the roles, the hierarchical levels and authority, the procedures in the staff manual, the timetable, etc.

People.   The people in a school organization are the teachers, their professionalism, their knowledge, experience, skills and attitudes; also the pupils and non-teaching staff.

Culture.   The character (or culture) of the organization covers such intangibles as its tone, its value system, the standards by which merit is judged, personal relationships, habits, unwritten rules of conduct and the practice of educational judgement.

The arrows in the diagram indicate that all the elements interact. The management of organizations involves not only the management of each of the elements but also of the balance or harmony between them.

Organization managers are apt to under-rate the importance of character as a formative influence on the people, the technology and the appropriate structure, and therefore give too little attention to shaping it. Instead, they constantly tighten up the structure. Goldsmith and Clutterbuck (1984, p. 162) show from their study of successful British firms that organizations can and do change their character radically: attitudes and culture are constantly evolving. Managers seek to build a unity of perception of what the company stands for, and culture changes take place, not as a result of edict, but as people observe behaviour and attitudes at work and assimilate them into their own way of thinking and doing. They conclude (ibid.): 'One of the strengths of many of the company leaders we have featured in this book has been their ability to adapt their own behaviour to stimulate cultural change.'

Rutter *et al.* (1979) showed how the ethos of Inner London Education Authority schools affected the outcome of the pupils' education. Indeed, in few organizations is the influence of ethos or culture on the product greater than in a school, or its consequences for society more profound. Mant, an

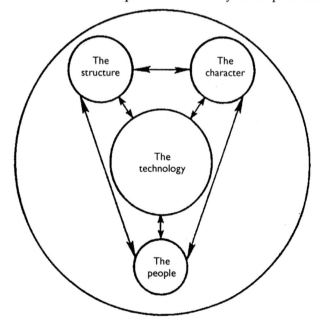

Figure 9.7   Elements of organizations

experienced management consultant, devotes a whole chapter ('School for scoundrels') to this (Mant, 1983). He writes that the problem about school goes to its very heart: what's it *for*? The good school keeps asking this question. If we don't really know, the school and its functionaries are without clear authority. The good school is an *authority structure* rather than a *power system* where survival is all.

In too many schools all that children learn is to survive in a naughty world. They explicitly reject the basis of the school's authority and the teachers begin to see schools as anti-educational child-minding institutions, in which the children's peer groups determine attitudes for life more effectively than do the teachers. By contrast, the good schools are sculpted with a respect for the intrinsic value of ideas and materials and not simply because they will help you 'get on'. With good schools you can almost smell the calm and quiet purposefulness when you walk in the door. Their heads reflect some higher purpose than the 'getting ahead' mentality. They confront their staff as to standards, notwithstanding 'academic freedom', and are highly intolerant of the irredeemably incapable teacher.

In a well-known independent school that we visited, a teacher who had spent much of his career in industry was as critical of the culture of his present school as Mant is of some state schools. He was shocked by the school's organization structure and culture, because they depended so much on command and the wielding of power. The head exerted more coercive power than company chairpersons, and this characteristic ran right through the organization. As a result, the boys, who were given very little responsibility, even as prefects, modelled their view of how organizations are run on an unrealistic concept. Thus the school was still preparing boys to work in or manage in organizations in which people did as they were told. What was needed, the teacher said, was a major cultural shift in the school regime to prepare boys for entering tomorrow's real world, in which management is by consent that is earned. Needless to say, his colleagues thought him eccentric!

Evidently this school was an example of the 'power' culture identified as one of four organizational stereotypes by Harrison (1972) and discussed by Handy (1993). The others are 'role' culture, 'task' culture and 'person' culture. Power-culture organizations are proud and strong; their managers are power oriented, politically minded and risk-taking. They put a lot of faith in the individual manager, and judge by results. They may or may not be successful: so much depends on the person at the top.

In the task culture, influence is more widely dispersed; individuals identify with the objectives of the organization; and they often work in transient teams. It is the culture most in tune with current approaches to change and adaptation, individual freedom and low status differentials (Peters and Waterman, 1995). But it is not always the appropriate culture for the technology of the organization. It would not be appropriate for schools that see their basic purpose as primarily custodial, for example.

PERSONAL APPLICATION

How would you characterize the culture of your school? What effect does it have on the behaviour of the people in it, including the pupils? Does it influence the educational process? Does the structure reflect it? Are the four elements in harmony, and consistent with the *raison d'être* of the school?

INTERLOCKING SYSTEMS

One aspect of systems theory deserving a brief mention is the way in which systems interlock. The pioneer work of the Tavistock Institute for Human Relations on organizations (Trist, 1960; Rice, 1971) distinguished between two systems, the social and the technical, which together constituted the arrangements for getting tasks performed. We prefer to add a third system, the economic system, overlapping with the other two as in Figure 9.8. The idea is to show that where the groups in the social system overlap with the plant (buildings, etc.) in the technical system, there is work; where the technical system (say, a factory) overlaps with the economic system, wealth is generated; and at the remaining interface, between the economic and the social system, we find reward.

The manager has to operate in all three systems, and solutions to problems in one of them which ignore the effect on the other two are no solutions at all. The systems interlock. Failure to recognize this, e.g. trying to save money without allowing for the effect of this on people's livelihoods, or settling disputes by paying people more money without asking where it is to come from, is simply to transfer the locus of the problem without solving it.

It may be objected that schools are not factories generating wealth by making goods and therefore this is irrelevant. We do not think so. Although the bulk of a school's resources are invested in people, the 'plant' is worth a tidy sum and is costly to maintain. It is important to turn these physical assets to account as fully and efficiently as possible. A school is of economic value to the community, too, because it adds economic worth to children by educating them. Those who see schools simply as drains into which taxpayers' money is poured ignore the investment element in such expenditure. Heads, however, should be very aware of the economic contribution that schools make to society, albeit indirectly, and should be able to defend their use of resources within the economic system.

Such an argument becomes more convincing, and applications for funds become more likely to succeed, if it can be shown that money is being used cost-effectively, i.e. good value is being obtained from the resources used by the school. The government has recently been emphasizing this in the 'best value' requirements imposed on local government and the health service, which aim to direct funds to wherever they are most effectively used. We do not suggest that the drive to improve the productivity of capital and labour should be as central a concern as in a factory, but good stewardship in any organization requires attention to the effectiveness with which all resources are used.

Stakeholders in the school who are more familiar with the economic system than are some teachers are more likely to be impressed by pleas for additional resources if they sense that the school appreciates and cares about good economic and technical management, as well as good management of the people in the social system.

We are sometimes shocked by the waste in schools which is caused by failure to spend money. An antiquated telephone system, a dilapidated photocopier, operated not by clerical staff but by professionals trained at great public expense to teach, are not efficient uses of resources. A transfer of resources from the economic to the technical system can greatly enhance the effectiveness of resource utilization in the social system. The good steward (organizational manager) keeps the three systems in balance.

In those schools that have bursars with experience in commerce or industry, we have encountered particularly good stewardship of resources in the three interlocking systems, to the benefit of all the organization's stakeholders. Not all schools need bursars, but heads without them can usefully take note of what good bursars do.

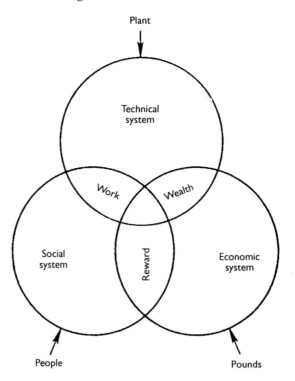

Figure 9.8 Interlocking systems

HALLMARKS OF EFFECTIVE SCHOOLS

There have been many studies of the organizational effectiveness of schools and in a major survey 719 factors were found to be associated with effectiveness. These have been reduced to eleven salient factors (Mortimore and MacBeath, 2003):

(1) professional leadership;
(2) shared vision and goals;
(3) a learning environment;
(4) concentration on learning and teaching;
(5) high expectations;
(6) positive reinforcement;
(7) monitoring progress;
(8) pupil rights and responsibilities;
(9) purposeful teaching;
(10) a learning organization;
(11) home–school partnership.

PERSONAL APPLICATION

Rate your school organization on a 1–5 scale (5 = excellent) against the eleven hallmarks above. Where do you think there is most scope for improvement? What are your next steps?

MacGilchrist *et al.* (1997) correctly emphasize the importance of synthesis in putting these discrete but interdependent factors together. In *The Intelligent School* they use Gardner's notion of 'multiple intelligences' to combine the different capacities that, taken together, constitute the 'corporate intelligence' that characterizes successful schools. Continuous learning – for everyone – is central to the notion of the intelligent school.

DISCUSSION TOPICS

(1) 'There is no such thing as society' – Margaret Thatcher. What warning, relevant to managers, underlies this aphorism?
(2) Read the quotation from the Education Reform Act 1988 on p. 178. How can schools be expected to promote the development of society? To what extent are they a microcosm of society? What does this imply?
(3) To improve organizational effectiveness, Handy recommends schools to distinguish between leadership and administration and between policymaking and execution. What is achieved thereby? Is he right?
(4) The School Teachers' Review Body reports express concern about 'the negligible amount of non-contact time available to most primary teachers within the timetabled week'. What measures should a head take to ensure that sufficient time is allotted to managing the school as an organization?

FURTHER READING

Argyris, C. (1999) *On Organizational Learning*, Blackwell, Oxford.

Davies, B. and West-Burnham, J. (2003) *Handbook of Education Leadership and Management*, Pearson, London.

Dutton, J. and Kleiner, G. (2000) *Schools That Learn: a Fifth Discipline Fieldbook for Educators, Parents and Everyone Who Cares about Education*, Doubleday Currency, New York.

Handy, C.B. (1993) *Understanding Organizations*, Oxford University Press, Oxford.

Senge, P.M. (1993) *The Fifth Discipline: The Art and Practice of the Learning Organisation*, Random House Business Books, London.

10

Teams

THE NATURE OF TEAMS

We turn now to a different aspect of organizations, the building-block which we call 'the team'. A team is a group of people with common objectives that can effectively tackle any task which it has been set up to do. 'Effectively' means that the quality of the task accomplishment is the best achievable within the time available and makes full and economic use of the resources (internal and external) available to the team. The contribution drawn from each member is of the highest possible quality, and is one which could not have been called into play other than in the context of a supportive team.

There is always dynamic interaction between the individual member and the team, such that each continuously adapts to optimize the quality of the team's work. This optimization consists of matching the individual and the team to the progressively developing technical requirements of the task.

Although this is how a team should work, it is often found that a group of people brought together to form a team (such as a head and his or her deputies) do not really 'gel', and a good deal of time is wasted because tasks are not handled effectively. When many groups in the school (departments, heads of department committees, pastoral teams, etc.) fail to work at peak efficiency, then the effectiveness of the whole organization suffers. If groups cannot work effectively by themselves, they are not likely to relate effectively to other teams with which they have to do business.

The head of an organization plays a key role in making the best choices of whom to bring together to make what happen for the good of the organization. He or she then has to ensure that these groups work effectively and collaborate with one another synergistically to achieve the task of the organization. ('Synergistically' means that they enhance one another's contribution, so that the whole is greater than the sum of the parts.) The head's role may be compared to that of the conductor of an orchestra, drawing from each group and player the highest possible quality of performance.

There are two complementary components in the building of an effective team: the selection of the members and the training of the team. Training begins either with some kind of instruction so that members know what makes for an effective team, or with some task that enables them to discover it for themselves. Then they practise and repeatedly review their own progress, so that they finally become proficient at any new skills required. Collaboration between teams can also be improved through practice and review, so that a process for developing effectiveness is at work throughout the organization (Figure 10.1).

Although in industry a good deal of team-building training has been systematically carried out along these lines over the last forty years (see below), it is only in the last twenty that the selection of team members has got much beyond the point of intuitive judgement. It was Meredith Belbin, a Cambridge psychologist, who made the breakthrough, in what has been described as one of the most imaginative and original pieces of research in management for two decades. His book *Management Teams: Why They Succeed or Fail* (1981) is a classic.

Team roles

The essence of Belbin's research findings is that the mix of personal characteristics in members of a team is a major determinant of the team's success. It is not simply the technical expertise that the members bring, for

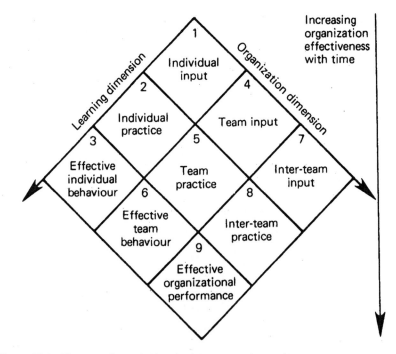

Figure 10.1   Training and organization development matrix

this can be of second-order importance – it is the way they interact. Moreover, astonishingly accurate predictions can be made of whether a particular team will succeed or fail. Although the research was mainly carried out in a business setting (the bulk of it at the Management College at Henley), it has been successfully applied in school management training. Some of the problems that schools repeatedly encounter in getting effective group working can probably be ascribed to injudicious selection of members.

The development of these ideas is a fascinating story in itself, comparable to the history of certain discoveries in physical science, but space does not allow us to go into it here – you must get it direct from the book if you are interested. What we shall do in this chapter is to summarize the main findings of relevance to managers in schools and reproduce (with permission) excerpts from the book and the website www.belbin.com..

The conventional wisdom in building teams in industry is that if you contrive to put together, for example, your best accountant, researcher, production person, salesperson *et al.* under a competent chairperson, you have probably got the best possible team. Technical merit and expertise reign supreme. What Belbin found was that this was a recipe for failure. In many cases the less brilliant exponents of their profession worked more successfully in a team. When very clever people are put together they tend to suffer from 'analysis paralysis'; anyone putting forward an idea finds it gets hacked to bits by his or her colleagues, and no progress is made.

By contrast, the meticulous observation of winning teams shows that the members individually adopt one or more of certain team roles, defined as 'a tendency to behave, contribute and interrelate with others in a particular way', which are indispensable to the successful completion of the task. Belbin now recognizes nine such roles (Belbin, 1995). Belbin's original eight roles are listed in Figure 10.2, together with the typical features, positive qualities and allowable weaknesses of the role incumbents. A short description of each role and associated common traits is given below.

ACTION-ORIENTED

Implementer.   Turns concepts and plans into practical working procedures, and carries out agreed plans systematically and efficiently. Traits: stable and controlled.

Shaper.   Shapes the way in which the team effort is applied; directs attention generally to the setting of objectives and priorities; and seeks to impose some shape or pattern on group discussion and on the outcome of group activities. Traits: anxious, dominant, extrovert.

Completer.   Ensures that the team is protected as far as possible from mistakes of both commission and omission; actively searches for aspects of work which need a more than usual degree of attention; and maintains a sense of urgency within the team. Traits: active, introvert.

PEOPLE-ORIENTED

Co-ordinator.　Controls the way in which a team moves towards the group objectives by making the best use of team resources; recognizes where the team's strengths and weaknesses lie; and ensures that the best use is made of each team member's potential. Traits: stable, dominant, extrovert.

Teamworker.　Supports members in their strengths (e.g. building on suggestions); underpins members in their shortcomings; and improves communications between members, fostering team spirit generally. Traits: stable, extrovert, not dominant.

Resource investigator.　Explores and reports on ideas, developments and resources outside the group; creates external contacts that may be useful to the team; and conducts any subsequent negotiations. Traits: stable, dominant, extrovert.

Type	Symbol	Typical features	Positive qualities	Allowable weaknesses
Implementer	IM	Conservative, dutiful, predictable	Organizing ability, practical common sense, hard-working, self-discipline	Lack of flexibility, unresponsiveness to unproven ideas
Co-ordinator	CO	Calm, self-confident, controlled	A capacity for treating and welcoming all potential contributors on their merits and without prejudice. A strong sense of objectives	No more than ordinary in terms of intellect or creative ability
Shaper	SH	Highly strung, outgoing, dynamic	Drive and a readiness to challenge inertia, ineffectiveness, complacency or self-deception	Proneness to provocation, irritation and impatience
Plant	PL	Individualistic, serious-minded, unorthodox	Genius, imagination, intellect, knowledge	Up in the clouds, inclined to disregard practical details or protocol
Resource investigator	RI	Extroverted, enthusiastic, curious, communicative	A capacity for contacting people and exploring anything new. An ability to respond to challenge	Liable to lose interest once the initial fascination has passed
Monitor-evaluator	ME	Sober, unemotional, prudent	Judgement, discretion, hard-headedness	Lacks inspiration or the ability to motivate others
Team-worker	TW	Socially orientated, rather mild, sensitive	An ability to respond to people and to situations, and to promote team spirit	Indecisiveness at moments of crisis
Completer	CF	Painstaking, orderly, conscientious, anxious	A capacity for follow-through. Perfectionism	A tendency to worry about small things. A reluctance to 'let go'

Figure 10.2 Useful people to have in teams

CEREBRAL ROLES

Plant.   Advances new ideas and strategies with special attention to major issues, and tries to initiate breakthroughs in the team's approach to the problems with which it is confronted. Traits: dominant, intelligent, introvert.

Monitor-evaluator.   Analyses problems and evaluates ideas and suggestions so that the team is better placed to take balanced decisions. Traits: intelligent, stable, introvert.

Specialist.   Provides team with scarce knowledge and skills. Traits: single-minded, self-starting, dedicated.

The two most crucial roles are probably those of co-ordinator and plant, and the incumbents need to relate to one another well: if they don't, the plant's ideas never bear any fruit. The essence of skilfully employing a plant (a role which some people prefer to think of as that of creative catalyst) lies in recognizing the member's potential, giving him or her scope and not allowing him or her to pursue unrewarding lines of thought. Successful co-ordinators do not have to be brainy: their characteristics are commonplace, but they are put together in an uncommon way, which earns the respect of everyone in the team. Often they are good shapers as well.

Different people are good at different team roles; although they may have one dominant role, they may still be reasonably competent in another one. In teams smaller than eight in number, people may have to play more than one role. By contrast, two dominant shapers, two plants or too many monitor-evaluators are apt to cause problems. Bowring-Carr and West-Burnham (1994) have noted that members of school management teams score low on both the monitor-evaluator and the completer roles: so beware of gaps as well as duplication.

Associated with these team roles are personality characteristics such as intelligence, dominance, introversion/extroversion and anxiety/stability. Stable extroverts, who often excel in jobs that place a high premium on liaison work and where co-operation is sought from others, are generally good team members. Anxious introverts, on the other hand, usually lack cohesion in a group, yet as individuals they are often very creative; they distinguish themselves in jobs (such as teaching?) which call for self-direction and self-sustaining persistence.

Anxious extroverts are commonly found in places where people need to work at a high pace and exert pressure on others: they form good teams in rapidly changing situations. Stable introverts plan well, are strong in organization, but are slow-moving and tend to be blind to new factors in a situation. They excel in bureaucratic occupations.

While co-operative stable extroverts form the most effective homogeneous teams (i.e. in which all team members are of the same personality type), they are excelled by heterogeneous teams (composed of different personality types) because stable extroverts on their own are prone to complacency and euphoria. The best teams also have a mix of mental abilities, usually with the highest belonging to the plant, then the co-ordinator. The advantage of having people of relatively low mental ability appears to lie in the fact that these members tend to be willing to adopt the less 'dynamic' team roles.

Another type of successful team is one dominated by a co-ordinator who has unrivalled superiority in intellectual or creative ability over his or her colleagues, and whose office and natural talents reinforce each other in establishing ascendancy. It is not a recommended formula because of the gulf left when the co-ordinator leaves the team.

Whatever the composition of the team, all its members must learn 'teamspeopleship'. This goes beyond fitness for any particular team role. Good 'teamspeople' time their interventions, vary their role, limit their contributions (often difficult for teachers), create roles for others and do some of the jobs that others deliberately avoid. Most of these behaviours can be learned through training.

One of the problems in a hierarchical organization is that it is not always easy to bring the most suitable people into teams. The wise manager avoids building teams solely on the basis of ex-officio membership. Meetings of heads of department, for instance, often lead to disappointing results. It is often better to set up project or study teams of a mixed composition of people at different levels in the hierarchy; what such a team may lack in structural authority, it may gain in effectiveness, if the team roles have been well chosen. To give it authority, let it report to a project steering group, e.g. heads of department, which meets occasionally to advise on guidelines and objectives; or let both report to the head independently.

Finally, you can rate your own preferred team role on-line by visiting www.belbin.com, or by investing in e-Interplace, a programme that is widely used in fitting people to jobs.

Knowledge of one's colleagues' preferred team roles, and of the roles that have to be played in effective teams, assists the manager both in composing teams and in helping them to work more effectively once they are formed. For instance, if it is noticed that the team is missing its deadlines, it could look to its completer to inject a greater sense of urgency.

TEAM-BUILDING

Team-building is the most widely used approach to the development of individuals and organizations (Everard, 1995a). One widely used approach is Coverdale training in 'the practice of teamwork' (Babington Smith and Sharp, 1990); as at 1996 over a quarter of a million delegates had undergone this training and more than thirty LEAs had been clients. For the last thirty years, one of the authors (Morris) has been training teams in both business and educational contexts.

Teamwork depends on effective meetings, effective decision-taking, effective communication, the identification of team roles and effective delegation. Members of a team must be able to trust each other. The most important work of a team will be done by individuals between meetings. It is therefore vital to be clear on the three 'W's – Who must do What by When. Team-building programmes will therefore enable participants to practise and discuss their skills together before embarking on one or more major exercises, success in which will depend on using these skills.

Because so much of the work of teachers is done alone with children in the classroom, there may appear to be fewer opportunities for practising team-work than is usual among professionals in industry. Moreover, there is less of a tradition of using consultants or short courses for developing effective teamwork. However, teamwork should not be confused with group therapy. Its test is whether the individual members follow agreed team objectives when they are apart! Teams are an essential part of healthy organizations, especially those undergoing rapid change, and heads would do well to encourage the formation of more teams such as task groups and working parties to get new things done. Such teams must learn to 'gel' quickly. Most large schools operate with a top management team, which is an obvious place to start trying to improve effectiveness.

Newly formed teams have been observed to pass through five stages of development as they gain experience of working together (Tuckman, 1965). These are depicted in Figure 10.3. Awareness by the team members of these natural stages of team development helps to depersonalize conduct sometimes misdiagnosed as members' personality defects. Teams and their members should bear in mind that

(1) progress is not continuous – a team that is 'norming' or 'reforming' can easily fall back into 'storming' on a particular issue;
(2) if there is a change in team membership there will invariably be some regression – otherwise a new member may be excluded; and
(3) most importantly, senior management should not change a team that is storming' in the mistaken belief that this group will 'never manage to work together'.

Like all models, this one is no more than an approximation to the truth, but it does set a direction for development.

Teams are trained by encouraging them to follow a systematic approach to getting things done. Individuals who have the talent and skill to solve problems intuitively may feel that they do not need to follow a systematic approach. Intuitive thinkers tend to solve a problem by devising solutions and testing them until they are satisfied with the quality of their decisions. Most individuals, however, are more effective when their thought processes and actions are systematic; even intuitive thinkers meet situations when they need a systematic approach.

It is when people are working in groups that a commonly understood systematic approach becomes essential, since an intuitive approach cannot be followed and understood by other members of the group. A simple

Stages in Team Development

TEAM DEVELOPMENT →

FORMING (Ritual sniffing)	STORMING (Infighting)	NORMING (Experimenting)	RE-FORMING (Effectiveness)	PERFORMING (Maturity & Excellence)
* Unclear objectives	* Lack of unity	* Question performance	* Change/re-affirm goals & obj.	* Leadership according to situation
* Central authority	* Lack of method	* Review goals & objectives	* Re-structure	* Flexibility
* Conforming	* Relationships significant	* Review team & individual performance	* Change/confirm roles	* Openness
* Caution	* Cliques	* Open up risky issues	* Improve working methods	* Effective boundary management
* Feelings hidden	* Strength & weaknesses known	* Question assumptions & commitment	* Build on strengths	* Individual & team needs compatible
* Anxiety	* Leadership questioned	* Leadership discussed	* Resolve weaknesses	* Risk-taking
* Poor listening	* Tension, anger, cynicism, scapegoats	* Deal with animosities	* Develop team	* Pride
* Little care for others	* Confusion	* Greater clarity	* Willingness to experiment	* Excitement
* Initial pairing	* Failure	* Relief	* Better listening	* Learning
* Weaknesses covered up	* Hidden agendas		* Involvement	* Achievement
* Enthusiasm vs wait and see	* Disillusion			*Trust
	* Team's needs emerge			

Figure 10.3 Understanding teams

systematic approach provides a foundation for teamwork, and a basis from which to develop ways of meeting the needs of the team when tackling problems.

Such an approach consists of a logical series of steps that are followed in order to achieve a given task or deal with a particular problem. We met an example of this when considering decision-taking in Chapter 4. The main steps in problem-solving and team-building are similar:

(1) Define *what we are seeking to achieve* in the specific situation to solve the problem, including the criteria by which we shall judge success.
(2) Identify *why* we are seeking to achieve this.
(3) Generate *alternative means* of achieving this.
(4) Decide *which means* to adopt.
(5) *Act* on the decision.
(6) *Review* successes and failures in order to improve performance.

The acronym TOSIPAR helps to fix these stages in the memory:

Tuning in to the problem;
Objective-setting;
Success criteria;
Information and ideas;
Plan;
Action;
Review.

Time spent on the 'TOS' stages is time saved later on. Everyone needs to know exactly what the team's product is for and how it will be used.

The last stage is also very important in team-building. Teams should set some time aside before the end of each meeting so that they can review the way in which they work together to accomplish tasks. Such a 'process review' provides an opportunity for members to make observations about the behaviour of a group (e.g. uneven frequency of members' contributions), from which it can deduce reasons for successes and difficulties. When important points emerge, they should be processed into group decisions, e.g. on how to remedy the situation or to consolidate good practice. Then a plan is needed to implement each decision, i.e. a specific statement of who does what, when.

All systematic approaches lay stress on the importance of the team defining and agreeing its objectives (what has to be achieved), for no team can work effectively unless everyone in it knows where it is going. This may sound trite, but the authors have repeatedly found that teachers are not good at defining what has to be done and formulating sound objectives, either for themselves or for groups or organizations in which they work. Others too have observed that few heads are systematic at problem-solving (Leithwood and Montgomery, 1986).

Soundly framed objectives are SMART: as far as possible they should be

Specific, Measurable, Achievable, Realistic and Time-bound. They tend to be quantitative rather than qualitative, results-centred rather than activity-centred, and realistic rather than pessimistic. A small degree of over-reach helps to motivate those who respond to challenge; a minimum objective, likely to be met anyway, provides little stimulus.

Objectives can be broadened by asking the question 'In order to achieve what?' and can be narrowed down by asking 'What has to be achieved to attain this?' Objectives that appear vague and woolly should be narrowed down.

Another device for increasing specificity is the definition of 'success criteria': these define the situation that will exist when the objective has been attained.

An example of an objective that is too broad to lead to effective action is 'To maintain sound communication in the school'. A soundly framed objective, dealing with the same problem, would be: 'To have introduced a two-page weekly staff bulletin, which all staff use and read, by half-term, edited by Miss X'. The success criterion for this objective might be: 'During the second half of the term, no more than five staff will complain to the head that something has been done without their being told'.

These techniques need to be assiduously practised before it becomes second nature for teams to use them. Exercise 11 at the end of this chapter, for use by teams, will help to improve objective-setting skills.

Apart from unclear objectives and other manifestations of failure to define the problem, teams sometimes waste time by not listening actively to what is being said, with the result that one contribution does not build on another. One way of following the process of discussion is to use a form down the vertical axis of which are listed various categories of contribution, and along the top are listed the names of the team members (see Rackham *et al.*, 1971). Categories of contribution can include the following:

Seeking suggestions. This label is used when someone invites others to contribute their ideas, suggestions or proposals.

Suggesting. Can take a number of forms, e.g. 'I suggest we do so and so', 'Let's do the following', 'Shall we do X, Y and Z?', 'Can I take your idea a stage further?'

Agreeing. Covers all types of supporting or backing what has just been said; this includes nodding.

Disagreeing. Covers all ways of opposing or withholding support for what has just been said: i.e. not only an outright disagreement ('No, I can't go along with that!') but also stating a difficulty, whether valid or not: 'The snag with that is...' or 'We are running short of time again.'

Seeking clarification. Whenever anyone asks for a recap or checks that he or she has understood what was intended: e.g. 'Do you mean', 'What happens if A and B coincide?'

Clarifying.   Responses to requests for explanations; also spontaneous summaries of a discussion.

Interrupting.   Whenever someone breaks in to stop a member from finishing his or her contribution; or when everyone seems to be speaking at once.

Miscellaneous.   In practice, it is difficult to assess all contributions quickly enough to categorize them, so any unspecified contribution can be put in this category rather than go unrecorded.

In order to analyse the discussion in this way it is necessary to detach from the group an observer, who does not take part in the discussion, but is given the task of leading a process review later, to help the team discover how effectively it is operating. With a bit of practice, observers not only get quicker at recognizing categories of contribution but can also study sequences of contributions from which they can deduce what types help and hinder the team in particular situations. They can observe, for example, how ideas get lost when the next contributor after a suggestion is made completely ignores the contribution; or the effect of timing of a proposal, and the style or tone in which it is made; or the different ways in which different individuals habitually contribute, e.g. by making positive proposals, asking relevant questions, encouraging action, controlling use of time.

Other aspects of teamwork can also be brought out: the degree of openness and trust in the team; the quality of leadership; the use of resources; the clarity of tasks and decisions; non-verbal communication; the extent to which values are explicit and shared; the degree of commitment; and whether action follows discussion.

Teams (including school management teams) sometimes invite an outsider to be a consultant to the group, and to coach it in improving effectiveness. A consultant, such as an industrial trainer or college lecturer, experienced in group processes, can bring a useful amount of objectivity and detachment into the proceedings, and get the team to confront issues that, left to itself, it would probably suppress.

The main object of these techniques is to heighten the team's awareness of the process by which it tackles its task, then to make use of the insights in order to improve. It certainly entails some members changing their behaviour, which can feel threatening, but the only way a team can improve is by individuals continually adapting their behaviour to meet the needs of the team.

MANAGING TEAM PERFORMANCE

The effective management of team performance is central to school improvement. There has to be a clear and consistent focus on achieving *results,* both short- and long-term. Short-term results help success to breed success; long-term results are important in creating an enduring school culture of continuous improvement. The two are connected: Schmoker (1999, p. 67) points out that 'current organizational habits that avoid focusing on short-term, measurable gains are the major obstacles impeding not only isolated improvements but also system-wide transformation. Palpable gains are the key to leveraging change in the system...'

Actions agreed at each team meeting must be followed up at the next, to find out what worked and what didn't. Belbin 'implementers' help here, while 'teamworkers' help to sustain zest and 'shapers' relentlessly keep the team's eye on the ball (task orientation). Teams sometimes become engrossed in 'process' issues in their attempts to develop, but managing process is but a means to an end. The most important end for a school is *student* achievement, not just team or departmental performance, so there needs to be a logical link to some measure of this.

Team performance can also be impaired by biting off more than the team can chew. Especially if members are already experiencing a sense of overload. it pays to *prioritize* objectives and avoid working on too many at a time. By concentrating effort, teams can get relatively quick results, which is motivational. However, there can be a downside to tying a team down, because this weakens a potential excuse for subsequent non-achievement ('there was just too much to do') and it can feel threatening to have no bolt-hole.

Heads have a special role in managing the performance of teams in their schools: to recognize, celebrate and reward achievement. Teams, be they departmental or organization-wide, which can demonstrate that they have achieved an objective unmistakably related to improving students' learning deserve a public pat on the back. Praise should be tied to specific successes – not just general performance. The more that the whole school community knows about the many incremental improvements that are occurring all over the place, the more the culture of continuous development and improvement will be reinforced. Heads may have something to learn from the way that military commanders foster *esprit de corps* by consistently celebrating success. It's all part of leadership.

PERSONAL APPLICATION

Next time you attend a meeting of a task group to which you belong, try to focus for some of the time on the process by which the group tackles its task. Does it start with clear, agreed objectives? Is use of time properly planned? Do some members impede the work of the group? Is a systematic approach consciously followed? Do ideas get lost? How do you rate the degree of openness and candour in the group? Do people listen to one another? Are the resources available to the group well used? Does it hold a process review? If not, try getting it to agree at the next meeting to set ten minutes aside to reflect together on how effectively it operates.

DISCUSSION TOPICS

(1) 'Managers are paid to take decisions; why should I be co-opted on to this working party to decide a school discipline policy?' What are the arguments in favour of detaching teachers from their classroom work to contribute to whole-school policy and its implementation?

(2) Does the fact that teachers are tied to their classrooms because pupils cannot be left on their own imply that teams are less important in schools than in industry?

(3) How can you apply Belbin's research on team composition when the dominant criteria for selecting members are usually their work roles, subject knowledge and availability?

FURTHER READING

Adair, J. (1987) *Effective Teambuilding*, Pan, London.

Belbin, M. (1981) *Management Teams: Why They Succeed or Fail*, Heinemann, Oxford.

Bell, L. (1992) *Managing Teams in Secondary Schools*, Routledge, London.

Hastings, C., Bixby, P. and Chaudhry-Lawton, R. (1986) *Superteams*, HarperCollins, London.

MCI (1996) *Effective Manager: Teambuilding and Leadership*, Management Charter Initiative, London.

Schmoker, M. (1999) *Results: The Key to Continuous School Improvement* (2nd edn), Association for Supervision and Curriculum Development, Alexandria, Va.

EXERCISE 11: *Formulating Objectives*

In 15 minutes, as individuals, write legibly on flipchart sheets

(1) a personal objective in your job, for improving your competence or effectiveness; and

(2) an organizational objective for your school, for improving its effectiveness.

For each objective, establish success criteria and write them immediately beneath the objective to which they apply.

In one hour, working as a group,

(1) display the flipcharts and read them;

(2) by marking the sheets in silence, each individual should distribute five points only, among up to five objectives and related success criteria (other than your own), so as to identify those that come nearest to being soundly formulated (SMART). You are *not* judging whether the objectives are intrinsically worth while: only how well they are formulated;

(3) in discussion, agree in your team and list succinctly on a flipchart the criteria you used in judging how to distribute your five points each;

(4) still as a team, take the objective and related success criteria that scored the most points and use the listed criteria to improve them (in case of a tie, take either or both); and

(5) if time permits, form pairs to improve one another's objectives and success criteria, again applying the agreed group criteria.

11

Managing and Adapting the Curriculum

MATCHING THE CURRICULUM TO THE NEED

The Education Reform Act 1988 defined for the first time a National Curriculum that would serve everyone at school. Hailed as an 'entitlement', it smacked of what is now known as a 'one size fits all' approach, introducing inflexibilities that have since been recognized as unhelpful. Besides, it was too crowded. Sir Ron Dearing was brought in to ease the requirements and this process has continued (for example, students in Years 10 and 11 may currently be disapplied from having to study science).

It is increasingly realized that different individuals and categories of learners have different needs, as regards not only curriculum content but also mode of delivery, depending on their preferred learning styles and aptitudes.

Moreover, different stakeholders have different perceptions of the learners' needs. The government, for example, is focused on ensuring that the UK is internationally competitive, so it sets high store on standards accredited by a nationally recognized certificate of some sort, and on national targets of achievement by various cohorts of the population. These are used as criteria of effectiveness of the education system. Learners, on the other hand, have their own criteria, such as the avoidance of boredom. Parents generally want their children to 'do well', leaving school with good grades attesting to (especially) academic achievement, and leading to good jobs.

Employers, however, have significantly different ideas about curricular outcomes and continue to complain that the education system does not deliver on 'employability' criteria. The Royal Society of Arts has followed up its 'Education for Capability' manifesto with a project entitled 'Redefining the Curriculum' or 'Opening Minds', which takes account of the 'knowledge revolution' and seeks to prepare people for work organizations of the 21st century by proposing a competence-based curriculum (Bayliss, 2003a). Associated initiatives, such as the 'Campaign for Learning' aim to promote positive attitudes to learning and its facilitation.

At the same time, the growth of childcare, playwork, experiential learning and early years education generally has challenged some of the old assumptions about the nature of education ('filling empty vessels with knowledge') and reminded us of Thring's definition of a teacher as 'an artificer of the mind'. Child development theory and research, and the different pedagogical approaches of nursery nurses and of trainers in commerce and industry are other influences that are driving nails into the coffin of the traditional knowledge-based school curriculum.

Teacher training institutions and the 'education establishment' have been generally slow to take these developments on board, so it is left to progressive school heads to make the running, notwithstanding the strait-jacket of the National Curriculum and the entrenched attitudes of many experienced teachers. Guidance on addressing the problems of curricular change is given in Part III. This chapter deals with specific areas of curriculum management.

THE NATIONAL CURRICULUM

The introduction of the National Curriculum represented a major change in our approach to education. While the 'core' and 'foundation' subjects prescribed by the Education Reform Act 1988 are not substantially different from those set out in the 1904 regulations, the advent of 'key stages', 'compulsory assessment', 'standards of attainment', and 'national norms' introduced a common structure that schools in the United Kingdom had never previously known. To many teachers and heads, the National Curriculum appeared as yet another unwarranted restriction of professional freedom, and resistance to the changes was understandably heightened by inadequate preparation for the introduction of such radical reform and an increase in workload. Obvious benefits, however, are the greater ease of transfer between schools and the creation of standards against which parents, pupils and teachers can measure and agree progress.

There were fears that, in complying with the National Curriculum, teachers might lose sight of the fundamental purposes of education. These were restated in Clause I (2) of the Education Reform Act (and in subsequent legislation) where it is said that:

> The curriculum for a maintained school satisfies the requirements of this section if it is a balanced and broadly based curriculum which:
> (a) promotes the spiritual, moral, cultural, mental and physical development of pupils at the school and of society; and
> (b) prepares pupils for the opportunities, responsibilities and experiences of adult life.

We were therefore gratified to find in the 1990s that Ofsted inspectors are specifically required to report on 'pupils' spiritual, moral, social and cultural development' as well as on 'standards, quality and efficiency'.

Fears were expressed that project work and interdisciplinary work would suffer as a result of the new requirements. However, while schools needed to refocus some of their efforts in order to ensure that mundane yet necessary skills (e.g. spelling) are acquired, work in primary schools suggests that there is no problem in meeting most of the demands of the National Curriculum through the more imaginative approaches that have been developed.

MEETING THE NEEDS OF TOMORROW'S CITIZENS

One of the more certain things about the world in which today's schoolchildren will spend their lives is that the pace of change is likely to continue or even increase. We may expect therefore that

(1) any 'vocational' knowledge and skills acquired may well be out of date by the time the pupil seeks a job. Indeed, in scientific or technical subjects, what is being taught in the schools and universities has already been superseded as it is being taught;
(2) the future for children holds fewer 'careers' of a structured kind. Career 'ladders' have been replaced by 'scrambling nets' or even 'climbing walls'. Using another metaphor, those who are to succeed will have to jump from raft to raft of new skills as their existing skills and knowledge become redundant. This applies as much to the shop assistant or the typist as to the technologist or the teacher, or the lawyer or industrial manager; and
(3) employment patterns are changing: 97 per cent of UK businesses have fewer than 20 employees, 15 per cent of the workforce are self-employed, 2.5 million people work from home and 70 per cent of job vacancies are not advertised. All these figures are growing, suggesting that enterprise is becoming ever more important for school-leavers.

It follows that the most essential needs of tomorrow's citizens (as, indeed, of today's) will be those core skills which are of general application (e.g. personal and interpersonal skills, problem-solving, creativity, communication, numeracy) together with positive and flexible attitudes. Above all, they will need the ability to learn, in order to cope better with unstructured situations. While 'work'-oriented skills are of some value in preparing pupils for their first job, that is probably the limit of their usefulness.

Industry has often been accused of being reactionary in the demands it makes of education (e.g. in insisting on correct spelling, punctuation and clear, concise English expression as opposed to 'creative writing'). However, the report of the CBI *Greater Expectations, Priorities for the Future Curriculum* (CBI, 1998), contained the following statements:

> ... learning for life is a continuous process and developing employability is not a narrow, marginal or separate activity.

> Pupils' understanding of how to learn is more likely to be captured if there are different types of learning available.

> The evidence does not suggest that there is a pressing need to permanently cut back on other subjects to give more time for literacy and numeracy.

> The development of personal qualities and personal skills is one of the main purposes of schooling ... This development needs to be paramount if young people are to be self-reliant and flexible enough to meet the challenges of the future.

> Development of key skills (communication, application of number, IT, working with others, improving own learning and performance, problem solving) should be a priority for the new curriculum, at all Key Stages.

There is strong and widespread support for these sentiments (Dearing, 1995), and some of them were embodied in the National Education and Training Targets, accepted by government, employers and trade unions (NACETT, 1995). NACETT's third aim is 'All education and training develops self-reliance, flexibility and breadth, in particular through fostering competence in core skills' (now known as 'key skills'), as listed above.

CREATING POSITIVE ATTITUDES

Positive managers, whether heads or heads of department, will recognize that their role is to steer their school, college or department on a positive course through the sea of change. Furthermore, they will need the support of the 'stakeholders' – parents, potential employers, local authority and pupils.

If we look at the 'force field' acting on the curriculum, it appears as in Figure 11.1. Ofsted inspections, the National Curriculum and key-stage assessments could be added to either side of the field. Currently we would see them as weighing heavily on the positive side, but others' perspectives may be different.

In a negative environment, the school staff may be so preoccupied by legislative demands, cut-backs, lack of resources, 'difficult' pupils and the varying demands of the other stakeholders that an atmosphere of hopelessness develops among both pupils and staff. No one is happy in an organization which has lost its sense of direction and in which the constraints seem overbearing. Energy is directed against the constraints instead of towards a purpose (see Figure 11.2).

The first problem is to develop within the staff the attitude advocated by Reinhold Niebuhr: 'to accept with serenity the things that cannot be changed, the courage to change the things which should be changed, and the wisdom to distinguish the one from the other' (Bartlett, 1987).

The positive organization is one in which the constraints are defined and accepted but which tries to redefine and fulfil its purpose within those constraints (see Figure 11.3).

The task of the school manager, and it is not easy, is not only to ensure that a sense of purpose is maintained but also to ensure that the energy is being focused in the right direction for today's pupils.

There is no one simple formula for building a positive ethos within the organization. It is less likely to be achieved through a dramatic programme

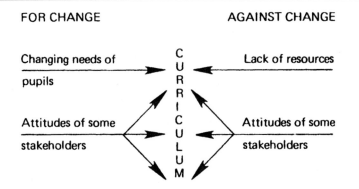

Figure 11.1   Curriculum force field

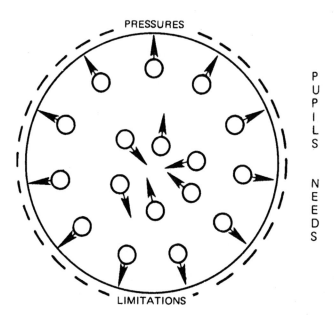

Figure 11.2   The frustrated organization

than by a consistent attitude and a series of carefully planned steps which will probably include the following:

(1) Sounding discussions with sympathetic members of staff.
(2) Sounding discussions with influential members of staff, especially the most frustrated and recalcitrant. (Listen and note their responses and, however negative the replies, do not argue but keep asking their views on what should be done.)

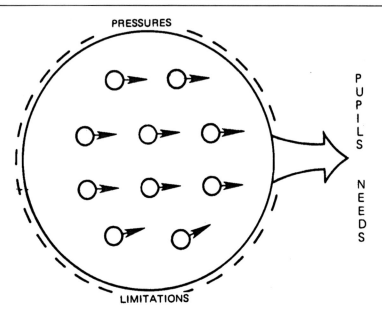

Figure 11.3   The purposeful organization

(3) Establishment of a small curriculum advisory committee (possibly heads
     of department, but this is also a good chance to develop some up-and-
     coming staff). Such a committee should be clear about its duty to sound
     out all members of staff systematically, to recommend ways of taking
     into account the views of the other stakeholders and to report its findings
     regularly for discussion by the total staff.
(4) Well structured discussion at staff meetings, based on an understanding
     that the aim of the discussion is to suggest what can be done within the
     constraints rather than to complain about them. (A realistic suggestion
     about how to overcome an apparent constraint is always to be
     encouraged.)

INVOLVING THE STAKEHOLDERS

The basic principles involved in curriculum development are no different from
those set out in the chapter on decision-taking. While the ultimate decision
rests with the school and ultimately the head, the wise head or head of
department will take every opportunity to ensure that, on such a vital issue
as curriculum, not only the staff but also the other stakeholders are actively
involved. PTA meetings, meetings with industrialists, and especially
discussions with older pupils, all present opportunities for involvement. The
governors are responsible for drawing up a general statement on the
curriculum of the school, and they must be involved in strategic decisions

about the curriculum (but do not take decisions relating to methods of teaching and learning). Suggestions can be invited, recorded and used. Education is not alone in having to adapt to the pressures of economic, technical, social and political change. Some widely accepted structures have evolved for 'corporate planning' and these can be adapted as well to education as to any other profession, to government or to industry. They provide a sound framework for thought, and discussion at meetings with staff and others.

CORPORATE PLANNING

The main questions to which stakeholders should be invited to respond are as follows:

(1) What are our aims and values as a school or college?
(2) In what order of priority do we rank our aims?
(3) What economic, technical and social changes do we anticipate over the coming years?
(4) What are the implications for the lives of the children in our schools? What are the threats and what are the opportunities? (The mark of a healthy organization or individual is a focus on the opportunities in change rather than the threats.)
(5) How do we need to adapt the curriculum?
(6) Given the needs which we have identified, how do our resources match these? What are the strengths and weaknesses of our resources?
(7) How do we need to develop or adapt our resources?
(8) What should be our action plan?

While it is useful to begin by discussing the questions in sequence, we should be prepared to amend our response to an earlier question (e.g. question 1) as a result of our analysis in response to a later question (e.g. question 3 or 4).

AIMS AND VALUE SYSTEMS

Few would disagree that the overall purpose of an educational institution is to prepare its pupils for life. However, as soon as we ask what this entails we find a variety of deeply held convictions, including our own. These convictions are the product of 'values', i.e. our perception of what is important, right or good. People do not justify their values in logical terms; they are the fundamental beliefs or premises from which other arguments are deduced.

Our values are conditioned by upbringing and by the group or groups to which we belong; many teachers are therefore likely to have certain values in common which will be different from the common values of many industrialists or pupils. However, while there may on occasion be fundamental disagreement about a particular value (some will believe that children should be taught to conform; others will not), the real problem comes with priorities. How do we rank in order of importance, for example, the ability to get employment, the ability to set up and run one's own business, the achievement of an academic qualification, a career in a profession, the use of leisure, an appreciation of the arts, the acquisition of knowledge, the acquisition of skills? The question is less one of individual educational values than of value *systems*.

Reconciliation of value systems is a need which is specially important to the educational and training role. Schools and colleges share the problem with churches, industrial training organizations and political parties. However, in the last three cases, a 'client' who is troubled by incompatibilities has the option of going elsewhere. Despite parental choice, this may not be such an easy option with schools.

For educational managers, particularly headteachers, an understanding of the value systems which affect their school is fundamental. How do staff see their priorities, how do pupils see priorities, how do parents see priorities, how do local industrialists see priorities? Are there important discrepancies which will produce tensions, a feeling that what the school is doing may not be 'relevant' and, consequently, discontent and misbehaviour in pupils, whose lack of faith may be reinforced by parental attitudes?

Though value systems are the underlying 'beliefs' on which arguments and actions are based, this does not mean that they are incapable of modification or even radical change. People are converted to and from religions, change philosophies radically, can move from idealistic to cynical systems, from spiritually based to materially based attitudes, and vice versa. Such shifts often occur because experience of life calls one's assumptions into question.

The important task for the educational institution is the reconciliation of value systems so as to achieve a clear statement of aims and beliefs to which a large majority of the stakeholders can subscribe and to which they feel commitment because they are satisfied that the process through which the aims have been defined has taken account of the main streams of fact and opinion. The statement of aims and beliefs should not of course be a watered-down compromise trying to be all things to all people, but one which clearly states priorities and commits itself to behavioural objectives of the form: 'A person who has been educated at this school should...'

One of us (Everard, 1993) has written a short practical guide to handling values issues, based on the work of Beck (1990). It is important in curriculum management to steer clear of indoctrination, but to enable students' values to be shaped in such a way as to prepare them for life after school.

PERSONAL APPLICATION

List the stakeholders in your school's curriculum. What do you believe to be the most important values or expectations of each in regard to the school? How do these relate to the government's requirements?

CURRICULUM DEVELOPMENT IN PRACTICE

As in all decision-making processes the objective in curriculum development is to collect and use positive inputs while reserving the right to decide.

As we have indicated, the sequence of input will normally begin with the staff and should probably end with the staff. Useful techniques which can be used with the staff or any other of the interested groups are as follows:

(1) Brainstorming on each of the first five corporate planning questions followed by a period in which subgroups respond to questions 1, 2 and 5.

(2) A curriculum representative committee to include representatives of staff, governors, parents and older pupils. Such a committee can stimulate, co-ordinate and use the findings of a wider circle of meetings.

(3) Questionnaires (possibly based on 'ideas' meetings) which contain a mixture of structured questions (e.g. the request to list a number of possibilities in order of priority) and open questions. These can be sent to staff, parents, governors, pupils and possibly a local employers' panel. They are particularly valuable in ensuring that a proper sample is taken, and the analysed answers show the weight of opinion in various directions.

(4) Classroom discussions with pupils from which the results are systematically collected. Such discussions are usually very fruitful and are motivating for the pupils, who may arrive at a better understanding of the possible purposes of education.

Whatever the method, it is important that results and findings are openly available to those who contribute. Transparency is the name of the game.

At the end of the process, it is up to the head, with the help of the staff curriculum group, to put together a final document for the consideration of the governors, which summarizes

(1) the aims, values and priorities of the school;
(2) the curriculum towards which the school will move; and
(3) the rationale behind these.

Though the head is the final arbiter, it goes without saying that the decisions should reflect the inputs rather than personal or staff prejudices. If this is not the case, credibility and motivation will be lost.

The whole process should have been carried out in the framework of the resource constraints and legislative requirements of which the school is aware. The force field, it is hoped, has now changed shape to Figure 11.4.

The procedure should have lined up the attitudes of a majority of stakeholders, though some will always remain opposed. However, the problem which still remains is that of adapting our resources. (See Chapter 13.)

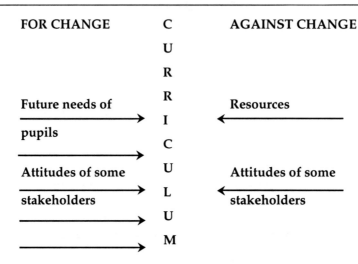

Figure 11.4   Revised curriculum force field

MANAGEMENT OF EARLY YEARS EDUCATION, CHILDCARE AND PLAYWORK

Since this book was first published, there has been a huge growth throughout the UK in the provision of early years education (i.e. up to 8), including childcare (a term often used generically), playwork, nurseries, after-school clubs and holiday schemes. This has been driven by the government's national childcare strategy, designed to encourage more parents of young children into employment, but it has also presented a golden opportunity for purposeful child development (as distinct from child-*minding*). About £1.5 billion per annum of public and lottery funds are currently being allocated to this sector.

Many primary schools have opened up pre-school nurseries and after-school and holiday clubs, often outsourcing their management. The private sector (both commercial and charitable organizations) is a major provider. Primary school heads need to understand the likely influence of this growth industry on curriculum strategy, and those who establish and manage child-care centres need to meet acceptable standards of effectiveness.

The prevailing pedagogical approach of most proponents and providers of childcare (but excepting nursery school education, which is more curriculum-oriented) is significantly different from that of mainstream education. It is more child-centred and less subject-centred, relying more on creating a rich and supportive learning environment and leaving the rest to children's natural curiosity and resourcefulness, than on teaching to a curriculum or to standard attainment tests. The key principle is that children are inherently active learners who learn best from activities that they plan and carry out themselves, and then reflect on. The emphasis is on the development of personal and social skills, including learning and problem-solving skills, but also involving familiarization with the alphabet, numbers and sometimes keyboard skills.

Well-founded longitudinal research has established that the beneficial effects of using this approach extend into adulthood, improving academic attainment and reducing the incidence of criminal risk behaviours, teenage pregnancies, etc. (www.highscope.org; Ball, 1994).

This approach requires the staff of a childcare centre to possess professional facilitation skills more than instructional skills, together with the relevant underpinning knowledge, understanding and values. Typically, they will be nursery nurses rather than qualified teachers, or have a National Vocational Qualification in Early Years Education or Playwork. Until 2002 social services departments regulated centres, but Ofsted has now taken over this function.

The features that differentiate the management of childcare centres from that of mainstream schools are:

- The regulatory framework specifies generous staff:children ratios of up to 1:8, whereas a sole primary school teacher is allowed to look after a class of 30 or more.
- The consequent inflation of staffing costs is partly offset by steep salary differentials between qualified teachers and nursery nurses, playworkers *et al.*
- Staff turnover is usually much higher – typically about 30 per cent p.a. – which inflates training costs.
- It is generally more difficult to devise reliable measures of experiential learning progress than it is with subject-oriented teaching, because such learning is more heuristic and opportunistic rather than focused on specific pre-planned outcomes.
- Because many Ofsted inspectors come from a teaching background, managers have to try to resist the 'structuralization' or 'academicization' of childcare, which would be counterproductive.
- Traditional teachers are apt to disparage informal education as mere 'play', and confuse childcare with childminding, whereas in fact 'play' (or 'playwork' to use the preferred technical term) is a serious, purposeful developmental process that stimulates children to use their imagination, be creative, learn about themselves and take risks.
- Professional development is usually best done on the job, so childcare centres are more likely than primary schools to be accredited for assessing NVQ candidates.
- The qualifications framework is less ordered than with teaching qualifications (QCA, 1999).
- Child-protection regulations place an even bigger burden on childcare centres than on schools, because of higher staff ratios and turnover.
- Because funding is predominantly by way of grants and fees, managers need to have the skills to identify potential funding streams and put

forward bids based on a 'business case', which can be a complex and challenging procedure, constrained by sometimes narrow windows of opportunity.

There are comparatively few textbooks on the management of early years education and childcare, but a useful manual, sponsored by the DfES, was compiled by the YMCA, which is the largest childcare provider in the USA and one of the largest in the UK (YMCA, 2000; see also Jameson and Watson, 1998; Whalley, 2004).

Primary school heads may notice pupils who have attended well-run childcare centres behaving differently from their peers in reception classes, by taking on more responsibility for utilizing learning resources and for organizing group-work. This can be mistaken for undue precocity, leading to the pupils being 'put down'.

LEADERSHIP AND MANAGEMENT IN THE CURRICULUM

The government now expects schools to foster leadership skills through the 14–19 curriculum by making more opportunities available to *all* pupils to experience activities that develop their management and leadership (DfES/DTI, 2002, section 46). Active Citizenship and 'Outward Bound' programmes are suggested as examples of such activities. Some of the text and exercises (e.g. Exercises 2 and 6) in this book could be adapted for this purpose.

MANAGING PUPIL ASSESSMENT

The growth in formal assessment following the introduction of the National Curriculum has been astounding. The system of national testing involves the biggest annual mailing in England – 4.2 million test papers in 80,000 packages, at a cost in 2003 of over £200m per year. The system of 'high stakes' testing, linked to the publication of the results and the production (in England) of 'league tables' has placed great demands on the leaders of schools, and their teachers. So great has this pressure become that, regrettably, there have been a few cases of headteachers cheating by falsifying results or opening papers early. One of the greatest challenges facing leaders is to reconcile the demand for accountability through national test results with the development of a curriculum which continues to give due weight to other aspects of learning which are not formally tested. The DfES policy document for primary schools 'Excellence and Enjoyment' (2003) shows that the government has begun to recognise that primary schools should be allowed to have a greater control of their curricula and be more innovative. A relaxation of the requirements to set targets at Key Stage 2 also points to the understanding that the climate of over-accountabilty has distorted the balance of the primary curriculum.

Assessment has a number of purposes, including diagnosing learning needs, helping pupils to improve and comparing schools. There is little at present that you can do as a school manager to change the use of assessment data for external purposes, but you can ensure that your school is using assessment for the purposes of learning. It is essential that consensus is reached, through the techniques described above, on the purposes and methods of marking, the use of criteria and the process of target-setting for individual pupils. Paul Black and Dylan Wiliam published a very influential booklet (*Inside the Black Box*) in 1998 which persuasively argued the case for teachers to use formative assessment rather than summative. This idea has now received official blessing through the inclusion of assessment for learning in the government's Key Stage 3 strategy.

Four elements of teachers' work need to be discussed and improved: questioning, feedback through marking, peer- and self-assessment, and the formative use of summative tests. A key message of assessment for learning is that 'giving marks or grades to pupils' work has a negative effect in that pupils ignore comments when marks are also given' (Black *et al.*, 2003). The technique of pupils assessing their own work or that of their peers has also been shown to be very effective, especially when they have been made familiar with grade or level descriptions. These need to be written in 'pupil-friendly' language – even teachers can have difficulty in comprehending the arcane language used by the examination boards in their syllabuses!

Many of these changes will present a challenge to many teachers and you will need to draw on all the skills of managing change outlined elsewhere in this book. It is best not to attempt to make all the changes at once, but to start with, say, improving questioning techniques and move on from there. You can help the process by setting up working groups of teachers to engage in mutual support and observation, and encouraging them to report back to departmental and staff meetings. Parents and governors will need to be informed about any changes and about ways they can help to use assessment to raise achievement.

SPECIAL NEEDS AND THE INCLUSION AGENDA

There has been an increasing emphasis in recent years on requiring 'mainstream' schools to include pupils who would formerly have been educated separately in special schools. Mainstream schools have long been expected to make provision for those pupils who have some special needs (such as relatively low reading ages) through the provision of extra support or specific procedures to be followed by the classroom teacher. In addition, many schools have been successful in including pupils with physical disabilities, and the requirements of the Disability Discrimination Act will increase such provision. However, pupils with, for example, severe learning difficulties, or emotional and behavioural difficulties, are now increasingly being directed to mainstream schools. There is considerable debate as to whether this results in effective education, and there is a lack of empirical evidence on the success of such policies. The teacher unions have been suspicious, demanding considerable extra resources in mainstream schools and pointing out that most teachers have not been trained to use effective pedagogy for children with special educational needs. There is also a tension between a drive for inclusion and the current emphasis on simple 'output' targets.

School leaders in such situations will have to try to ensure that resources are adequate, and that funding for teaching assistants is provided. This may well require you to use your skills of negotiation (see Chapters 7 and 14) to secure these from the LEA. Staff will need to be trained how to differentiate effectively and the pastoral systems will need to be aware of a wider range of emotional needs.

Headteachers of special schools have to look for staff who are good generalists, with high levels of teaching skills and creativity. These teachers understand different learning styles, and how different special needs affect learning or lack of it. SEN pedagogy and process come first, with subject expertise and knowledge second. Mainstream school leaders may have to adapt their recruitment criteria when seeking staff who will spend a large part of their teaching commitment with pupils with SEN. There are many examples of excellent practice in special schools and mainstream school leaders should ensure that their staff are provided with opportunities to learn from their colleagues in those schools.

An alternative approach which is being pioneered in some areas is to try to create a continuum of provision, with collaboration and flexibility being encouraged.

Case Study – West Hill (Special School) and Therfield (Comprehensive)

A shared commitment by the headteachers of the schools to meeting the needs of pupils with SEN led them to identify a way to collaborate which meets the needs of pupils at risk of disaffection (or already disaffected) in Year 10. This collaboration means shared costs, shared resources (staff, minibus) and inclusion of pupils from both schools into each other other's establishment. Some staff work in both schools, and there is a high level of liaison.

The project involves a group from West Hill who are taught separately. On one day per week, they link with pupils from Therfield for sport, social skills and the Duke of Edinburgh Award. This programme is taught off-site. A Project Trident employability programme, teaching practical building skills, is also included, as is work experience.

The benefits of the project include:

- motivation to attend school and to learn;
- a reduction of the negative effects on the education of other students;
- a more appropriate curriculum.

SPECIALIST SCHOOLS

Specialist schools are secondary schools which focus on their chosen subject area but must meet the full National Curriculum requirements and deliver a broad and balanced education. The scheme has been rapidly expanded in the last few years and the government has announced that eventually it expects each secondary school in England to be a specialist school. Schools may choose a specialism from arts, science, technology, business and enterprise, sport, music, humanities, languages, maths and computing, and engineering. They may also choose to specialize in a combination of two subjects. The school must work with a named 'family of schools' and with the wider community. A sum of £50,000 in sponsorship has to be raised from private-sector sponsors (which may include parents) and the DfES adds £100,000 to this for expenditure on a capital project related to the specialism.

The school has to draw up a four-year development plan for improvements in teaching and learning and for involving other schools and the wider community. In return, the school receives a grant per pupil (currently £123) for each of the four years.

The process of applying to become a specialist school is arduous and needs to be undertaken with careful planning. Governors, parents and staff need to be convinced of the benefits, and staff in areas other than the chosen specialism will understandably be initially suspicious that their subjects will be downgraded in importance or that they will see no benefit from the extra funding. It is common for a deputy head or other senior teacher to take the lead in drawing up the application, and the time commitment involved should not be underestimated. Obtaining the necessary sponsorship can be difficult, especially in rural or deprived areas, although sources of funding are available through the Specialist Schools Trust. However, many schools report that the process of auditing current strengths and weaknesses, and devising action plans to improve teaching and learning is valuable in itself, regardless of whether they are granted specialist status.

DISCUSSION TOPIC

To what extent has the introduction of the National Curriculum reduced or increased the school's scope for curriculum development?

FURTHER READING

Bayliss, V. (1999) *Opening Minds: Education for the 21st Century*, Royal Society of Arts, London.

Black, P. and William, D. (1998) *Inside the Black Box*, King's College, London.

Black, P. *et al.* (2002) *Working Inside the Black Box*, King's College, London.

Everard, K.B. (1993) *A Guide to Handling Some Values Issues*, NAVET, Aberdeen.

Garwood, M. and Dowden, M. (2001) *Curriculum Management and Assessment Manual: A Practical Guide to Managing, Monitoring and Target-Setting,* Pearson Education, Harlow.

Lyus, V. (1998) *Management in Early Years,* Hodder and Stoughton, London.

Powell, R. (1997) *Raising Achievement,* Robert Powell Publications, Stafford.

Whalley, M. (2004) *Management in Early Childhood Settings,* Sage, London.

12

Managing Quality, Risk, Health and Safety

Teachers are under constant pressure to achieve more without any increase – and often with a reduction – in resources. The euphemistic term for this is 'productivity'.

In such circumstances, considerations of quality, health and safety in particular can easily fall by the wayside. If they do, however, the result is almost invariably an increase in pressure on the school and, in extreme cases, severe disruption of school life with criminal penalties imposed on staff – especially senior staff – and heavy compensation payments to be made by the school. It is true that compensation claims may be met by insurers but there are often 'excess' clauses and insurers, whose business is to make money, will recover their losses eventually through increased premiums. Indeed, some risks have become uninsurable.

Quality, health and safety all depend on developing positive attitudes in both staff and children. Since 1999, schools have had a statutory duty to teach risk management (QCA/HSE, 1999). All in the school need to be aware of where risks may lie and of the disciplines needed to identify and control the risks. Hazard-spotting and troubleshooting can be fun, and these skills will be increasingly important in the adult life of the children we teach.

All that we have said so far is common to all elements of quality, risk, health and safety. It is useful now to look at each in turn.

QUALITY

The concept of quality and the means to achieve it have gone through some interesting gyrations over recent years.

The definition of quality as 'excellence' was replaced in the early 1980s by 'reasonably fit for the purpose' and since the late 1980s has swung back to be generally accepted as 'meeting or exceeding the expectations of the customer'.

These swings in thinking are well illustrated by the engineering industry. 'Murphy's law' – 'If it can possibly go wrong it will and it will happen at the worst possible time' – was not just a cynical view of inanimate objects, but was the principle which US engineers were supposed to bear in mind while maintaining aircraft during the Second World War. They should, in fact, repair or replace anything that could 'possibly go wrong'. Excellence was the name of the game.

Compare this approach with a discussion that one of your authors had in 1985 with the Quality Audit Manager (note the job title) of a major aircraft manufacturer. The manager said that one of his problems was that the design department prescribed the same tight tolerances in specifying all components. In consequence these tolerances were not always respected. What he therefore wanted the designers to do was to slacken the tolerances in cases where they were not really necessary, so that quality audit could ensure respect for all tolerances and in particular therefore ensure that tight tolerances were kept on those components where there was real need.

The logic in the above example is sound, but consider the story of a Japanese car manufacturer who built gearboxes in the UK as well as in Japan. Those built in Japan proved more reliable. The reason, it was discovered, was that, whereas the UK production workers aimed to create components that fell somewhere within the specified tolerances, the Japanese constantly aimed to produce as nearly as possible to the ideal dimension.

Since the late 1980s an increasing number of organizations worldwide have endeavoured to practise 'Total Quality Management' (TQM). In so doing they have drawn heavily on the theories, principles and practical work of the three best-known quality 'gurus', Philip B. Crosby, J.M. Juran and W. Edwards Deming. The three 'gurus' are not always in agreement, and the approaches taken by organizations are far from identical. However, there is fairly general concurrence on a number of key principles, and these principles are just as applicable and useful to schools as they are to commercial organizations, government departments, hospitals or universities. They are as follows.

Customer focus

Quality is 'meeting or exceeding the expectations of the customer'. Therefore you need to find out what those expectations are and constantly monitor the extent to which you are satisfying them. We have mentioned elsewhere that a school has a variety of customers or 'stakeholders' – parents, pupils, employers, government – and the importance of monitoring their expectations and our satisfaction of these expectations cannot be overstated.

An irony about meeting or exceeding expectations is, of course, that any improvement that we make rapidly becomes the new 'norm'. Further improvements will be looked for and any slipping back to the old standards will create dissatisfaction. Furthermore, the direction and emphasis of customer expectations will change.

Internal and external customers and suppliers

TQM defines our 'customer' as 'anyone who expects or receives a service from us' and our 'supplier' as 'anyone from whom we receive or expect a service'. Customers and suppliers may therefore be those whom we normally consider as such – i.e. people 'external' to our own organization. However, they may also be people within the same organization. Thus if the head expects a member of staff to produce a report, the head is the customer and the member of staff the supplier. Conversely, if the member of staff requires some information from the head in order to produce the report, the customer–supplier roles are reversed as regards that piece of information.

In a 'quality' organization it is, of course, expected that the 'supplier', whether member of staff or head, will endeavour to meet or exceed the expectations of the 'customer'. However, the next principle also applies.

Communication of expectations and capabilities

Whether in any given situation you are the 'customer' or 'supplier' you should try to ensure that

(1) the 'supplier' fully understands the expectations of the 'customer'; and
(2) the 'customer' fully understands the capacity of the 'supplier' to meet his or her expectations. If there are any constraints or question marks, these should be communicated as soon as their existence is known, otherwise the 'customer' may be 'let down'.

Get it right first time

A lot of time and effort are needed to correct mistakes. This truth applies not only to marking pupils' work but also to all fields of human endeavour including the running of schools. If incorrect information is circulated, if there is a clash of dates, if a flawed timetable is published, it is often not simply a matter of redoing the same work. Special efforts may be needed to ensure that all affected or misinformed parties are contacted and some ruffled feathers may need to be smoothed.

Research has shown that if you get something particularly right, one or two people may hear about it; whereas if you get it wrong, the number is likely to be anything from ten to over a hundred.

How do we 'get it right first time' then? Here the next two maxims apply.

INVEST EFFORT IN PREPARATION INSTEAD OF IN CORRECTION

The human tendency, especially under pressure, is to 'get on with the job', to 'get it out of the way'. This is particularly true if deadlines are looming. We therefore tend to spend very little effort in planning and preparing, a moderate amount in 'doing' and we may consequently need to expend a great deal of time and effort in checking and correcting. The need is to reverse the allocations.

CONCENTRATE ON THE PROCESS RATHER THAN THE RESULT

This principle is best illustrated by a production line, though it is equally true of secretarial work, classroom work, the organization of school events or any part of school routine.

On a production line there would traditionally be one or more 'quality controllers' or 'checkers' at the end of the total line and/or each process along the line. These checkers would scan the goods being produced and/or take samples in order to spot any defective product. If defects occurred on a fairly infrequent basis, the offending items would simply be removed by the checker and either scrapped or 'reworked'. If, of course, defects suddenly rose beyond an acceptable level, the line would be stopped in order to check for a fault.

The TQM approach is to say that no level of product defect is 'acceptable'. If *any* defective items are being produced there is something wrong with the process. Certainly there should be no need for 'checkers'. Instead, every worker and machine on the line should be ensuring that the process is being carried out in a way that eliminates errors.

The approach is, of course, the one followed by good teachers who do not simply correct pupils' work but try to ensure that pupils' understanding will be such that they make as few errors as possible in the first place but certainly do not frequently repeat the same error.

Carrying the principle over into school management tasks, the message is that we should not simply 'do' the timetable, 'run' the school sports day or 'put on' a school play but should first think through the various steps that will be involved, who will take them and when they will need to be taken. In setting up this 'process' we will need to 'consult' with those who will need to play a role (our 'suppliers') and communicate to them exactly what are our expectations. We may also need to train them.

However, the most important thing of all is that having made the effort to set up a process, we get the maximum benefit from it. When the activity needs to be repeated by ourselves or by others we want therefore to be sure that we

(1) do not have to reinvent the wheel; and
(2) learn from any problems that may have been encountered on previous occasions and update the process to reduce or eliminate these problems.

When human beings have solved a problem, they are apt to be so anxious to tackle other problems that await them that they completely forget to learn or communicate the lessons they should have drawn from the first problem.

The result is that the same mistakes are repeated again and again. Clearly defined, recorded and applied processes are the basis of the 'standards' discussed in the next section.

BS5750 and ISO9000

BS5750 and ISO9000 are quality standards that have been adopted by organizations of many kinds – industry, government departments, local authorities, retailers and hospitals. So far we have heard of only a few schools that have adopted these standards.

The standards are set by the British Standards Institute and the International Standards Organization respectively. Governments, including that of the UK, have promoted the use of these standards and many government departments and other organizations insist that their suppliers of goods or services should have been approved to one or other of the standards, which are very similar except, of course, that ISO is internationally recognized and is therefore increasingly preferred to BSI.

A 'standard' is a set of requirements to which an organization must conform in order to be given accreditation by the appropriate institute. Essentially the requirements are that the main procedures used in the organization are effective, well documented, known by those who use them or are affected by them and applied in practice. A most important requirement is that there should be a systematic review and update of the procedures. The organization is regularly monitored to ensure that the standards are being maintained.

The immediate objections which teachers – or any other managers – will raise to this approach are

(1) it creates unnecessary paper and bureaucracy;
(2) to implement the standards is very time-consuming; and
(3) the fact that you have described a procedure or 'process' does not mean that it will be followed.

The responses to these objections are as follows:

(1) In most schools there is already no lack of paperwork about, for example, organizing school trips, timetabling, dealing with absenteeism, detentions, discipline, dinner duties. The problem is often that it is created as problems arise and then forgotten or lost until the next time there is a problem. The procedures operating within a school can be a source of mystery to newly appointed staff.

What the systematic approach of BS5750 or ISO9000 does is to ensure that documentation describing the various procedures or 'processes' is organized into a manual or manuals which are easily accessible, must be updated as needed and can be referred to by established or new staff. These manuals are excellent induction training material.

(2) There is no argument that the creation of or systematization of documentation on 'processes' is time-consuming. This is an aspect of the constant management dilemma that to save time and effort in the long term you have to invest time and effort in the short term. We have discussed this elsewhere (p. 123).

(3) It is again true that to document 'processes' does not mean that they will be followed. We are indeed wasting our time unless we
    (a) focus staff's attention on the processes;
    (b) train newcomers in their use;
    (c) monitor compliance; and
    (d) update as necessary.

The application of TQM in school management

It will not have escaped the notice of our readers that TQM is largely a new language for restating many of the well established principles of management which we have discussed elsewhere in this book. A great deal of the value of TQM lies precisely in this fact, since the learning of this new language helps us to rethink our behaviour and to re-examine our criteria for effectiveness. By discussing TQM with others we achieve a useful common language.

Particularly novel and useful in a school context are the concepts of internal customer/supplier relationships and of describing and recording systematically the 'processes' within the school. This latter activity not only stimulates an improvement in the way we do things but is also an excellent preparation for Ofsted inspections and can save an awful lot of frenzied activity as the invasion approaches!

PERSONAL APPLICATIONS

(1) (a) List your 'internal customers' (i.e. those who expect you to 'produce' things for them and in particular those who depend on what you produce in order to do their own job effectively).

(b) Choose one or more of these 'customers', list some of the more important things that they expect you to produce and against each of them write in order of importance what you believe to be the criteria (e.g. punctuality, content, presentation) against which your 'customer' judges the 'quality' of your product.

(c) Discuss your findings with your 'customer' and the extent to which you are meeting/exceeding expectations.

(2) (a) Similarly list your internal 'suppliers' (i.e. those who are expected to produce things for you and on whom you depend for your effectiveness).

(b) Choose one or more of them, list what you expect them to produce and the criteria by which you judge their 'products'.

(c) Discuss your conclusions with your 'supplier'.

(3) Choose one 'process' for which you are primarily responsible (e.g. establishing your departmental budget) and one in which you are involved (e.g. organizing parents' evening, preparing the timetable). Describe each

'process' as it currently happens. List any problems the last time the 'process' was run. Amend the 'process' so as to reduce or eliminate these problems. How would you ensure that the amended 'process' was followed?

RISK

Since 2001 charities have been required by law to submit risk-management statements with their annual reports, confirming that the major risks to which the charity is exposed, as identified by the trustees, have been reviewed and systems have been established to mitigate those risks. Although it is only compulsory for schools in the charitable sector, it is good management practice for all schools to take stock annually of the risks they face. This enables heads to focus attention on mitigating the most serious risks, and is helpful as a defence if negligence is alleged after a serious untoward incident.

Although legal responsibility rests with the governors (trustees) or the LEA, advice will be required from heads and senior staff. The first step is to identify all risks that the school faces from any source whatsoever; this is best done by assembling groups to brainstorm them. Examples of risks are: fraud or embezzlement, expenditure exceeds income with no reserves to draw on, failure of IT systems, loss of key staff, accidents, a child abuse incident, litigation and loss of reputation. They can then be placed in categories, so that similar risks can be combined if necessary. Next comes a process of scoring (say, out of 10); judgments are made of the *impact* of the risk if the worst should happen, also of the *likelihood* of it occurring. The product is the 'risk score'. Ways of addressing the risk are then identified, and any explanatory notes added. The results are tabulated as in Figure 12.1.

High-impact, low-likelihood risks may be insurable. Low-impact, high-likelihood risks require alert day-to-day management attention. High-impact, high-likelihood risks (say, scores greater than 30, depending on the school's risk tolerance) require specific attention and regular monitoring. Focus on what really matters and don't waste time agonizing about minor risks. Can the risk be avoided by ceasing an activity? Can it be transferred by outsourcing the activity? Can it be controlled by introducing new procedures? Are the benefits of accepting the risk commensurate with the drawbacks of running the risk? Remember that life is inherently a risky business and excessive risk aversion can be damaging. Thus prohibiting conkers and skipping to reduce the risk of children hurting themselves courts ridicule and prevents the school from fulfilling its statutory obligation to teach children to look after themselves by learning the technique of risk management.

HEALTH AND SAFETY

In a book of this kind it is not appropriate to go into the many detailed regulations covering health and safety in schools. For these we would refer

Score	Category	Details of risk	Likelihood	Impact	How to address	Notes
24	Health & Safety	Arson	3 *Sample*	8	Install movement-activated CCTV system & alarm	School 2 m away set alight
	Financial Staff Pupils Inspection Operational Governance					

Figure 12.1   Risk assessment report – by risk score

you to the sources listed at the end of the chapter and, for a readable overview, to David Brierley's *Health and Safety in Schools* (1991) of which details are also given at the end of this chapter. Since its publication, inspectors have started to devote more attention to emotional health (work-induced stress). Our purpose here can only be to discuss some of the key issues and principles involved in the *management* of risk, health and safety in schools.

Liability at civil law

If a pupil, a member of staff or, indeed, any person suffers injury or loss as a result of the act or omission of any other person or persons, the injured person may be able to sue the person whose act or omission has caused the injury or loss, for compensation or 'damages'. Whether or not an action will succeed depends on whether the defendant is deemed to have been 'negligent' and/or 'in breach of statutory duty'.

For a person to be deemed 'negligent' it is necessary to show that the person being sued might reasonably have foreseen that his or her act or omission could cause loss or injury of the kind actually caused to the sort of person of the kind actually injured. Furthermore, people are expected to take special account of the sometimes irresponsible behaviour of children according to their age.

'Breach of statutory duty' occurs if the defendant has failed to comply with one of the many regulations which exist and, in consequence, injury or loss is caused to a person of the kind the regulation was intended to protect.

In either of the above cases the person causing the loss or injury will be required to compensate the injured party to the extent required to restore as nearly as possible the injured party to the situation and quality of life that he or she enjoyed before the accident. In the case of physical injury, damages can be enormous, though they may be reduced to the extent that the injured person caused the injury by his or her own folly ('contributory negligence').

The good – or rather better – news for schoolteachers is that, provided that they are acting in the course of their employment, the injured party may, instead of suing them personally, sue his or her employer (i.e. LEA, school governors or school owner), and this the injured party will usually do, because the employer will be insured and will, in any case, be more able to pay than the teacher.

Liability at criminal law

The Health and Safety at Work etc. Act 1974 places a duty on every employer to ensure, so *far as is reasonably practicable*, the health, safety and welfare at work of employees. It requires the employer to prepare a written policy statement on safety and to bring it to the notice of employees, to train employees, to provide safe equipment and a safe system of work and to meet with safety representatives appointed by a union. In the school context, this means that the safety of teachers must be protected.

The Act goes on to say that an employer must 'conduct his under-taking in such a way as to ensure, as far as is reasonably practical, that persons not in his employment who may be affected thereby are not exposed to risks to their health and safety'. This section (5.3) of the Act therefore means that the school must be run so as to protect the safety of children, parents and the general public.

In case this is not enough Section 4 of the Act says that controllers of any non-domestic premises must ensure that they are safe.

So far the person made liable is, in a school context, the LEA. However, the teacher is caught by Section 7 which requires an employee 'to take reasonable care for the health and safety of himself and others who may be affected by his acts or omissions at work' and to 'co-operate' with the employers in carrying out his or her duties.

If the employer and/or the employee fails in these duties, *whether or not there is an accident,* they may be prosecuted and fined.

The law is enforced by inspectors of the Health and Safety Executive who have wide powers to visit and investigate. They may also issue 'improvement' or 'prohibition' notices if they find anything to be unsafe.

Until recently the Health and Safety Executive left schools in relative peace, but there have now been several prosecutions of schools and school staff, notably for failure to take adequate precautions in science laboratories and use available safety equipment. There have also been prosecutions for more general safety failures such as unsafe wiring or allowing young children to use scissors with points.

MANAGING SCHOOL SAFETY

As we have already said, a book such as this cannot go into the detailed regulations and guidance pertaining to the many and varied aspects of school life. What we can do is to suggest a framework for health and safety which involves

(1) publication of a school safety policy or policies;
(2) training of staff and pupils;
(3) consultation with safety representatives;
(4) allocation of safety responsibilities;
(5) hazard-spotting and risk analysis; and
(6) emergency procedures.

The active use of such a framework will not only make the school a safer place but will also go a long way to satisfying the requirements of the Health and Safety Executive and Ofsted inspectors.

Let us now look at each of the framework elements in turn.

Safety policies

As we have already mentioned, the Health and Safety at Work Act requires:

> Every employer to prepare (and as often as may be appropriate revise) a written statement of his general policy with respect to
>   (a) the health and safety at work of his employees; and
>   (b) the organization and arrangements for the time being for carrying out that policy;
> and bring the statement and any revision of it to the notice of all his employees.

This is all the guidance that the Act gives, but for practical purposes there will be a policy published by the LEA and there should also be a separate policy for each school. Both these policies should be displayed on a notice-board, included in any literature given to staff for their guidance and discussed during any health and safety training sessions. We suggest that the content of the policy should express a general commitment to the health and safety of staff and pupils and go on to cover the other items in our 'framework'.

Training of staff and pupils

The school should ensure that all staff are familiar with the safety policy and know how to carry it out. They should also recognize that they have a duty to teach children how to recognize hazards, assess and control risks and behave safely (QCA/HSE, 1999). Ofsted inspectors will require proof of this. A useful leaflet entitled *Preparing Young People for a Safer Life* was issued in 2000 (HSE/IOSH/CCC, 2000).

The Social Security Act 1975 requires that an accident book be kept. Training should include the procedure for logging all accidents and for the reporting of more serious accidents to the local office of the Health and Safety Executive on form 2508 *by the quickest means available* (i.e. e-mail or fax). Staff should also be taught – and given a choice to practise – 'hazard-spotting' and 'risk assessment'.

Consultation with safety representatives

A recognized trade union has a legal right to appoint one or more safety representatives to

(1) represent the interests of employees;
(2) receive information from the employer; and
(3) carry out inspections or investigations.

Whether or not a union has exercised this right we would strongly advise any school to ensure that one or more members of staff have specific responsibility for co-ordinating health and safety matters and bringing issues up in management and staff meetings. These representatives may also organize training and the dissemination of information.

Safety responsibilities

No one person should alone be responsible for safety throughout a school and its activities. Responsibility and accountability should be allocated among the members of staff ensuring that everyone knows who is primarily responsible for safety in respect of

(1) each part of the school premises (office, classroom, laboratory, playing fields);
(2) each school activity (drama, school trips, parents' evenings); and
(3) each piece of school equipment.

Particular attention should be paid to areas of overlap (e.g. a trip organized by the drama group or music department) or gaps between two areas (staircases, corridors). It should also be clear how responsibility is shared among the LEA, the governors and the school staff.

Although one person cannot cover all these areas, one person should certainly have clear responsibility for ensuring that they are adequately covered by appropriate members of staff, and this person could also organize training. Ofsted inspectors will ask specifically whether such a person has been appointed.

Hazard-spotting and risk analysis

The fundamental task of anyone who is accountable for an area, an activity or equipment is to identify actual or potential hazards associated with his or her sphere of accountability. This 'hazard-spotting' can be a fun activity for children.

Hazards can be of two kinds:

(1) Physical (electric cables, slippery floors, torn carpets).
(2) Behavioural (running in corridors, throwing objects, cutting wood towards one's fingers, balancing books on top of lockers).

Often hazards have both a physical and behavioural aspect, especially where pupils are concerned.

One very important means of identifying hazards is to read the accident book. If several minor accidents have happened for the same reason and nothing has been done about it, you will be wide open to prosecution under the Health and Safety at Work Act – and rightly so!

How big is the 'risk' associated with a particular hazard is a multiple of two factors:

(1) The probability that an accident will occur.
(2) The potential seriousness of an accident.

The greater the risk, the more important it is that some action is taken to eliminate or reduce it.

The Management of Health and Safety at Work Regulations 1992, which are the result of a European directive, prescribe (regulation 3) that 'every employer shall make a suitable and sufficient assessment' of risks. The employer should then try (in turn) the following means of combating the risk:

(1) Eliminate it or find a harmless substitute (e.g. replace all spirit-based marker pens by water-based).
(2) Where possible adapt the workplace to the individual and not vice versa.
(3) Try to reduce the risk (rounded not pointed scissors, tape down electric cables).
(4) Prevent access to the risk (rope off newly washed floor, lock laboratories).
(5) If all else fails, provide protective equipment (e.g. goggles) for individuals who may be exposed.

In all events give warning of the risks!

A suggested form for carrying out risk assessments is shown in Figure 12.2, and these should be used and kept for any major hazards that are identified.

Emergency procedures

Finally, there should be clear procedures for dealing with accidents, illness and emergencies when these occur. These procedures should include

(1) alarm procedures;
(2) evacuating the building and assembling for roll call;
(3) use of emergency equipment;
(4) first aid in the event of accidents (who is trained?);
(5) summoning emergency services; and
(6) controlling the scene of an accident (probably the task of the staff member responsible for co-ordinating safety).

(NB Use a rating scale of 1 (low) to 10 (high) where appropriate)

Location

Hazard

Possible or known consequences – and to whom

Risk
- Frequency rating
- Seriousness rating

Existing controls

Suggested further action(s)

Resources needed and cost

Figure 12.1   Risk assessment

All these procedures should be made known to all staff and to the children as appropriate, and practised.

SOME AREAS OF GENERAL CONCERN

Although we cannot go into the many regulations affecting the various aspects of school life, it is useful to look in greater detail at three areas of current interest which affect all teachers:

(1) Control of Substances Hazardous to Health Regulations.
(2) Display Screen Equipment Regulations.
(3) Out-of-school activities.

Control of Substances Hazardous to Health (COSHH)

The COSHH regulations date from 1988 and concern substances such as solvents, cleaning fluids, paints, chemicals and even Tipp-Ex. Various objects containing such substances (e.g. permanent marker pens) are included.

It is a legal requirement that a written 'risk assessment' should be prepared for any such substance that is used on school premises. The Health and Safety Executive suggests that an assessment should involve the following questions:

(1) What substances are present? In what form?
(2) What harmful effects are possible?
(3) Where and how are the substances actually used or handled?
(4) What harmful substances are given off, etc.?

(5) Who could be affected, to what extent and for how long?
(6) Under what circumstances?
(7) How likely is it that exposure will happen?
(8) What precautions need to be taken to comply with the rest of the COSHH regulations?

We would also suggest that the assessment should include the immediate action to be taken in case of an accident involving the substance.

The best way of dealing with hazardous substances is, of course, to exclude them or replace them by a non-hazardous alternative.

Health and Safety (Display Screen Equipment) Regulations 1992

These regulations, which were created to protect habitual computer users, combined with other 1992 regulations to determine the running of offices. Though few dramatic accidents occur in offices, hazards often include trailing wires, guillotines, innumerable boxes over which people can trip, typist chairs which are unstable or cause back injury over time, loose carpet, precariously poised kettles and solvents.

The Display Screen Equipment regulations call for a risk analysis of 'workstations' – i.e. not just the computer but also desks, chairs, space, lighting, heat, reflection and glare and humidity. Things that should be checked include the trunking of wires, whether typists' swivel chairs have five feet and *not* four.

Furthermore, it is a requirement that the employer should provide eyesight tests at the request of any habitual user of display-screen equipment and provide corrective appliances for display-screen use where 'normal corrective appliances cannot be used' and the test finds special appliances to be necessary (e.g. persons wearing bifocal spectacles often need a special pair for computer use and these the employer must pay for).

Finally there is a requirement that people using display-screen equipment should have 'periodic breaks or changes in activity'.

PERSONAL APPLICATION

(1) Define what you understand to be your accountability for safety in terms of
    (a) areas of school premises;
    (b) equipment; and
    (c) activities.
(2) List any 'grey' areas where responsibility is unclear.
(3) For either 'a' or 'b' or 'c' above make lists of
    (a) behavioural hazards; and
    (b) physical hazards.
(4) Carry out a risk analysis for one or more of these hazards.

Out-of-school activities

For educational visits the same general principles apply as for in-school activities, and these are the subject of guidelines issued by the DfES (DfES, 1998 and 2002). The 2002 supplements to this *Good Practice Guide*, available from www.teachernet.gov.uk/visits, are particularly helpful.

One supplement deals with managing safety in outdoor adventurous activities, which are part of the National Curriculum and are compulsory at Key Stage 2. If such activities are to present the kind of challenge that underpins effective learning, there must be an element of risk attached. Part of the skill of conducting such activities is to enable children to experience the thrill associated with high *perceived* risk, while responsibly containing the *real* risk at acceptable levels. As most children are adventurous creatures anyway, it is safer to expose them to controlled risk situations than to let them take unsupervised risks on their own.

Some schools allow their teachers to supervise such activities and even have their own outdoor activity centres. Others take children to specialist centres, run either by the LEA or by charitable or commercial organizations.

If schools provide their own activities, the head must ensure that they are conducted safely in compliance with the 1974 Act and 1992 Regulations. Teachers have been sent to prison for infringing these. LEA outdoor education advisers or other specialist advisers should always be consulted. It is imperative to check that, where the activities come within the scope of a national governing body of sport (such as Mountain Training UK or the British Canoe Union), the teachers in charge have the requisite NGB qualification at a level appropriate to the activity and context, and that the qualification has not expired. Most serious accidents occur with unqualified staff in charge, and a BEd or PGCE is no guarantee of competence in the outdoors. However, a Scottish or National Vocational Qualification in Outdoor Education, Development Training and Recreation provides better evidence of competence because several of the constituent units cover health and safety in the outdoors and are linked to NGB requirements. Another useful qualification, Accredited Practitioner of the Institute for Outdoor Learning (APIOL), is just being piloted.

Contrary to public perception, most specialist outdoor activity centres maintain high safety standards, according to the Health and Safety Executive, which carried out 200 inspections in 1994 and 1995. This remains the case in 2003, when the Health and Safety Commission wrote: 'Given the number of people participating in adventurous activities, the sector is considered to be of low risk in comparison to other industries' (HSC/03/38: www.hsc.gov.uk). Additional assurance is provided by their membership of the British Activity Holiday Association (BAHA: comprising mostly commercial organizations) or of the Development Training Employers Group (DTEG, of which Everard is chair, is a consortium of 11 leading educational charities specializing in outdoor learning). However, the best assurance derives from the regulations that were developed by the Health and Safety Executive following the passage of the Activity Centres (Young Persons' Safety) Act 1995. These are administered by the Adventurous Activities Licensing Authority which inspects centres' safety provision and issues licences to those that comply (www.aala.org.uk). Not all centres, and not all activities within centres, are subject to this registration and inspection scheme, but those that are cannot trade legally without a licence.

Although the management of safety in outdoor activities is loaded with regulations, it is important to put the actual risk into perspective. More children get hurt travelling to outdoor centres than once they get there. And always remember the words of the Health and Safety Executive's publication on *Safety Principles for Nuclear Plants:* 'A safety culture should be established which will enhance and support the safety actions and interactions of all managers'; so with schools, in every department and activity.

DISCUSSION TOPICS

(1) 'Teachers have their work cut out simply teaching the curriculum; quality, health and safety management must come second.' Why is this wrong?

(2) What else can be done in your school to get quality and safety management 'into the bloodstream'?

(3) Employers who have endangered mental health and emotional safety have been brought to justice. What are the implications of this for school managers?

FURTHER READING

Brierley, D. (1991) *Health and Safety in Schools*, Paul Chapman Publishing, London.

Crosby, P.B. (1993) *Quality is Free: Making Quality Certain in Uncertain Times*, McGraw-Hill, Maidenhead.

Crosby, P.B. (1995a) *Quality without Tears: Art of Hassle-free Management*, McGraw-Hill, Maidenhead.

Crosby, P.B. (1995b) *Reflections on Quality*, McGraw-Hill, Maidenhead.

Deming, W.E. (1992) *The Deming Management Method: The Complete Guide to QM*, Mercury Business Books, Burien.

Health and Safety Executive (1995) *Managing Health and Safety in Schools*, HSE Books, Sudbury.

Juran, J.M. (1994) *Managerial Breakthrough: The Classic Book on Improving Management Performance*, McGraw-Hill, Maidenhead.

Ofsted (1994) *Handbook for the Inspection of Schools*, Consolidated Edition, HMSO, London.

West-Burnham, J. (1997) *Managing Quality in Schools*, Financial Times Prentice Hall, London.

13

Managing Resources

RESOURCE DRIVEN OR NEED DRIVEN?

Our ability to develop the curriculum in the way that we wish to achieve our objectives as a college, school or department will, of course, depend on the resources that are available to us. However, it is extremely important to ensure that the tail does not wag the dog, that the content of the education that we offer is not determined by the resources most easily available to us, rather than by the needs of our pupils.

Unfortunately, resources always seem to be most freely available in the areas where they are least needed. This is particularly true of teaching staff, who are most readily available for those subjects of which commercial employers have the least need. If we advertise for historians or English specialists we probably have a number of applicants of high calibre, but to recruit an ICT specialist, mathematician, linguist, physicist or engineer may not prove so easy. In consequence the best teachers in many staff-rooms are those whose subjects are least useful commercially. These teachers are likely to be the most persuasive both in curriculum discussions and in influencing pupils' choice of options. Does a pupil choose a subject because he or she has an innate bent for it, or because the subject has been well taught, has been made interesting and is likely to be taught in such a way as to achieve exam success? The risk in such a situation is that we produce more and more people with the least-needed skills.

A similar phenomenon occurs with equipment, and schools can easily become the repositories for cheap junk or, even worse, expensive junk sold to education authorities at 'bargain' prices. A powerful, high-quality computer whose manufacturer has gone out of business and for which there is very limited software may be of doubtful benefit even at a knock-down price.

We must therefore be clear in our resolve to define the needs of our pupils and therefore our educational goals. Though resources may mean that the swing towards these goals has to be moderate, we must nevertheless attempt to make the transition and develop our resources very deliberately in the desired direction. When staff or equipment have to be replaced, we should see an opportunity for change and question whether we really wish to replace like with like.

WOMEN AND EDUCATIONAL MANAGEMENT

One valuable resource which tends to be underutilized in schools is women. Since the first edition of this book was published, the feminist movement has strongly infiltrated education, but there is further to go before women are adequately valued in management roles. Women headteachers are under-represented in relation to the proportion of women teachers, yet there is no doubting their competence in senior management roles, both within education and outside. History, tradition and male prejudice, rather than objective rationality, underpin this state of affairs; strategic planning is needed to redress it, if resources are not to be squandered.

Adler *et al.* (1993) and Ouston (1993) have investigated the problem and identified a number of causes: stereotypes of women and managers; shortage of role models; women's comparative lack of confidence; interference with family life; and clients' expectations.

Some ways of improving the position of women in education are equal opportunities policies, monitoring selection procedures, equal access to INSET, mentoring, networking and support groups. The gradual shift from authoritarian to participative school cultures, and the adoption of styles of management that better match the prevailing values of women, will also help. We do not think it useful to regard (as some authors have done) some management approaches as gender specific. In our experience, some men are just as capable of adopting a so-called 'feminine' style of management as some women adopt a 'masculine' style. It is always important to suit behaviour to circumstances, and there will be times when heads need to display a Thatcherite resoluteness or a Ghandian gentleness, whatever their gender.

INVESTING MONEY

Resources are usually classified as

(1) human;
(2) material; and
(3) financial.

As far as educational establishments are concerned, the prime concern is how we share limited finance between the human and material in order to achieve our goals more effectively. The investment can take the form of maintaining or developing existing resources or of acquiring new resources. Investment may also take the form of buying in goods or services from contractors. The question is, or should be, how do we invest limited financial resources so as to maximize the benefit to the school? The question is doubly pertinent when the money available to schools is not increased, or is even reduced, from year to year despite increasing costs of equipment and salaries. Difficult choices have to be made, including those of making staff redundant in order to remain viable. It is also a distasteful fact of life that less experienced but lower-paid staff may well be a better bargain than experienced staff. Industry has long known this and remuneration tends therefore to be linked only to competence whatever the age or experience.

LOCAL MANAGEMENT OF SCHOOLS

Independent schools have long had to manage their own finances, including how they obtain those finances. 'Local management of schools' (LMS) has given to maintained schools the freedom to apply financial resources in the way that the governors and head believe to be most appropriate, and they are now able to switch expenditure according to need.

Under LMS schools control

(1) costs of teaching and non-teaching staffs;
(2) heating, cleaning and decorating of premises;
(3) supplies, services, books and equipment;
(4) some elements of capital expenditure;
(5) the use of any income they can raise; and
(6) relative spending under each of the above headings.

They are able to carry a limited amount of overspending or underspending forward to the next year, and can modify their spending plans to deal with unforeseen problems such as staff sickness *provided that* they stay within their cash limits.

LEAs may decide whether or not to delegate additional responsibilities including those for

(1) school meals (unless the school can show that it can provide these more cheaply);
(2) particular services (e.g. psychologists);
(3) major repairs and maintenance of premises; and
(4) special staff costs (e.g. long-term supply cover).

What LEAs are not able to delegate are

(1) 'major capital' expenditure (i.e. major investments with a life of more than one year, for example in land and buildings);
(2) LEA administration and inspection;
(3) home-to-school transport; and
(4) government or EU grant-aided project costs.

While the introduction of LMS has given schools freedom, the exercise of this freedom has meant that heads and senior staff have had to master the techniques of costing, budgeting, negotiating, contracting and financial control.

While the support of a bursar or other specialist administrator can be of help, all the experience of independent schools, industry and small business goes to show that to leave finance completely to the specialist is a recipe for frustration, conflict and disaster.

COST/BENEFIT ANALYSIS

The effective manager of resources will constantly be asking two questions:

(1) Looking at the present and past, am I making effective use of the resources available to me?
(2) Looking at the future, what is the most cost-effective way of achieving my goals?

While 'benefit' in education will not usually be measurable in financial terms, it is usually possible, and convenient, to reduce the resources used to a common denominator of money.

Some areas in which cost/benefit analysis can pay off in a school or college are

(1) the use of time;
(2) teaching staff/equipment/ancillary staff choices; and
(3) training decisions.

The cost of time

Calculating the cost of time is a salutary exercise for most organizations. A person does not simply cost the organization his or her salary but also

(1) employer's contribution to National Insurance;
(2) employer's contribution to superannuation;
(3) a proportion of common-room costs (furnishings, heating, lighting, etc.);
(4) stationery, textbooks, etc., for personal use;
(5) meals (if supplied), etc.; and
(6) INSET including supply cover.

These costs, if aggregated, mean that the real annual cost of a teacher is something between 1.5 and 2 times his or her salary. Allowing for holidays and weekends, teachers work for 195 days a year in the maintained sector and between a six- and eight-hour day depending on the time we allow for out-of-school activities.

If we assume a salary of £20,000 a year, therefore, some simple arithmetic tells us that the cost of an hour's time is something between £20 and £25. A two-hour staff meeting of twenty people, therefore, costs between £800 and £1,000. This may, of course, be money well spent, and it may be argued that some staff would not be doing anything else if they were not at the meeting. However, we should constantly be aware that we are using a valuable resource and ask whether we are getting the benefit which should flow from the investment.

Teaching staff/equipment/ancillary staff choices

In choosing equipment for the office or classroom, cost/benefit analysis should be a normal routine. Will a new telephone system really bring savings in staff time and/or some benefit that we can use in terms of our goals? If we get an interactive whiteboard, how will it improve the quality of our teaching, either directly or by freeing staff time? In the case of equipment, it should not be forgotten that the true figure for comparison will usually be the cost over a period of, say, a year. This will be a 'depreciation' cost (usually about a quarter of the capital cost) plus a maintenance cost.

There is, of course, no justification for saving staff time, unless that time can be put to other productive use or unless the net result is that we can cut staff numbers. Turning the argument the other way, of course, if staff cuts are imposed, an investment in equipment may be needed to maintain the quality of teaching.

Training decisions

Training should be seen as an investment and it should be remembered that the greatest cost element in training someone is his or her time, or that of the equivalent supply teacher. On this basis it is false economy to save money on course fees if pupils will then be taught less efficiently.

In all the above examples, the point is not that cost/benefit analysis will yield a result one way or the other. What matters is that we get into the habit of assessing proposals in terms of their cost and benefits, however difficult it may be to estimate the latter. Ofsted standards and the emphasis on best value should help.

BEST VALUE

The four principles of best value have become central to the work of the Audit Commission in evaluating whether public money is being well spent. The same principles are used by Ofsted inspectors, who are required to answer the question 'Are the principles of best value central to the school's management and use of resources?'

The four principles are

(1) Challenge, e.g. do we need to do this/buy this at all? What are we trying to achieve?
(2) Compare, e.g. prices, different approaches.
(3) Consult, e.g. those who would be affected by a decision to buy new computers.

(4) Compete – obtain/provide the best possible service at the best possible price by, e.g., a tendering process.

Ofsted will make a judgement as to how well these principles pervade not just the provision of material resources, but also all management activities and decision-making. There is no need for increased bureaucracy and paperwork, and most schools are used to applying principles 2 and 4, and to a lesser extent 3. However, we would suggest that the principle of challenge is not widely used and school managers would benefit their schools by applying it consistently.

BUDGETING AND FINANCIAL CONTROL

Fundamental to the success of investment decisions is that they are planned through the process of budgeting. Budgeting should start with the school development plan (see Chapter 11):

(1) What do we wish to achieve?
(2) What are our priorities?
(3) What do we need to do in order to reach our objectives?

What we then need to do is to see how we can best use the 'budgets' available to us. This process is an ideal application for a spreadsheet computer model with headings of cost down the side, months of the year across the top and, of course, the appropriate formulae to total by type of cost and by month.

Last year's costs will be a good starting point, but it is dangerous simply to extrapolate, and real value comes from challenging every item of cost to see whether it is really appropriate at that level for the coming year or whether a better result may be achieved by cutting one item and increasing another.

Assumptions made should be written down in a plan, e.g. 'We shall reduce the cost of cleaning by employing Easisweep Contractors.' 'The maintenance budget is increased by £X to allow for the re-painting of ...'

In going through the budget, thought should be given also to increasing revenue through, for example

(1) fund-raising;
(2) selling off unwanted equipment; and
(3) hiring out the school premises (not, of course, forgetting any additional costs).

All this effort in drawing up a budget is, of course, to no avail unless actual expenditure is monitored against it on a periodic basis, normally a calendar or lunar month. The latter concept (i.e. 13 × four-week periods) often gives a better comparison since we are comparing like with like.

Figure 13.1 gives a typical spreadsheet for budgetary control. For some of the main headings you may need to have subsidiary spreadsheets (e.g. teaching salaries by department).

	Period 1			Period 2			Cumulative to date		
	Budget	Actual	Variance	Budget	Actual	Variance	....	Budget	Actual	Variance
Teaching staff salaries										
Employment costs										
Other salaries										
Employment costs										
Heating										
Lighting										
Maintenance										
Total										

Figure 13.1   Budget monitoring

In order to help control, the figures used should be those for costs which are *incurred* for that period, i.e. though we may not have paid a bill or indeed received a bill, we must include any money that we have used for that period. This latter process is known as 'accruing', and we do it because the last thing that we want is a nasty shock when the bills catch up with us as they inevitably will.

Most crucial of all is that at the end of each period the head should review variances with the governors and senior staff and decide what action, if any, needs to be taken.

RESOURCE CONTROL

We have dealt with the control of human resources at some length in Chapters 1, 6 and 10. The control of our material resources must also be considered. It involves the following:

(1) Making sure that our material resources are actually present by keeping up-to-date inventories which are periodically checked.
(2) Ensuring that someone is clearly responsible for the control and maintenance of each piece of equipment.
(3) Reviewing the use to which resources are being put. This procedure has the benefits of
   (a) making us realize where equipment or space is available for some other use;
   (b) causing us to think about clearing out (preferably selling) redundant equipment; and
   (c) sometimes reminding staff that there is a resource available about whose potential they have forgotten.

ADAPTING EXISTING RESOURCES TO FIT THE NEED

A problem faced by schools is that resources in which we have previously invested may not fit the needs that have now been defined for the year ahead. Whether we actually achieve our aim depends on an ability to match our resources to it. Cost/benefit analysis, budgeting and resource control are tools which help us to invest money wisely and to avoid waste. However, in times of limited resources, success calls for 'helicopter' thinking and imagination. Necessity is the mother of invention. Again commitment will depend on involving staff via techniques which have been discussed in Part I of this book, but every attempt should be made to avoid conventional thinking.

The basis for discussion should be a factual analysis of what exists and how the resources are being used. We need

(1) a profile of staff against subjects taught and numbers of pupils;

(2) an inventory of all staff skills including those which are not currently being used. Such an inventory should include not only subjects but also teaching approaches;

(3) an inventory of equipment and how it is used;

(4) a review of available space and how it is being used; and

(5) an assessment of available and potential sources of finance.

Much of this information is required by Ofsted, and care should be taken not to duplicate work or forms unnecessarily. Against the view of the present, we can usefully set a view of the curriculum three years ahead with corresponding profiles and inventories.

A more radical approach is that of 're-engineering'. This is very much in vogue in the USA and involves imagining that we are starting from nothing to create the best possible means of meeting future needs. These analyses are excellent development projects for younger members of staff.

Finally, we need to look at how we can possibly move from the present to the future. The widest 'gaps' can be identified and brainstorming used to consider how these may be bridged. As a preliminary to the 'gap-bridging' brainstorm it may be useful to state some previously held assumptions about education and ask that these and others are deliberately set aside during the session. Typical such assumptions may be that

(1) teachers can only teach subjects that they know. (Can they not guide their pupils in learning about what is unknown to both?);

(2) knowledge is more important than mental skills. (Perhaps we can achieve school aims through any subject, if thinking skills are better understood); and

(3) classes should be of uniform size and consist of regular groups. (Should we not instead vary class sizes, so that very large groups attend 'input' sessions – i.e. lectures, videos, films – with the result that more teachers are made available to run smaller, interactive discussion sessions?)

At the end of such a session the curriculum group will, of course, have to reconcile their bright ideas with the realities of staff attitudes and what can be done in one year. The outcome will be a compromise, but it should take the form of an action plan to decide in which direction the 'push' should go, with practical steps for moving in that direction and clear responsibility within the school for making the moves and reporting back.

Typical actions could be to

(1) explore the possibilities of selling/buying unused/necessary equipment;

(2) make approaches for funds for a defined purpose; and

(3) ask a member of staff to consider how he or she might help pupils to learn a new subject or to learn in a different way.

PERSONAL APPLICATION

Given the financial constraints that apply to your school, consider how you would ideally like to see the school staffed and equipped so as to best meet governmental requirements and the needs of the pupils.

DISCUSSION TOPICS

What are the pros and cons of financial autonomy for a school? What are the key requirements for control?

THE ROLE OF THE BURSAR AND FUND-RAISING

The introduction of LMS led many maintained secondary schools to follow the practice of independent schools in appointing a bursar. Some larger primary schools now have bursars, and it is becoming increasingly common for smaller schools to share a bursar or financial administrator. The growth in the number of bursars has led to the formation of a professional association and to training by LEAs and external providers. The job description will vary, but typically bursars oversee financial expenditure, the management of the site and the non-teaching staff. Some are given a major role in the preparation of the school budget, but, as already pointed out, to leave finance completely to the specialist is very unwise. All financial decisions must be based on educational principles, and all senior staff should have at least a working knowledge of budget preparation and monitoring (these aspects are covered in the NPQH). Conversely, it is not sensible to expect the bursar to implement decisions without understanding their rationale, and for this reason many bursars are members of school senior leadership teams. A good bursar plays a very valuable role in helping a school achieve its aims, and should be given a correspondingly high level of salary, status and professional development.

Expenditure on schools has increased in real terms in recent years, but there have been, and will continue to be, short-term problems of funding. There will also be desirable projects which cannot be funded from delegated funds. Schools need to be aware of all the many sources of alternative funds, which include lottery funding, charitable funds, special grants from bodies such as Sport England, and sponsorship from local or national companies. Directories of grant-making bodies are useful sources of funds, and some LEAs have officers to advise on lottery bids. A member of the senior leadership team could have the responsibility to be aware of all funding opportunities, and to prepare bids. If a major project is being contemplated, it might be worth engaging a professional fund-raiser. You must ensure that he or she belongs to a reputable firm with a track record of working with schools, whose needs can be quite specific, and you should insist on talking to other schools with which the company has worked. Will the fees be based on the amount raised or be fixed? Will the fund-raiser be based in school?

How easily can the contract be ended if you are dissatisfied? For smaller sums, you should consider forming a working party of staff, governors and parents.

INDEPENDENT CONTRACTORS AND COMPETITIVE TENDERING

The use of independent contractors offers many attractions, particularly in situations where unions or individuals have become so powerful that costs have soared and the 'tail wags the dog'. This has been known to happen with caretakers, cleaners and kitchen staff! Among the advantages of using independent contractors can be

(1) lower costs;
(2) fewer management problems, since the school deals principally with the contractor alone and expects him or her to sort out any major issues;
(3) shedding of the problems and costs associated with employment of staff; and
(4) the ability to terminate the services of the contractor at whatever notice has been agreed.

On the other hand

(1) the school head may not have as much direct influence over staff;
(2) the management of health and safety may be more of a problem; and
(3) there can be difficulties in managing the contract.

Whether any of these last three problems actually occur will depend on the quality of the contractor and of the contract.

The school may be required to, and certainly should in any event, ask at least three contractors to tender for any contract. What is then important is not to choose a supplier on price alone but on best value. The selection process should certainly include an interview with whoever will manage the contract, the taking up of references and a careful study of what is offered, what guarantees are given and what mechanisms will be used to ensure customer satisfaction. The health and safety policy of the contractor should be studied and its conformity to the school's policy and requirements, of which the contractor must be informed. Last but not least, always insist on a probationary period and remember that 'cheap' contractors can be very expensive!

FURTHER READING

Adler, S., Lang, J. and Packer, M. (1993) *Managing Women*, Open University Press, Buckingham.
Coleman, M. (2000) *Managing Finance and Resources in Education*, Paul Chapman Publishing, London.

HMSO (1994) *Buying for Quality: A Practical Guide for Schools to Purchasing Services*, Her Majesty's Stationery Office, London.

Hywel, T. and Martin, J. (1995) *Effectiveness of Schools and Education Resource Management*, University of Birmingham, Birmingham.

Knight, B. (1993) *Financial Management for Schools*, Heinemann, Oxford.

Ouston, J. (ed.) (1993) *Women in Education Management*, Longman, Harlow.

14

Managing the Environment

THE NATURAL ENVIRONMENT

Although most of this chapter relates to the socio-political environment, it is worth noting that both public opinion and legislation are facing managers with increasing expectations that their schools will espouse 'green' values and set an example of environmental protection. Educating children on how to dispose tidily of litter is a continuing problem. Less well known is the duty to ensure that all waste that has been in contact with bodily fluids (such as wound dressings and tampons) should be separately stored in yellow plastic bags and identified as hazardous.

The need to reduce the emission of greenhouse gases has led to initiatives to save energy; even the national standards for managers include a unit to 'identify improvements in energy efficiency'. Competence in sport and recreation facility management is assessed against the backcloth of a number of values including:

> Respond to global environmental issues by economising in the use of energy and non-sustainable resources, by avoiding destruction of natural resources, by controlling pollution and by careful management of waste.

The Institute for Outdoor Learning, some of whose members supervise school trips, have a fifteen-point policy for environmental sustainability as part of their code of conduct, which enjoins members to conserve the natural environment, be sensitive to the impact of their operations on the local community and cultural setting and encourage knowledge, understanding and respect.

Many heads ensure that such values and codes are instilled into the school ethos and set an example by habitually picking up litter, switching off unnecessary power consumption and making the physical environment of their school something to be proud of. Others, alas, seem not to care, thereby spoiling the public's image of the school and adding to the negative forces that influence pupil behaviour.

EXTERNAL RELATIONS

In Chapter 9 we emphasized the importance of thinking of schools in the context of their environment (Figure 9.3) and said that heads are having to spend more time managing transactions across the boundary between their school and its environment. Recent legislation has intensified this need. Governing bodies have new powers and parents more rights. Although LEAs now wield less political influence over schools, they are still significant stakeholders, except for independent and foundation schools. Employers are also an important constituency and can influence education both directly and through bodies such as Learning and Skills Councils. It is therefore incumbent on heads actively to shape community expectations of schools, to solicit co-operation and support for their activities and to build a public image.

For many heads, dealing with these outsiders is among the least enjoyable aspects of their jobs (Jones, 1987). However, schools are not, and cannot be, closed systems; their boundaries must be semi-permeable if they are to thrive and respond to environmental change. The aim of heads and senior managers should be to direct traffic across the boundary and to forge inter-dependent partnerships and understandings across it.

To assert this is not to deny the uneasy relationships that sometimes exist with some parents, some governors and some elected LEA members. All can interfere, disrupt and consume time and energy. But the coin has two sides: they can also offer support, contribute and argue the school's case. The question is what heads can do to engender helpful behaviour, discourage unhelpful and, where there is conflict, to manage it constructively.

Ignorance often lies at the root of conflict and misunderstanding; parents, employers and teachers harbour myths about each other. The more we retreat behind our boundaries, the less we comprehend each other's worlds. Schools, like industry, have to project an image and actively manage their public relations; otherwise outsiders will form their own (probably mistaken) impression of what they are like inside. A school where visitors feel welcome and comfortable is less likely to engender antagonistic attitudes.

THE ANGRY PARENT

Even so, angry parents or neighbours will cross the boundary and heads will be faced with managing conflict. The guidelines in Chapter 7 (which dealt with internal conflict) still generally apply to conflict across the boundary: thus heads should aim to lower the emotional temperature, steer away from a win–lose situation towards a problem-solving approach and not start arguing or driving parents into feeling that they have to make a stand for the sake of honour. Self-control, listening skills and empathy are vital. Never assume that the immediate problem has caused their anger; on many occasions you will find that there is another, possibly more long-held, dissatisfaction with the school, and today's problem has been the last straw. Pause to think about and then reflect back what has been said, to show you have listened, and summarize at the end, including whatever action is agreed.

Always respect the position and feelings of parents; even if tempted to think them stupid, show them the opposite, remembering that you would probably feel the same way if you started from the same imperfect knowledge base. For instance, some parents have been conditioned by their experience of others in authority to tar heads with the same brush. Animosity should therefore not be taken personally, but seen as directed towards the authority role.

PARENTS AS PARTNERS

Running through the legislation is the notion of parents and teachers jointly involved in children's education: 'pupils are to be educated in accordance with the wishes of their parents' (Education Act 1944). The 1981 Act and Circular 1/83 see professionals and parents as partners in decision-making about pupils with special educational needs (20 per cent according to the Warnock Report). The 1988 Act requires parents to be involved in decisions about departures from the National Curriculum.

Quite apart from the law, good practice requires heads to cultivate fruitful relationships with the parent body. Problems are more easily resolved by parents and teachers together than by either alone. Parents' attitudes strongly influence their children's progress; so schools that set out to educate parents can enhance the classroom experience. Moreover, reservoirs of talent and goodwill exist among parents, and many surveys suggest that they would like to be more involved with the life of the school. At primary level it is known that parental involvement is a determinant of school effectiveness (Mortimore et al., 1988). The Sussex Project showed that parents who gained access to the classroom showed increased confidence in teachers. Joan Sallis talks of 'collaborative equality': there should be consensus about objectives, exchange of information about methods and dialogue to discuss the success of what has been done (Glatter et al., 1988, p. 150). Such involvement works; Everard witnessed in a project aimed at improving special needs provision impressive contributions of 'ordinary' parents not only at the technical level but also in the management of change. While teachers may have the edge over parents in pedagogy, in management many parents can contribute on more equal terms. The same goes for local employers.

GOVERNORS

Much the same also applies to the governing body as to the parent body, yet the establishment of effective governing bodies is identified as one of the three weakest areas of school management in an Ofsted report on leadership and management (Ofsted, 2003). Again there is a legislative framework (especially the 1986 and 1988 Acts): 'In a well-managed school, the head and governing body will work in a close and balanced partnership' (DES, 1988). The necessary changes in role relationships have taken some time to work through. The transfer of power and responsibility within the LEA–governing body–school system is a good example of strategic change, and several of the techniques described in Part III are relevant to building a healthy working relationship.

Heads have a duty to advise and assist the governing body to discharge its functions and many new governors pay tribute to the help they receive. However, some heads try to keep governing bodies at arm's length. Governors can only help to the extent that they understand what the head is trying to do and how he or she is doing it. This means sharing problems and concerns as well as achievements, and soliciting help and advice. Reports to governors should not be confined to factual reports of past activities; they should also deal with philosophy, strategy and forward planning. Many heads use the school development plan as a framework for their reports, using it to comment on progress towards its objectives, and to generate discussion on future opportunities.

A common complaint from businesspeople who become involved in education is that the papers they get are prolix and not user-friendly. Since schools are in the communication business by definition, they need to set high standards in communicating with busy people unfamiliar with teachers' jargon. Another complaint is that meetings with educationists are unproductive and inconclusive; although it is the responsibility of the chair to conduct meetings, heads can offer valuable guidance, avoiding the traps of overlong agendas and ill-prepared items (Chapter 5).

It is in the management of change that governors can be particularly helpful, acting as sounding boards and evaluating the effects. Governors are a potential resource for change and because of their position in the local community may be more powerful advocates of the school and its needs than the head himself or herself. Hence it pays to cultivate the friendship and support of governors and to involve them in the work of the school. Unfortunately, as Anne Jones (1987) found, this is seldom done well: 'what appears to be lacking between heads and governors is professional respect and any sense of working together in a common cause.'

SKILLS REQUIRED FOR DEALING WITH PARENTS, GOVERNORS AND EMPLOYERS

At the skills level, heads have much to learn from the methods used by reputable sales representatives in industry for fostering beneficial relationships with customers and getting them to buy products and ideas – sometimes called the skills of persuasion. They are not as alien to the school culture as might be supposed, for they are firmly based on consideration for others.

The key principle is empathy with the other party. Show respect for them and their opinions. Present your ideas and proposals from their standpoint. Understand their world. Consider their self-interest and what they are trying to achieve by relating to the school (you may have to ask questions to find out). Ask yourself how acceptance of your proposal can help them. Think of the benefits to them, rather than letting them infer these from the features of your proposal; you can turn a feature into a benefit by answering the question 'so what?' Also list the drawbacks to them of rejecting your proposal. Avoid, however, a long monologue; instead, use questions to establish in their minds the problems and drawbacks which your proposal will help to mitigate. Give time for points to sink in. Test reactions with questions and watch non-verbal behaviour.

Since both emotion and logic influence decision-making, try to get the other party into the right mood. Ascertain mood with a friendly question. Establish enduring rapport and create an emotional bond. Look for ways of offering a small service.

If you need a decision (e.g. agreement to provide resources), never end an encounter without one, even if it is only agreement to make one at a specified future meeting. Timing is of the essence in moving people towards agreement. They may need nudging. Once there, sum up what has been agreed.

If the other party raises obstacles and difficulties, handle the situation as you would manage conflict (see above and Chapter 7). Awkward or antagonistic customers who always raise difficulties present a special challenge. Try to soften your attitude towards them. Understand their mood, use tact and work through their objectives. Such negative people tend to lack friends, so if you can get through to them emotionally, you are home and dry.

Follow these precepts with sincerity and you will acquire a reputation as firm, considerate and 'someone I can do business with'. Your propositions and ideas will become more 'yes-able', though you may not clinch them all.

PERSONAL APPLICATION

(An exercise in empathy) List some adjectives and phrases or draw some cartoons that you think governors would use to caricature your school. Then construct in the same way your image of the governing body. How do you want each image to change? What should be your first steps in bringing about the change?

MANAGING AN OFSTED INSPECTION

An Ofsted inspection may be seen as a working relationship between two teams with the common ultimate objective of school development. The framework of inspection provides the guidelines for each team to follow. The Ofsted team (the 'joiners') will want to garner information as effectively as possible; the school team (the 'steerers') to present this information in the best possible light.

Some of the general principles that apply to inter-team interactions are identified in Coverdale training (Babington Smith and Sharp, 1990):

(1) Do not over-concentrate on the content of the inspection, but think about the processes and the relationships.
(2) Prepare well and agree the main procedures with the inspection team.
(3) Ensure that the inspection team understands the school's situation and the work already done by the school (e.g. a development plan). Forms S1–S4 are crucial in ensuring that the inspection team are given accurate information about the school's context. Wide consultation with staff, governors and other stakeholders will ensure that when the team arrives, everyone is well prepared to answer their questions.
(4) Agree what has to be done and the priorities, and a rough timetable.
(5) If the school team is to contribute willingly and effectively, they must be able to understand clearly and identify with the aims being pursued.
(6) The more people see their abilities, experience and ideas being respected and valued, the more willing to help they tend to be.

The independent review of inspection quality (Ofsted, 1995) showed a high degree of professionalism among those in both teams, and three-quarters of the schools surveyed were broadly satisfied with the inspection process. Schools prepare very thoroughly for inspection and most heads report that this is an effective team-building exercise. By following the systematic approach (Chapter 10) self-appraisal, review and evaluation are reinforced, so try to see inspection in this light. Good relationships were usually established (principle 1 above). Over two-thirds of headteachers were satisfied with the management of the process (principles 1–4). Less well handled was the involvement of staff in professional dialogues, and some support staff felt marginalized. Not enough is done to allay the apprehension of the staff before an inspection, which results in the 'freezing' of the school's normal development processes. The fact that no less than 90 per cent of schools report that inspections are conducted efficiently, sensitively and constructively can be used to allay such apprehension. Remember also that Ofsted encourages feedback about their inspection teams and has its own process of quality improvement, so they are on a learning curve as well as the school team.

Clearly heads must work to establish in their staff teams a positive attitude towards inspection, emphasizing opportunities and strengths to counteract the natural feelings of threat and fear of weaknesses – just as students are advised before exams to focus on the hills of erudition rather than the pits of ignorance. Ormston and Shaw (1994) express this as follows: 'We believe that the healthiest approach to inspection is one where school leaders inculcate in staff an expectation that they will be confidently operating at the highest level of quality assurances, rather than reacting to externally imposed quality control resulting from the inspection.'

The identification of weaknesses is not the end of the world; in a school that has developed a capacity for change (Chapter 16), it is a positive advantage to acquire independent data, set against national benchmarks, showing where there is scope for school improvement. A problem-solving task group can then be set up to implement the necessary changes.

Although over 80 per cent of secondary heads are satisfied with the inspection team's overall judgements, there will be instances where these judgements are called into question. Inspection is not an exact science, and judgements have to be made against numerous criteria in limited time. Some rough justice is inescapable in these circumstances. Heads may well have to smooth ruffled feathers and encourage staff to apply their energies to improvements that *both* teams agree to be necessary, and time may have to elapse before defensiveness plays itself out and the justification for a contested, adverse judgement sinks in. The fact that over four-fifths of schools are broadly satisfied with the key issues for action in the inspection report, as a basis for school development, indicates that well managed school inspection has a useful part to play in the improvement process. Secondary schools in particular have a high expectation of the potential for improvement and development afforded by inspection.

In common with other inspection processes (e.g. NVQ centre approval and verification), school inspection generates much paperwork and is therefore criticized as 'bureaucratic'. This is indeed a problem, and needs managing. You may need to deter those who have to complete the forms from being over-zealous, and you may be able to negotiate with the registered inspector some simplification of the paperwork. On no account assume he or she is inflexible until you have tested it out. Speaking as an NVQ 'inspector', I (Everard) like to believe that I am open to reason!

Inspectors have become more experienced in evaluating the quality of management and leadership in schools, using the following criteria.

For management, they assess the extent to which there is:

- rigorous self-evaluation and effective use of findings;
- monitoring of performance data, then appropriate action;
- thorough and effective performance management of staff, including support staff, in bringing about improvement;
- commitment to staff development;
- good management of recruitment, retention and deployment;
- acknowledgement of educational priorities in finance and resource management;
- application of the principles of 'best value'.

For leadership, they look for:

- clear vision, sense of purpose, high aspirations and relentless focus on pupil achievements;
- strategic planning;
- leaders inspiring, motivating and influencing staff and pupils;
- creation of effective teams;
- knowledgeable and innovative leadership of teaching and curriculum;
- commitment to an equitable and inclusive school where each individual matters;

• good role models.

(Ofsted 2003)

These criteria, and the greater emphasis in the latest Framework (2003) on inspecting a schools's own self-evaluation processes, mean that preparation for an inspection should not be undertaken in a great rush once the dreaded 'brown envelope' arrives in school. Good schools use the Ofsted Handbook (2003) as an aid to better monitoring and evaluation in their normal planning cycle. A useful exercise is to complete the self-evaluation form S4 each year. Governors and middle managers should be asked to complete their own versions, before drawing up a final version, in order to answer Ofsted's question, 'does self-evaluation penetrate to the heart of the school?'

Special measures and superheads

At the end of Ofsted inspection, the team will decide whether it is necessary to put the school into one of three categories:

(1) The school is failing, or likely to fail, to give its pupils an acceptable standard of education, and thus requires special measures.
(2) Although providing an acceptable standard of education, nevertheless it has serious weaknesses in one or more areas of its activities.
(3) Although not requiring special measures or having serious weaknesses, it is underachieving.

If the school has a sixth form, it is judged to be 'inadequate' if it falls into one of the first two categories above, and this judgement is separate from that on the main school.

HMI are asked to corroborate that a school requires special measures and may well visit the school to test whether the inspection team's judgement is well founded. HMI corroboration is not needed in the cases of serious weaknesses or underachieving, but in all cases HMI will visit the school to monitor progress in rectifying the problems. The LEA is required to support schools in special measures or with serious weaknesses.

We sincerely hope that you never find yourself in the situation of having to cope with the aftermath of such devastating Ofsted judgements and indeed if you and other leaders follow the advice of this book, you are very unlikely to. It is quite common for LEAs and/or governing bodies to pressurize head-teachers of schools in special measures to resign, and to replace them with headteachers seconded from other schools (often nicknamed 'superheads'). In extreme cases of schools failing to come out of special measures, they have been closed and re-opened (sometimes with a change of name) under 'Fresh Start' procedures. A school judged to need special measures or to have serious weaknesses will be in shock, perhaps with staff denying that there are serious problems, or becoming very demoralized. Stoll and Myers (1998) include some very useful case studies of how schools in such situations were turned around, and these and other studies indicate that a process similar to coping with bereavement is common. The leaders in such schools have a short time-frame (usually a maximum of two years) in which to bring the school to an acceptable standard. This implies planning for a mixture of changes which are highly visible and which restore the belief of staff, parents and governors that someone knows what is to be done, with other changes that take longer because they deal with the need to change ethos, values and structures.

THE SCHOOL IN THE COMMUNITY

There are now some impressive examples of how schools can play a leading role in developing their local community, thus fulfilling the oft-neglected requirement in the Education Reform Act 1988 and subsequent legislation, for schools to promote the development not only of pupils but also of society. Government initiatives such as Education Action Zones and the requirement placed on councils to establish Local Strategic Partnerships (on which schools can be represented) have provided new opportunities for school leadership to extend beyond school boundaries. Partnerships involving schools are helping to build communities and establish community cohesion. A government programme on 'Extended Schools – Schools at the Heart of their Community' is supported by a DfES team and £100m funding over three years (www.teachernet.gov.uk/extendedschools). A case study of this from Barrow-in-Furness illustrates what can be achieved with imaginative leadership.

Case Study: Barrow Community Learning Partnership

The Director of the BCLP project, who is an ex-headteacher, and his deputy, a former drama advisory teacher and head of arts faculty, have applied their creative thinking to 'promoting education which challenges, intrigues and empowers'. Two senior educational psychologists left their LEA posts to work within the partnership.

The team's first days together were spent developing a shared vision, using leadership development analysis to identify their strengths and individual problem-solving approaches. This early vision was subsequently developed and adapted as the team trialled various initiatives and projects within and with partnership schools. This was accompanied by continuous and enthusiastic investigation of the latest research into effective educational change (with the support and advice of Lancaster University Centre for the Study of Education and Training colleagues, Murray Saunders and Paul Davies) and developments in learning and teaching methodology. Throughout the life of the partnership the team has continued to adapt and reflect upon the process of change and how experiences can be used to determine progression and effectiveness – and subsequently raise self-esteem, expectations and achievement. Many of the processes that they used match those described in Part III of this book.

BCLP is a 'whole change project' aimed at effecting gradual, but sustainable, cultural change in the Barrow community, driven by a 'values'-led vision. Initiatives have been sustained which demonstrated those values and criteria identified as likely to encourage this cultural development rather than a quick-fix, results-driven, short-term approach.

The team eventually worked towards developing a methodology, which would encompass all these initiatives – 'BarroWise' - which is about building wise learning communities, developing a wise set of principles permeating all aspects of school life – and the wider community – balancing the practical, creative and cognitive with the social and emotional needs of individuals and the community.

These principles are turned into action within a range of school and community groups through

- thinking and reflection (cognitive domain);
- feeling good about ourselves (emotional domain);
- working, living and playing together (social domain);
- making wise choices (balancing these domains).

New teaching methodologies have been widely introduced, such as brain-based learning, critical skills, the behaviour curriculum, philosophy for children (P4C: www.sapere.net) and communities and inter-generational work. The work of leading researchers such as Howard Gardner, Robert Sternberg, Guy Claxton and Michael Fullan is being used within a context of local research. A new dynamic relationship between teachers (facilitators) and learners is instrumental in changing classrooms and schools.

BCLP has now developed its sphere of influence beyond the initial EAZ 5–16 education brief, through the establishment of two Network Learning Communities and substantial strategic leadership in a range of local and nationally funded projects – such as Furness Strategic Partnership, Furness Education Consortium, Furness Education Business Partnership, Children's Fund, Cumbria 14–19 Pathfinder, etc.

This approach is beginning to bear fruit. An Ofsted inspection in 2003 gave a series of 'outstanding' grades for lessons conducted by a teacher using Critical Skills and P4C techniques, who has subsequently become one of only three qualified Critical Skills trainers in the UK. Lancaster University's Centre for the Study of Education and Training is gathering extensive independent evidence of the success of the projects in terms of participation, engagement, impact and transferability. Evaluation is focused on the promotion of cultural change, not only within schools, but also in the wider community.

Some 120 (25 per cent) of Barrow's teaching force have been trained in Critical Skills techniques, including the first FE college cohort in the UK. Five teachers from Barrow attained UK trainer status in January 2004. The

Critical Skills programme throughout the UK and USA now uses a demonstration video made in BCLP schools as evidence of this successful practice both as a teaching methodology and as an agent for change.

BCLP has also worked closely with the Brathay Hall Trust, Ambleside, a leading international provider of personal, educational and corporate development programmes on a range of youth, professional and leadership projects. These programmes include the setting up of peer coaching within the BCLP team and school Senior Leadership Teams and the development of leadership skills and strategies, with a former Unilever manager acting as coach and mentor. These leadership groups have been established to nurture professional development and create leadership roles, not only in schools but also among parents and in the local community, where teachers and support staff apply the skills necessary to embed new approaches and technologies.

All this is based on an achievable, community-wide educational vision for South Cumbria – an area associated with rural isolation and high levels of social and economic disadvantage – in which schools and colleges are central to the task of neighbourhood regeneration and renewal.

For more information contact mason.minnit@cumbriacc.gov.uk.

DISCUSSION TOPIC

If you send out signals that 'people out there' are enemies, they may be-have like enemies, whereas if your regard them as potential allies, you will often gain their support. Is this true? How can you get people to want to help you?

FURTHER READING

Clegg, D. and Billington, S. (1994) *Making the Most of Your Inspection*, Falmer, London.

Dean, J. (1993) *Managing the Secondary School* (2nd edn), Routledge, London (especially Chapter 12).

Dean, J. (1994) *Managing the Primary School* (2nd edn), Routledge, London.

Foskett, N. (ed.) (1999) *Managing External Relations in Schools*, Paul Chapman Publishing, London.

Glatter, R. (1989) *Educational Institutions and their Environments: Managing the Boundaries*, Open University, Milton Keynes.

Jones, A. (1987) *Leadership for Tomorrow's Schools*, Blackwell, Oxford.

Ormston, M. and Shaw, M. (1994) *Inspection: A Preparation Guide for Schools* (2nd edn), Longman, Harlow. Contains a useful set of practical actions at the end of each chapter.

Stoll, L. and Myers, K. (eds) (1998) *No Quick Fixes: Perspectives on Schools in Difficulty*, Falmer Press, London.

West-Burnham, J. and Gelsthorpe, T. (2002) *Educational Leadership in the Community: Strategies for School Improvement through Community Engagement*, Pearson Education, Harlow.

Whalley, M. (2000) *Involving Parents in their Children's Learning*, Paul Chapman Publishing, London.

Woods, D. and Orlick, S. (1994) *School Review and Inspection*, Kogan Page, London.

PART III

MANAGING CHANGE

Organizations are dynamically conservative: that is to say, they fight like mad to remain the same. Only when an organization cannot repel, ignore, contain or transform the threat, it responds to it. But the characteristic is that of least change: nominal or token change.

(Donald Schon, 1971 Reith Lecture)

15

Change Described

THE NATURE OF CHANGE

How often we are aware that something is crying out to be changed, yet somehow the sheer inertia of 'the system' proves too great to overcome. Since managers are there to get things to happen, how is it that they so often fail to achieve significant, timely or orderly change?

Industry, like education, has faced this problem for many years, and not only is it now more clearly understood but it is also one that has become the focus of a good deal of management training, with considerable success. In the past, most training has been aimed at helping managers to manage the status quo more efficiently but, as the environment becomes more turbulent, so it becomes more important to develop their skill in coping with change, and indeed in steering it. The Education Reform Act and subsequent legislation have put change at the top of the agenda in schools.

The main thrust in raising managers' capacity to manage change has come from a set of behavioural science theories and approaches called 'organization development', usually abbreviated to 'OD'. Schmuck *et al.* (1977) are one of its leading proponents in the context of education. Fullan *et al.* (1980), also proponents, have defined it thus:

> OD in school districts is a coherent, systematically planned, sustained effort at system self-study and improvement, focusing explicitly on change in formal and informal procedures, processes, norms or structures, using behavioural science concepts. The goals of OD include improving both the quality of life of individuals as well as organizational functioning and performance, with a direct or indirect focus on educational issues.

The meaning of the phrase has been changing somewhat over the years (Everard, 1989b), and the corpus of knowledge is now more popularly described as 'the management of change' or, outside the UK, 'school improvement' (Weindling, 1989).

Unsuccessful attempts to change organizations have been made throughout history: Caius Petronius, for example, a Roman consul, recorded his experience thus:

> We trained hard, but it seemed that every time we were beginning to form up into teams we would be reorganized. I was to learn later in life that we tend to meet any new situation by reorganizing; and a wonderful method it can be for creating the illusion of progress while producing confusion, inefficiency and demoralization.
>
> (Peter, 1996)

What are among the causes of success? Do the same factors account for success in educational change? Is it possible to make useful generalizations about effecting major change which can be applied to any new situation, and thus produce a 'tool-kit' for managers in schools to carry around with them? Unfortunately the subject is more complex than it might appear (Stoll, 2003; Fullan, 2003). In any case there is no way of learning how to manage change solely from a book: real proficiency comes from practical experience accompanied by reflective learning. Nevertheless, we can set out the important principles, offer useful techniques and give some practical guidance on systematic approaches to change.

Since one of the main difficulties in managing change is conceptualizing the process, we need to start by asking what we mean by 'change' and by related words such as 'innovation' and 'development'. For practical purposes we can ignore the semantic differences between these words.

Let us take some concrete examples of recent changes in many schools:

(1)   Introducing local management (LMS).
(2)   Improving the quality of school management or leadership.
(3)   Setting and implementing educational objectives for the school.
(4)   Developing a whole-school policy.
(5)   Introducing a formal system of staff appraisal and development.
(6)   Amalgamating two schools.
(7)   Opting out.
(8)   Building closer links with the community.
(9)   Bringing new information technology into school administration and the curriculum.
(10)   Implementing the National Curriculum and subsequent changes.

Why are such changes apt to be so fraught, and only rarely turn out to surpass our reasonable expectations of the benefits to result from them? The problem with change is that it is far more difficult to manage than people with limited experience of managing organizations think it should be. Those with particularly rational minds have major problems in encompassing the complexities of implementing change; the more obvious the need for it, in their view, the more exasperatingly obtuse are those responsible for failing to carry it out. However, to grasp the nature of change one has to understand the more subtle ingredients in human and organizational behaviour. Beckhard and Harris (1987, p. 116), from their wealth of experience of consulting with managers on their change efforts, conclude:

> One of the biggest traps ... is the failure of organizational leaders to resist the temptation to rush through the planning process to get to the 'action stage' ... it has been our experience that a great portion of large-system change efforts failed because of lack of understanding on the part of the organizational leadership of what the process of intervention and change involves. When the manager lacks an appreciation for and understanding of the complexity of the intervention process, it is predictable that the emphasis will be on 'action' or results.

Although this book aims to be practical and skills oriented, we cannot escape having a section on problems and concepts of the change process, before coming down to practical guidance. The nature of change is not well explained in many management books, nor in many management courses. Perhaps this is caused by failure to distinguish among theories of education (what we ought to be doing in schools), theories of organization (how we should be set up to do it), theories of change (what causes progress towards where we want to be) and theories of changing (what has to be done to influence those causes). Let us therefore try to unpick the problem.

The call for change may spring from outside the school or educational system, or from within. The growth of ethnic minorities in the UK's population, the alleged failure of education to prepare young people for working life and the erosion of the country's capacity to afford escalating public expenditure have all been cited as reasons for making changes in schools. But within schools themselves situations arise that cry out for change: a failure of discipline, dissatisfaction with exam results or a member of staff (including the head) wanting something done differently. In the discussion that follows we shall have in mind mainly change stemming from outside the school, but regardless of the source there are some fairly common factors:

(1) The individuals involved will start with different feelings about the desirability of the change, some seeing it as a threat or a source of insecurity and of concern about personal exposure and possible weakness. The change may involve having to learn new skills and attitudes and unlearning old ones and the 'not invented here' syndrome may apply. The co-operation of all cannot be assumed, yet it may be essential if the change is to be successful.
(2) It will not be clear at the beginning how things will look when the change has been implemented: there will be many unknowns and fear of the unknown. Even the few people around with a clear vision may find themselves confronted by a number of different visions and fantasies among their colleagues.
(3) Institutional politics will become important: individuals will align around common interest groups, both informal (e.g. a staff-room coalition) and formal (e.g. a union).
(4) There will be a number of internal consequences of the change: it will

impinge on various systems and interests inside the school (e.g. the exam system and pupils' interests).

(5) The school in which the change occurs is not isolated: the change itself may stem from, and the results impinge on, a part of the environment, such as the local education authority.

(6) The change is complex, or at least by no means straightforward, in that the correct action may be counterintuitive: it involves many people's behaviour over a period of time.

(7) There are a number of obstacles to the change: some are obvious, others latent. Examples are organizational impedimenta like status, demarcation, authority; lack of support and commitment, or of resources; the psychological or legal contract between the teacher and the school; all kinds of personal motives. In any organization there are always people who can be relied on to think of 101 reasons why something can't be done (see Figure 18.2, p. 281)!

(8) Several ways of implementing the change can be envisaged: there are, for example, degrees of freedom in the order in which necessary tasks are tackled, who does them, who is consulted and who is told – all of which may generate conflict.

(9) Those in managerial positions will sense that the change will involve them in a lot of conflict, bother and hard work. This they may dread, especially if they feel hard pressed already.

In other words, change of the kind we are describing engages both our intellect and our emotions; it may impinge on people's value systems; it affects not only individuals but also the organization, its structures, its norms and its environment. Consequently, it will not happen successfully unless it is promoted, steered or facilitated with all these crucial factors being taken into account.

PERSONAL APPLICATION

Think of some example of actual or needed change in your school. Do they match this general description? How would you like to amplify it? Do you recognize all the factors listed above? How far are they taken into account in managing the change?

APPRECIATING THE COMPLEXITY OF CHANGE

Dynamic conservatism is a social phenomenon. It stems more from the propensity of social systems to protect their integrity and thus to continue to provide a familiar framework within which individuals can order and make sense of their lives, than from the apparent stupidity of individuals who can't see what is good for them.

Few individuals in organizations appreciate how multidimensional change really is; we tend to espouse a comfortably simplistic notion of it. Sometimes this helps; we might not so readily accept some changes if we could foresee all the implications. But usually it hinders change, because it diverts us from dealing with reality. Once we apprehend that it is the *social system* that withstands change, we begin to realize some of the complexity; for there exist within such systems innumerable relationships, unwritten norms, vested interests and other characteristics that will probably be disturbed by a proposed change.

Heads and senior staff who want to implement change therefore have a sizeable educational task on their hands: they have to help everyone concerned to discover and conceptualize the true nature of change and how it impinges upon us all. (This is separate from the equally important need to develop the skills for coping with change.) Change will affect beliefs, assumptions and values, and be affected by them. Change will alter the way we are expected to do things. And change will alter the things we need to do them with.

This attempt to help people to conceptualize change is like tilling the ground before planting the seed; or to use another metaphor, it is like tuning the receiver to the carrier wave before the message of change is transmitted. It involves both helping people to understand change – any change – in the abstract, and helping them to apprehend the nature of the particular change being introduced. These matters have to be discussed face to face; it is insufficient to read about them – they must be tossed around and savoured. There must be a suitable outlet for the fears that the prospect of change evokes in everybody (however robust) – fears that one will not be able to cope, that one's sense of competence will be eroded and one's occupational identity will be dented.

It is no use pretending, in stiff upper-lip fashion, that these feelings do not occur when we confront the need for behavioural or conceptual adjustment: they do, and we might as well come to terms with it. Change usually leads to temporary incompetence, and that is uncomfortable. Some changes (TVEI and ERA, for example) challenged the core values we hold about the purpose of education, a purpose in which we have invested our careers. They may also shake vague, unarticulated beliefs which we have never quite understood, or discussed with professional colleagues. Fear of tampering with something unknown but still perceived as important can only be assuaged by trying to clarify what it is we are really worried about. So it helps to hammer out a set of beliefs that are shared with colleagues and regularly subjected to review and revision in the light of experience: beliefs about *both* education *and* change.

WHY PLANS FOR IMPLEMENTING CHANGE FAIL

The best laid schemes o' mice an' men Gang aft a-gley.

The first reason why those who initiate change often fail to secure a successful conclusion to their dreams is that they tend to be too rational. They develop in their minds a clear, coherent vision of where they want to be at, and they assume that all they have to do is to spell out the logic to the world in words of one syllable, and then everyone will be immediately motivated to follow the lead. The more vivid their mental picture of the goal, and the more conviction they have that it is the right goal, the more likely they are to stir up opposition, and the less successful they are likely to be in managing a process of change. As George Bernard Shaw once observed: 'Reformers have the idea that change can be achieved by brute sanity.'

Another reason is that reformers are operating at a different level of thought from that of the people to be affected by the change. Take, for instance, the implementation of the Education Act 1981, for which there could be six levels:

(1) *Philosophy*. Integration of children with special educational needs in mainstream schools.
(2) *Principle*. Education to be in least restrictive environment.
(3) *Concept*. Locational, social, functional integration.
(4) *Strategy*. Provide support staff and systems to achieve integration.
(5) *Design*. Set up multiskilled force of peripatetic professionals.
(6) *Action*. Establish new posts according to plan and eliminate some existing posts.

If the head of a special school, having been exposed by an education officer to the higher levels of thinking and having agreed to the strategy, were to spring straight into action with his or her staff, without first engaging at their level of thinking, they would undoubtedly resist.

Effecting change calls for open-mindedness and a readiness to understand the feelings and position of others. Truth and reality are multifaceted, and the reality of other people's worlds is different from yours. Most people act rationally and sensibly within the reality of the world *as they see it*. They make assumptions about the world, and about the causes of things, which differ from yours, because their experiences are different, and they even experience the same event in different ways. Hence innovators have to address themselves not just to the world they see but also to the world other people see, however misguided, perverse and distorted they may think the outlook of others to be.

Therefore, implementing change is not a question of defining an end and letting others get on with it: it is a process of interaction, dialogue, feedback, modifying objectives, recycling plans, coping with mixed feelings and values, pragmatism, micropolitics, frustration, patience and muddle. Yet, messy though the process is, adopting an objective, rational, systematic, scientific approach to implementing change is far more likely to be crowned with success than relying simply on intuition (though that has its part to play too). The point is that rationality has to be applied not only to defining the *end* of change but also the *means*.

Another fallacy is that those who have the positional power to inflict change on an organization will be successful in implementing enduring change: seldom are their sanctions adequate to do so, especially in the educational system above the level of pupil. They have to take into account the feelings, values, ideas and experiences of those affected by the change. This is not an ideological argument for democratic decision-making so much as a pragmatic one for managerial effectiveness: successful managers are observed to do this. The so-called scientific-rational mode of management has long been discredited and supplanted in successful organizations. (Failure by academics to appreciate this is usually at the heart of objections to schools learning anything from industry about management.)

Another trap in implementing change is to ascribe the problems that necessitate change to the shortcomings of individuals. Not only is personalization of the problems likely to lead to defensiveness but it is also often a misdiagnosis of the true cause. Most organizational defects are attributable to methods and systems.

The next reason why some plans for implementing change fail is that they are addressed to insoluble problems. However uncomfortable it may be for legislators and managers to admit to impotence, it has to be acknowledged that some undesirable conditions of society are so little understood or so complex to explain causally that in the present state of knowledge and expertise there is no solution to hand. Even if someone of outstanding conceptual ability could fully grasp the problem, it would be an impossible task to transfer that understanding to others who have a significant and indispensable part to play in solving the problem. *Felix qui potuit rerum cognoscere causas*, quoth Virgil ('happy is he who can find out the causes of things'); but we live in an unhappy world.

However, on a happier note, not all problems are intractable, and as time goes by we do learn how to improve our methods of solving problems and introducing change. Even tackling seemingly intractable problems is not impossible: the best way to eat an elephant is one bite at a time.

DISCUSSION TOPICS

(1)   Most managers' work is not about planning, organizing and making rational decisions: it is about chaotic situations, 'firefighting' to deal with crises and keeping the ship afloat amidst constantly threatening seas – Mintzberg. Should we seek a rational approach to dealing with chaos?

(2)   A dominant feature of planning in schools is the need to respond to a decision made at LEA or central government level which is likely to have been perceived as rational by those who made it but appears irrational or misguided to staff in school – Wallace. How does this come about, and how might it be prevented?

FURTHER READING

Boyson, J. (1999) *Managing Change in Schools Pack: a Practical Guide to Managing and Facilitating the Change Process*, Financial Times Prentice Hall, London.

Fullan, M. (1993) *Changing Forces: Probing the Depths of Educational Reform*, RoutledgeFalmer, London.

Fullan, M. (2001) *The New Meaning of Educational Change* (3rd edn), RoutledgeFalmer, London.

MacBeath, J. (1998) *Effective School Leadership: Responding to Change*, Paul Chapman Publishing, London.

16

Antecedents of Successful Change

ORGANIZATIONAL CONDITIONS CONDUCIVE TO SUCCESSFUL CHANGE

Fortunately, enough surveys have been made of organizations that do implement change successfully for us to give some useful guidelines to heads and senior staff wishing to bring their schools into this category.

Some of the surveys have focused on commercial organizations, others on schools. Some schools have tried to apply the results of the former surveys to themselves, and found that many of the criteria are transferable. Her Majesty's Inspectorate's *Ten Good Schools* (1977), Peters and Waterman's *In Search of Excellence* (1995), Goldsmith and Clutterbuck's *The Winning Streak* (1984) and the National Commission on Education's *Success Against the Odds* (1995b) are examples of such surveys.

Peters and Waterman believe (p. 110) that a major reason for excellence in the 75 most highly regarded American companies is the habitual acceptance of change, or 'intentionally seeded evolution': the excellent companies are *learning organizations*, which have developed a whole host of devices and management routines to stave off ossification. They experiment more with change, and encourage more tries. Likewise Goldsmith and Clutterbuck (p. 10) identify this as one of the eight distinctive characteristics of successful British companies: 'These companies have a continuous interest and commitment to things new, to the process of change.' All this is also patently true of the Barrow Community Learning Partnership (BCLP) which will be used as a case study (see page 229) to illustrate how the generic approach to the management of change described in this book is reflected in a real educational situation.

Professor Beckhard, of MIT, has stressed the critical importance of managerial strategy in keeping an organization healthy, and quick on its feet. The top managers need to have a model or a philosophy of how the organization should work, and how it can be changed; then they must constantly update this in the light of hard experience. They should strive to build an organization with distinctive approaches to purpose, structure, process, people, realism and the environment.

Purpose

Effective organizations tend to be purposeful and goal directed. Their managers, departments and the individual members work towards explicit goals and have a clear sense of direction. The development of purpose is a continuing activity providing a focus and a framework for understanding the whole and linking it together. Thus schools without explicit aims and a whole-school policy would not meet this criterion of effectiveness.

Structure

The structure is determined by work requirements, not by authority, power or conformity. Form follows function. Different departments may be differently organized, according to the nature of their work. Procedures may not be standardized: people can do things their way if it works. Thus, in a school, some learning would not be subject to the norm of a 45-minute period. Power to do things is dispersed to where it is needed; for instance, the power to get a defective pottery kiln repaired would reside in the department, rather than be invested in a deputy head.

Process

Decisions are made near to where the requisite information is, rather than referred up the hierarchy. Authority is delegated accordingly, as has happened in LMS. Communications are frank, open and relatively undistorted. Ideas are considered on their intrinsic merits, rather than according to their source in the hierarchy. Conflict and clash of ideas (not personalities) are encouraged, not suppressed or avoided, and everyone manages conflict constructively, using problem-solving methods. Collaboration is rewarded, where it is in the organization's best interests. Competition is minimized, but when it occurs it is because people are vying with one another to contribute to the organization's success.

People

Each individual's identity, integrity and freedom are respected, and work is organized as far as possible to this end. Attention is paid to intrinsic rewards. Everyone's work is valued (e.g. including that of the non-teaching staff in a school). People's interdependence is stressed. Individuals evaluate their performance against benchmarks, comparing themselves to others; they review one another's work, and celebrate achievement.

As Peters and Waterman report (1995, p. 277): 'The excellent companies have a deeply ingrained philosophy that says, in effect, "respect the individual", "make people winners", "let them stand out", "treat people as adults".' It is the same with BCLP, which is driven by similar values. 'Making people winners' can hardly be better illustrated than by the design of a

Barrow summer workshop for gifted and talented children: the prevailing 'wisdom' is that only 5–10 per cent of the overall school population fall in this category. BCLP, however, believes that all children have gifts and talents and that the task of schools is to discover, for each child, in what respect (Hymer and Michel, 2002). Therefore, selection for the summer workshop is random. This is splendid creative thinking 'outside the box'. The caption of a cartoon of a boy talking to a head says it all: 'I can suck up pudding through my nose and blow it out of the corners of my eyes, and you *still* won't put me in the gifted class'!

Central direction coexists with individual autonomy:

> Autonomy is a product of discipline. The discipline (a few shared values) provides the framework. It gives people confidence to experiment, for instance, stemming from stable expectations about what really counts. Thus a set of shared values and rules about discipline, details and execution can provide the framework in which practical autonomy takes place routinely.
>
> (Peters and Waterman, 1995, p. 322)

Goldsmith and Clutterbuck (1984) also identify the balance between autonomy and control as crucial. Without this discipline, teachers' autonomy in the classroom, or 'academic freedom', soon degenerates into licence. Lavelle (1984, p. 161) also places autonomy in context: quoting Stenhouse: 'Teacher autonomy is seen as the ethical base of professionalism and a cornerstone of tradition', he points out that this can lead to gross disjunctions of practice unless that autonomy is set within the framework of the school and its value system. Mant (1983) makes a similar point.

Realism

People deal with things as they are, with a minimum of 'game playing'. An 'action research' mode of management predominates: i.e. the organization has in-built feedback mechanisms to tell it how it is doing. Then it uses this valid and factual information about how things are in order to plan improvements. There is widespread awareness of the 'health' of the organization and its parts, just as the human body knows when it feels well or poorly.

Environment

The organization is seen as an open system embedded in a complex environment with which it constantly interacts. The changing demands of the environment are regularly tracked, and an appropriate response made. A school would have its eyes and ears open, alertly sensing what was going on in the community and in the corridors of power. In turn, the environment would inject a sense of reality and proportion into what might otherwise be a claustrophobic system.

Balance

All these factors are interdependent, and have to be balanced. For example, Everard was involved with a major change initiative in ICI, the 'Staff Development Programme' (Pettigrew, 1985). Its objectives, which are still as relevant as ever in schools today, were

(1) in the short term, the achievement of an exceptional and demonstrable improvement in organizational effectiveness; and
(2) in the longer term, the development of an environment in which major improvements occur naturally and continuously, without being enforced or imposed.

In conducting the programme it was essential to link the benefits to the organization in terms of improved effectiveness with benefits to the individual in terms of personal and professional development.

In educational settings, Fullan (1982, pp. 97 and 112) makes the same point, applauding leaders who not only plan the organization development associated with the change but also simultaneously foster staff or professional development. He argues that effective educational change cannot occur without improvements to the teachers' working life. Change must not simply aggravate teachers' problems.

The second ICI objective above is a reminder that the best change agents are catalysts: they do themselves out of a job by embedding their skills into the social system, so that it has an in-built capacity for continuous self-improvement.

Collegiate culture

There is one condition of successful change which seems more prevalent in industry than in schools: industrial managers and professional staff get together more often, whereas the cellular organization in schools means that teachers struggle privately with their problems and anxieties. It is unusual for teachers to observe and discuss their colleagues' work, and there is little attempt to build what Fullan (1982, p. 108) calls 'a common collegiate technical culture or analytic orientation' towards their work. The processes of teaching and learning are inadequately explored compared with the processes of manufacturing, marketing and management in industry.

One of Everard's most vivid experiences in the management of change was bringing together ten senior managers off-site to meet Professor Trist, an organizational consultant, with the request to come prepared to talk for five minutes each on 'the problems of the company'. For the first time, ten very different people, from different departments, shared their concerns, only to find that they were essentially the same. But they also shared a vision of how things could be, and the professor explained why things were as they were, and how they could be changed. The new, deeper understanding provided an immense store of energy for beneficial change, which was steered into channels that enabled organizational improvements to occur.

In schools that wish to change, regular opportunities for such encounters must be created, and the negative energy of disaffection must be transformed into a positive will to make a difference to the way things are, to the benefit of the teachers and the organization. You may not be able to get hold of a professor, but it helps to invite someone from outside the system who knows something about organizational, managerial or pedagogical processes.

Fullan *et al.* (1980), in their research on North American schools, report similar findings. The schools good at change are characterized by openness of communication, a high level of communication skills, a widespread desire for collaborative work, a supportive administration, good agreement on educational goals and previous experience of successful change.

In a later book, Fullan (2001) leaves his readers with a message that resembles what progressive companies have been trying to do in creating 'learning organizations':

(1) Redesign the workplace so that innovation and improvement are built into the daily activities of staff.
(2) Each individual should take responsibility for his or her own empowerment by becoming an expert in the change process.
(3) Collectively they should engage in continuous initiative, thereby preempting the imposition of change from outside.
(4) Establish a 'critical mass' of highly engaged individuals working on the creation of conditions for continuous renewal, while themselves being shaped by these very conditions.
(5) The way ahead is through melding individual *and* institutional renewal.

Fullan (1993) also offers some practical lessons from his studies of change in schools; they ring bells for us, although perhaps no. 4 is a little stark:

(1) You can't mandate what matters (the more complex the change, the less you can force it).
(2) Change is a journey, not a blueprint (change is non-linear, loaded with uncertainty and excitement and sometimes perverse).
(3) Problems are our friends (problems are inevitable and you can't learn without them).
(4) Vision and strategic planning come later (premature visions and planning blind).
(5) Individualism and collectivism must have equal power (there are no one-sided solutions to isolation and 'group-think').
(6) Neither centralization nor decentralization works (both top-down and bottom-up strategies are necessary).
(7) Connection with the wider environment is critical for success (the best organizations learn externally as well as internally).

(8) Every person is a change agent (change is too important to leave to the experts).

But it is the head who must start this ball rolling, notwithstanding the odd fact that creating the conditions for continuous improvement is not laid down as a specific professional duty under his or her terms of employment (DfES, 2003). It must surely, however, be accepted as an implicit part of the role of any leader. As the NCE survey (1995b) of eleven once-threatened but now-thriving schools noted, most had experienced inertia or had neglected to focus on, or even to recognize, the need for continual improvement. The importance of the head and his/her ability to foster a sense of shared purpose, emerged as key. The right sort of leadership is at the heart of effective schooling, and no evidence has emerged of effectiveness in a school with weak leadership. Some years ago Her Majesty's Inspectors concluded in *Ten Good Schools* (HMI, 1977):

> The schools see themselves as places designed for learning; they take trouble to make their philosophies explicit for themselves and to explain them to parents and pupils; the foundation of their work and corporate life is an acceptance of shared values.
>
> Emphasis is laid on consultation, team work and participation, but without exception the most important single factor in the success of these schools is the quality of leadership at the head. Without exception, the heads have the qualities of imagination and vision, tempered by realism, which have enabled them to sum up not only their present situation but also attainable future goals. They appreciate the need for specific educational aims, both social and intellectual, and have the capacity to communicate these to the staff, pupils and parents, to win their assent and to put their own policies into practice. Their sympathetic understanding of staff and pupils, their acceptability, good humour and sense of proportion and their dedication to their task have won them the respect of parents, teachers and taught. Conscious of the corruption of power, and though ready to take final responsibility, they have made power-sharing the keynote of their organization and administration. Such leadership is crucial for success and these schools are what their heads and staff have made them.

Twenty-five years later, the message is the same (Ofsted, 2003).

PERSONAL APPLICATION

Rate the conditions in your school along the dimensions listed in this section, using a 5-point scale (1 = favourable, 5 = unfavourable):

• Philosophy • Realism • Purpose • Environment • Structure • Collegiate culture • Process • Quality of leadership • People • Balance

Pick out the three least favourable conditions. What practical things can you do by the end of (next?) term to make these conditions in your school more conducive to the implementation of successful change?

MANAGERIAL QUALITIES NEEDED TO HANDLE CHANGE

'The ability to create and manage the future in the way that we wish is what differentiates the good manager from the bad' (Harvey-Jones, 2003, p. 96).

Observation of people who are more successful than others at managing complex organizations in which major changes have to be implemented shows that they tend to have a distinctive mix of knowledge, skills, personal attitudes and values, and the capacity to orchestrate these as they make a host of personal decisions that lie at the heart of organization management. By the very nature of their competence as educators, heads are well endowed with some of the qualities that are required – more so, perhaps, than their counterparts in industry. Other qualities, however, are more commonly found to flourish in a business environment. Few people in schools or industry are such paragons as to possess all the requisite qualities in full measure. However, an understanding of the kind of person who is good at handling change is helpful both in selecting senior staff and project leaders and in assessing what qualities we need to develop.

Before describing the key qualities that seem to be needed to implement change effectively, it is instructive to examine the characteristics that Peters and Waterman (1995) found in the leaders of successful companies. The two are related.

Such leaders listened to their employees and treated them as adults. They saw that leadership, unlike naked power-wielding, was inseparable from followers' needs and goals. Caring ran in the veins of managers of the 'excellent' companies. They did not allow intellect to overpower wisdom. They set and demanded high standards of excellence. As Henry Kissinger said: 'Leaders must invoke an alchemy of great vision.' But they had to combine visionary ideas at the highest level of abstraction with actions at the most mundane level of detail. They had the capacity to generate enthusiasm and excitement, to harness the social forces in the organization and to shape and guide its values: 'Clarifying the value system and breathing life into it are the greatest contribution a leader can make. Moreover, that's what the top people in excellent companies seem to worry about most.' (Peters and Waterman 1995, pp. 282, 291). A strong and coherent values base, coupled with a vision of a networked learning community, are also benchmarks of BCLP's excellence.

Yet success in instilling values appeared to have little to do with charismatic personality. None of the leaders studied relied on personal magnetism. All *made* themselves into effective leaders by persistent behaviour and high visibility.

How different these characteristics are from the teacher's stereotype of the business tycoon! And how similar to those of many a highly respected head! The heartening conclusion is that these people *make themselves* effective, although Mant (1983) argues that there has to be in effective leaders a basic orientation that enables them to see themselves as part of a higher purpose external to themselves.

Valerie Stewart (1983), a British psychologist and business consultant, has listed the following characteristics of people who are good at managing change:

(1)   They know clearly what they want to achieve.
(2)   They can translate desires into practical action.
(3)   They can see proposed changes not only from their own viewpoint but also from that of others.
(4)   They don't mind being out on a limb.
(5)   They show irreverence for tradition but respect for experience.
(6)   They plan flexibly, matching constancy of ends against a repertoire of available means.
(7)   They are not discouraged by setbacks.
(8)   They harness circumstances to enable change to be implemented.
(9)   They clearly explain change.
(10)   They involve their staff in the management of change and protect their security.
(11)   They don't pile one change on top of another, but await assimilation.
(12)   They present change as a rational decision.
(13)   They make change personally rewarding for people, wherever possible.
(14)   They share maximum information about possible outcomes.
(15)   They show that change is 'related to the business'.
(16)   They have a history of successful change behind them.

We have used for training purposes (with minor modifications) a list of qualities supplied by Beckhard in identifying successful managers of change and indicating what further development was required. The qualities

Knowledge of	*Rating*
(1) people and their motivational systems – what makes them tick;	
(2) organizations as social systems – what makes them healthy and effective, able to achieve objectives;	
(3) the environment surrounding the organization – the systems that impinge on and make demands of it;	
(4) managerial styles and their effects on work;	
(5) one's own personal managerial style and proclivities;	
(6) organizational processes such as decision-making, planning, control, communication, conflict management and reward systems;	
(7) the process of change;	
(8) educational and training methods and theory.	

Figure 16.1 Knowledge required for managing change

themselves range from those that are usually regarded as intrinsic in the personality to those – the majority – that are capable of being systematically developed. The most easily assimilated qualities are those of knowledge and comprehension.

Figure 16.1 lists some important categories of knowledge, with a column for self-rating (use a five-point scale, with 5 indicating deep knowledge and 1 superficial).

Figure 16.2 lists some of the skills that are important in managing change; all of them can be systematically learned, and some develop of their own accord, albeit patchily, as the manager gains experience of the job.

Skills in   *Rating*

(1)   analysing large complex systems;

(2)   collecting and processing large amounts of information and
        simplifying it for action;

(3)   goal-setting and planning;

(4)   getting consensus decisions;

(5)   conflict management;

(6)   empathy;

(7)   political behaviour;

(8)   public relations;

(9)   consulting and counselling;

(10) training and teaching.

Figure 16.2   Skills required for managing change

Various personality characteristics, attitudes and values are also important, and these are listed in Figure 16.3. They have been arranged roughly in order of decreasing inherence; i.e. those towards the bottom of the list respond best to training.

Caution is needed in rating oneself against these characteristics because of the possibilities of self-delusion. More reliable ratings can be obtained in a management group that agrees to assess each other candidly and discuss the results.

It is, of course, not these dissected qualities of knowledge, skills and other characteristics that alone determine whether a manager will prove effective: it is the way in which he or she is able to synthesize them into a synergistic whole, and call them forth in response to particular situations. 'Style' is a word sometimes used to describe how he or she does this, and is assessed by observing his or her behaviour (Chapter 2).

Rating

(1) a strong sense of personal ethics which helps to
     ensure consistent behaviour;

(2) something of an intellectual by both training and
     temperament;

(3) a strong penchant towards optimism;

(4) enjoyment of the intrinsic rewards of effectiveness,
     without the need for public approval;

(5) high willingness to take calculated risks and
     live with the consequences without experiencing
     undue stress;

(6) a capacity to accept conflict and enjoyment in managing it;

(7) a soft voice and low-key manner;

(8) a high degree of self-awareness – knowledge of self;

(9) a high tolerance of ambiguity and complexity;

(10) a tendency to avoid polarizing issues into black and white,
     right and wrong;

(11) high ability to listen.

Figure 16.3 Personality characteristics required for managing change

PERSONAL APPLICATION

Pick out from the ratings you have given yourself in the three figures those qualities
that you most need to develop. What can you do to start a change process in
yourself, leading to a greater capacity on your part to manage change?

DISCUSSION TOPICS

(1) If I were going there, I wouldn't start from here – Irishman asked the
     way. How far should pragmatism and expediency dictate whether to
     embark on a journey of change?

(2) What can a newly appointed head do to develop a culture conducive
     to change?

FURTHER READING

Bennett, N., Crawford, M. and Riches, C. (eds) (1992) *Managing Change in Education*,
     Paul Chapman Publishing, London, and the Open University.

17

A Systematic Approach to Change

INTRODUCTION TO THE APPROACH

So far we have considered the nature of change, its complexity, the conditions that help an organization to cope with change, and the qualities that managers need to bring about specific changes.

In no way can the management of change be reduced to something like the checklist that an airline pilot runs through prior to take-off. It is, and will remain, an art, though the 'artist' has at his or her disposal some tools and technology to help, and it is gradually becoming more of a science than an art.

We shall describe a general approach to major change, which has been found by experience to be effective in industrial, health service and educational settings, and is underpinned by theories of organizational behaviour. The value of this approach is in helping to identify all the bits of work that need doing in order to effect the change; unless a systematic approach is followed, it is almost inevitable that one will be caught unawares by snags that one has totally overlooked.

The approach described is largely based on the work of Beckhard and Harris (1987), modified by long experience of its use in ICI (and by ICI staff working with school heads), and amplified in the educational context by Fullan (1982; 2001). Everard has used it to produce a practical training guide to the implementation of the Education Act 1981, *Decision-making for Special Educational Needs* (Evans *et al.*, 1989), which was piloted in four local authorities in 1988–89. Although the examples relate to SEN, the core material (instructions, handouts, slides, worked examples, etc.) can readily be adapted for other change programmes.

The approach is mapped out in Figure 17.1. There are six key stages that have to be carried out sequentially, though some recycling may be needed in the later stages of the process. These stages are as follows:

(1) A preliminary *diagnosis* or reconnaissance, leading to a *decision* to undertake a change programme: is the change sound? Is it inherently likely to succeed?

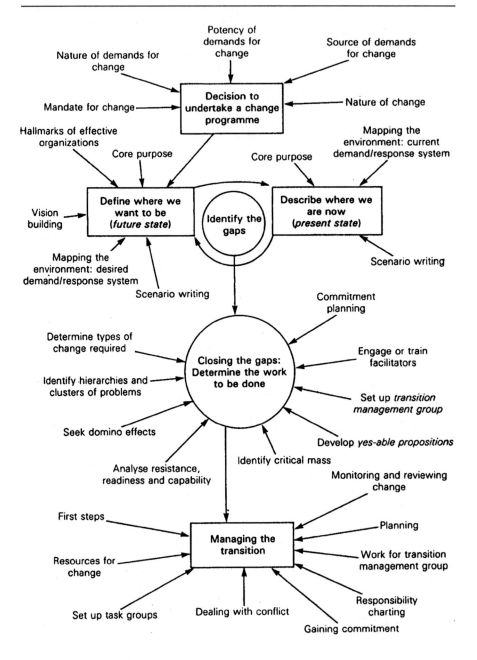

Figure 17.1   Stages in the process of change

(2) Determining the *future:* what do we want to happen? What will happen if we do nothing?
(3) Characterizing the *present:* what are we here for? What are the demands on us? What is stopping us? What is working for us?
(4) Identifying the *gaps* between present and future to determine the work to be done to close them: who is resistant? Who can help the change? Who should manage it?
(5) Managing the *transition* from present to future: who does what by when? How do we gain commitment?
(6) *Evaluating* and monitoring the change: was success achieved? Will the change endure? What has been learned?

A word of warning about using this approach is needed. It must not become a shackled approach. It needs to be used flexibly and with careful thought. A golfer may complete a successful round without using all his or her clubs. So do not worry if some of the elements in the approach do not speak to your situation. Do not labour any of the stages if common sense and intuition provide you with a short-cut, especially if the scale of the change is relatively modest. But do be wary of skipping an essential step in the logic. Equally, if you have tried other approaches successfully, or have read authors like Schmuck *et al.* (1977), Bolam *et al.* (1979), Stewart (1983), Plant (1987) and Caldwell and Spinks (1998), by all means adopt whatever approach works for you; the similarities outweigh the differences.

It is interesting how successful change programmes such as BCLP (p. 229) match this approach, although sometimes the emphasis is different. For example, BCLP makes a special point of celebrating achievement and success, which can inflame further progress. This can take the form of articles in the local press, ceremonies to reward achievement and the accreditation of new skills and competences through qualifications and certificates.

BCLP also comment on the importance of language in describing a change process; the word 'gap' implies a deficit model and suggests that people are failing to be fully professional. How true! One of us (Everard), fresh from industry, recalls how he innocently used the word 'improve' to describe the purpose of school management training. To a teacher, however, 'improve' carries a nuance: 'Johnny is showing signs of improvement' is a euphemism. The moral is to describe 'closing the gap' as 'moving from good to excellent' or 'improving still further on the current best'. Wisely, instead of using the DfES term 'Education Action Zone', the Barrow project was called a 'Community Learning Partnership', which emphasizes these three words as key drivers of worthwhile change.

ASSESSING THE SOUNDNESS OF A PROPOSED CHANGE

It should not be assumed that changes proposed from within or without the organization should be adopted without question: they may be unsound on educational grounds or on grounds of practicality, as judged by those who will have to bear the brunt of the change. After all, an unsuccessful change, however progressive the idea seemed, does not necessarily benefit the pupils; and it may harm them. A succession of unsuccessful attempts at change can have a devastating effect on school morale and evoke a sense of disillusionment and impotence that acts as an obstacle to future change, even that agreed to be desirable and practicable.

In other words, shrewd heads will be circumspect in their response to a proposal for change (including one to which they are personally attached, or even one enshrined in legislation). A proposal may seem eminently well intentioned, so that to reject it seems churlish and scarcely defensible; its adoption may seem inevitable in the long run; it may emanate with great conviction from a respected source; it may appear to carry the force of law: but it may still be wrong or untimely to adopt it, for the system may not be in a state of readiness to take in on board. The impulse of rejection must be allowed to play itself out; indeed, in the nineteenth century Thomas Carlyle said that we should *always* reject a proposition before accepting it. We shall return to this point later; meanwhile, let it not be construed as support for King Canute!

As managers we can, and should, attempt a dispassionate assessment of the quality or soundness of a proposed change regardless of whether we are in tune with it ourselves.

How do we assess the soundness of a proposed change? First, who is initiating it, and what is their motivation? Sadly, some people with strong career aspirations, be they in the political or the professional world, see advancement as conditional upon having made their mark, or having established a track-record of getting things done. Organizations and societies usually award 'Brownie points' to people who push through some reform or other; and everyone likes to receive esteem. So we need to beware of change initiated by someone (especially an outsider) mainly for career purposes, rather than because it has intrinsic merit. As Lavelle (1984) has pointed out, innovation is more likely to be successful when perceived as necessary by those in the school, rather than by outsiders. He sees the key to effective innovation as lying within the microdynamics of the school and the classroom, within areas in which heads and their staff wish strongly to exercise their personal autonomy.

We must be circumspect about changes that have some popular or topical appeal, but whose implications have not been thought through. No one can expect all the consequences of change to be worked out in advance, but it ill becomes an initiator of change to will the end without providing the means. Even if the goal of the change has been carefully and clearly defined (and not even this is commonly done, to the point where criteria are specified by which we can judge whether the goal has been attained: see Chapter 10), the means of implementation may be vague in the extreme. Or again, the magnitude of change may not be appreciated, so that the whole system stands to be overwhelmed. Successful change depends on having realistic aims.

Another point to consider before adopting change is the extent to which it is supported within the power system. Has it been initiated from the DfES? Does the local education authority support it? It is especially important to check the degree of political backing if additional resources will need to be negotiated at the implementation stage. Support may be needed from several levels in the hierarchy.

The teachers' unions' attitudes, the governors' support, the parents' attitudes and of course those of the teachers themselves, all need to be taken into account in judging the extent of demand or support for the change.

Government grants in support of a change may give the change a fair wind, and indeed may be vital for success, but the ingenuity with which people can gain access to funds yet divert them to other purposes is well known in all walks of life. As many teachers know, TVEI was a case in point. Government legislation may also indicate support and even appear to mandate adoption of a change, but again the propensity of a complex system for outwitting the intentions of the legislators (as in parts of the Butler Education Act 1944) is well documented. Accordingly, we should be careful not to read too much into grants, circulars and even legislation. Beware also of short-term funding for long-term programmes.

These are some of the factors that wise heads will take into consideration in deciding what stance they will take to a change instigated by another part of the education system. It is neither necessary nor practicable for all conditions to be ideal before a proposed change is adopted; but some judgement has to be made about the probable success of a decision to adopt, and if the head is convinced that the change, however well intentioned, is doomed to failure, then it may well be that he or she is right to resist that particular change at least for the time being. The school may not be ready for it. This is not to suggest that all changes should be resisted, nor that resistance invariably succeeds in fending off the attempt to change, nor that some token response may not be prudent.

PERSONAL APPLICATION

Think of some educational changes you have experienced in your career which have produced the least successful outcomes. Were any basically unsound? Why? How could they have been resisted?

THE RECONNAISSANCE

Having decided that a proposed change is sound, we have to conduct a reconnaissance. Much educational change is technically simple but socially complex, and the complexity arises not so much from dogged, mindless opposition of narrow-minded staff as from the difficulty of planning and organizing a multidimensional process involving many people, all with different perceptions and outlooks. The factors affecting implementation cannot be dealt with in isolation from each other, because they form a set of interacting variables which has to be seen as an entity. What are the factors?

First, there are the characteristics of the change itself: is it needed? Is it relevant to the particular school at this time? Has the relevance to be established? Is it complex? Is it feasible? Can it be presented as practical in the short run, not too costly and potentially helpful to the teachers?

The question of need is not an absolute one. We have to ask if it is needed more than other changes, the implementation of which will use the same (usually scarce) resources. It is quite possible to overload any system or organization with change, so the issue of priorities and sequencing changes is a vital strategic decision for any manager. When some LEAs saddled their schools with four major simultaneous changes – for example multicultural education, mixed-ability teaching, helping the underachiever and avoidance of gender discrimination – at a time when there were already unavoidable changes brought about by contraction, reorganization, etc., they could not expect all these changes to be enthusiastically or successfully handled. The changes required by the Education Reform Act 1988 also overloaded the system. So the effect of all the changes already taking place on the school's capacity to cope with yet another change will have important implications for the rate at which plans for implementation can be put into effect.

Lack of clarity about the goals and means of effecting change is a common problem which we addressed in preceding chapters. All who are affected by the change need a clear picture of what it will mean for them: what will they be doing differently, after the change has been implemented? They want to know specifically what it means *in practice* for them. Nor will they be content to be fobbed off with false clarity, in which the commanding heights of the future scenario are sketched starkly and boldly, but the terrain in their neck of the woods is left totally vague. Clarity is not something which can be prepackaged in some sort of blueprint; it is something that grows through dialogue and questioning. We must judge how long it will take to achieve clarity, and incorporate this process into the time planning. The legislative provisions for religious education and worship that is 'broadly Christian' exemplify this difficulty.

Complexity is an unwelcome but usually unavoidable factor, because worthwhile change often requires the bringing together of a set of inter-locking conditions into a critical mass powerful enough to break through a log-jam of problems. However, much more care is needed in complex change, to ensure that there is proper co-ordination of all the activities needed to implement the change successfully. Leadership is called for, in addition to tactical skills.

Then there is feasibility. If a new syllabus is to be introduced, are there opportunities and funds for any necessary in-service training? If physically handicapped pupils are to be integrated into an ordinary school, is it possible to equip the buildings accordingly, other than at inordinate cost? Is the timescale of the change realistic? You do not have to have the solution to every problem at hand before you accept that a change is feasible, but you do have to assess how imaginable solutions are.

The second set of factors affecting the implementation of change concerns the particular locality where the change is to take place. History is the first such factor: has the LEA a track-record of introducing or facilitating change successfully on previous occasions, or has a succession of bad experiences built up a negative climate of cynicism, disillusionment and apathy? Are there people there who can facilitate change, such as well respected advisers with time available? Are there any local problems that would be helped incidentally by tackling the larger change?

Thirdly, what is special about the school? Does it have a track-record of innovation? Are there problems that could be simultaneously helped by implementing the change? For instance, there may be a deputy head who has not been really stretched, and for whom the responsibility for carrying out a complex change programme would offer considerable career advantage. What is the head's attitude to change? This is an important question, because research shows that the head in any organization plays a disproportionate part in determining whether change is successful or unsuccessful. Active support is almost indispensable. Then there are the teacher inter-relationships: it is difficult to bring about successful change without a lot of human interaction. Professional discussion in a positive, supportive atmosphere helps change, whereas retreating to the familiar surroundings of one's classroom or office hinders it. Are the teachers relatively confident in their own ability, yet open to suggestions from colleagues on further improvement? If so, the school has fertile soil for implanting a programme for change.

Last, there are the factors deriving from the external environment. Is the change against the grain of parental outlooks, or of local or national government policies? Would future employers of the pupils think well of it? Would they even understand its significance? What will the chair of governors think?

If, after all this, it is decided to undertake a change programme, someone with the necessary authority should formally mandate it and a 'prime mover' should be appointed to take the next steps.

DESCRIBING THE FUTURE

The next piece of work to be done is to answer, with some precision, the question: 'What do we want to happen?' Later, we shall answer a related question: 'What will happen if we let matters drift?'

We need to define where we want the organization and its constituent elements (see Chapter 9) to be, how it should behave or what it would look like as though viewed from a helicopter or through a wide-angled lens, when the process of change has been fully completed. The jargon for such a word picture, probably projecting several years ahead, depicting exactly what shall have been achieved, is 'the future scenario'. When this vision is shared, it can become a powerhouse for change. The BCLP vision captured many hearts and minds.

Ignore, for the moment, detailed questions of feasibility (dealing with obstacles comes later); otherwise the mind gets entrapped by the constraints of the present, and creative thought is impaired. As Churchill once said: 'Don't argue the difficulties; the difficulties will argue for themselves.'

On the other hand, it pays to think operationally, so as to build a self-consistent picture that has a ring of reality about it, rather than to fantasize about a dream world in which unlimited resources are available and the laws of logic and arithmetic are repealed.

Take everything relevant into the scenario – finance, parents, governors, unions, local education authority, employers, etc. – and decide how these will be behaving differently in the desired future. What different demands will they be making on the school? How will the school ideally respond? Let your reach exceed your grasp. If there is a suggestion of cloud cuckoo land in your scenario, never mind: the object of the exercise is to find out what you value and want, and unless you know this you will not have a clear idea of the direction and goal of the desired change. To stimulate your thinking, read a few accounts by well-known forward thinkers of where schools are going, e.g. Anne Jones' *Leadership for Tomorrow's Schools* (1987) and David Hopkins' *Think Tank Report* (2001).

Try to be specific: will each child have a computer in the classroom? What kinds of INSET will be done? Will the influence of a competence-based curriculum (Bayliss, 2003a) have transformed classroom teaching? Will schools have enough young, creative teachers in shortage subjects? What will the universities be demanding? Don't forget that it is not just the schools that are changing: they are trying to track moving targets.

It is invariably necessary to take time off from the daily round in order to give oneself the opportunity to reflect and to muse about the future; there is no way in which scenario-building can be slotted into a busy, fragmented day. Some managers never actually get round to starting a change process until they have learned to manage their time better, and that may have to be a preliminary personal task in the total process.

Where there is a close-knit team at the top of an organization (e.g. the head and his or her deputies), the scenario-building is often most effectively carried out together off-site, say at a residential weekend event in a relaxed but work-oriented atmosphere, perhaps with the help of an experienced outsider to guide the process.

However, Fullan (1993) recommends that vision-building should be more of a corporate effort, taking into account the personal visions of the teaching staff, in order to get the organization's full commitment to implementing the vision. So, if the management team starts the process, it should plan to involve others long before an ideal scenario is cut and dried.

Having constructed the 'ideal' scenario, without too much additional work we can also project a second scenario which describes the situation that we think would probably come about if no steps were taken to change direction. This is sometimes dubbed the 'doom' scenario. Comparing 'where we want to be' with 'where we shall end up' if we let things go on as they are, is a helpful way of pinpointing what has to be done. More is said about what to include in a scenario in the next section.

PERSONAL APPLICATION

Without filling in all the detail, outline on a sheet of paper the desired scenario for your school five years hence. Then construct your 'doom' scenario.

DESCRIBING THE PRESENT

The next stage is to articulate the salient features of the present situation *in the context of the future*. BCLP carried out a detailed audit in 1999 to describe the state of the Barrow community, warts and all. Later they repeated the comparison of the future and present scenarios to ensure that they had identified all the gaps. In determining the work to be done, they had to adjust the objectives of the collective partnership to match what each school wanted to do.

Sometimes the order of stages 2 and 3 on p. 255 is reversed, but the future context is always important. The advantage of building the future scenario first is to free the imagination from the constraints of the present, then to allow the present to be viewed against some clear goals. Three questions should be answered:

(1) Where is the system now?
(2) What work is needed to move it?
(3) Where are we, the initiators, in all this?

The answers provide us with a list of *what has to be done*.

Davies and Ellison (2003) describe various ways of analysing the present state strategically, of which SWOT analysis is the most popular (Strengths, Weaknesses, Opportunities and Threats).

The core mission

In this stage we have to go right back to fundamentals: the starting point is a definition of the organization's reason for being. Why does it exist? What is its central *raison d'être* or 'core mission'? It is not as easy to answer this question as might at first be thought; it is still less easy to get unanimous agreement on what the answer should be. The reason for being is generally assumed rather than debated and defined explicitly. It might be, for a school, to

(1) educate children; or
(2) prepare children for life, citizenship and work; or
(3) be a lively centre for effective learning and development for the young; or even
(4) provide rewarding jobs for the staff teaching the children.

There may be several elements in a statement of core mission: if so, the order of priorities is important.

Environmental mapping

No organization exists in total isolation: it can only thrive if it interacts dynamically with its environment. Environments are never static and have proved for schools, as for industry, remarkably turbulent in recent years; this necessitates a process of continual adaptation to the changing demands of the environment if the organization is to survive. Those managing change, therefore, have to cultivate an outward-looking mentality (see Chapter 9). The more complex and turbulent the environment, the more important it is that those who run the organization should perceive what is going on 'out there' and understand the problems and opportunities it presents. A change in government, further developments in the National Curriculum and continuing pressures for vocational orientation are obvious factors to take into account in recording where the system is now (at the time of writing): there may well be other factors round the corner to recognize in building the scenarios.

Pressures emanate from different sectors of the total environment, so it is helpful to map these various sectors or 'domains' and identify the main demands, or changes in demand, stemming from each of them. Figure 17.2 is part of such a 'domainal map' for a mathematics department contemplating a major reorganization based on the introduction of computer-aided learning.

Concentrate on those domains, and the associated demands, that are most relevant and important to the change being planned. Then, for each demand, write down the organization's typical response pattern: what does the school do at present to cope with these demands?

Thus the response to the LEA in the example given might be not to solicit additional resources. The future scenario, however, might call for a more assertive response, and hence a set of goals and actions might emerge in order to bring about the desired state. At the same time, the demand from parents may be thought likely to intensify, as they gain more power on governing bodies, and the school's response may have to be a faster development of new teaching methods.

It may become apparent that, if nothing is done, the system is heading for conflict or even disaster (the 'doom' scenario). But no one wants to submit to the future: we want to shape it! So something must be done to alter the demand–response system. Either we have to ask what future demand we

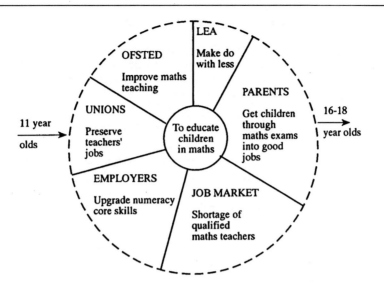

Figure 17.2 Domainal map for a mathematics department

would *like* to be made by each domain, and then plan to influence it; or we have to adjust our response. Often it turns out that influencing a domainal demand to fit an organization's response capability is a more attractive proposition than submitting to an unmanaged demand. An important aspect of the technique of domainal mapping is that it alerts us to the need to manage the environment as well as the organization. Many heads have been finding over the last few years that they are having to spend an increasing proportion of their time influencing the environment rather than running their school.

It is on the basis of this demand–response behaviour that a basic statement of the 'present scenario' is constructed, i.e. an answer to the question: 'Where is the system now in relation to the future desired scenario?'

In completing the present scenario, you may find that you do not know enough about the present system to be able to write down some of the important cause-and-effect relationships in the organization. It is, of course, essential to know how the system works before you start trying to influence it, so you may need to go around asking questions. What is important is how the system *actually* works, not how it is supposed to work. BCLP used the phrase 'epistemic fluency' to describe the skill of those who can see beyond the bullshit and spot the games that are actually being played.

PERSONAL APPLICATION

Draw up two domainal maps for a change that you foresee or want to bring about, showing respectively the current and the future demand–response relationships.

READINESS AND CAPABILITY

Further definition of the present scenario is needed under the heading 'readiness and capability to change'. Any organizational change will encounter resistance from people, forces and systems and will depend on finding countervailing influences that will help to promote the desired change. In the previous example of the maths department, the children, with their predilection for computer games, may be one such influence. Other key factors may be the head, staff-room opinion, Phyllis, the recruitment system, the exam system, etc. Remember that some of the factors that need to be influenced will be external to the school, because organizations are always embedded in an environment with which they interact.

Having identified the key individuals, groups, forces or systems that might influence the change, positively or negatively, we next consider

(1) how *ready* is he/she/it to change in the desired direction (high, medium, low)? Readiness is to do with willingness, motives and aims; and
(2) irrespective of readiness, how *capable* is he/she/it of making or helping the change? Capability is about power, influence, authority and resources like equipment and skills.

Figure 17.3 is sometimes useful in categorizing people or departments confronted with change. It indicates a distribution along the spectrum of resistance to or enthusiasm for change, with most people following the herd. This is fortunate, because it means a smaller 'critical mass' who have to be persuaded to accept change. It is seldom profitable to concentrate on the 'total resisters' or those who 'try anything'; given some choice in the matter, aim for the 'early change drivers', that is, people who have developed a reputation

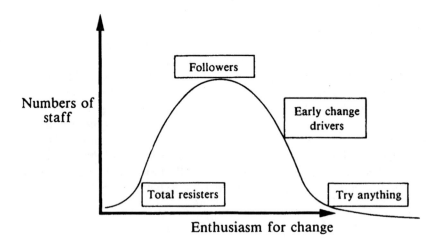

Figure 17.3 Distribution of resistance/enthusiasm

for being in the van of change, and who already have a track-record of successful innovation.

BCLP found that different schools were in different states of readiness and capability to change, with respect to different issues. So each had to start from where it was, to make a change that was achievable. In one school the head did not share the core vision and values and eventually chose to sideline the school.

PERSONAL APPLICATION

Fill in the chart in Figure 17.4 for any change that you have in mind. Enter key people, etc., in the left-hand column. This exercise helps you to focus on what work you will need to do to create the critical energy for change. Other techniques that are helpful in this context are 'force-field analysis' (see below) and the Gleicher formula (Chapter 18).

	Readiness			Capability		
	H	M	L	H	M	L
1						
2						
3						
4						
5						
6						

Figure 17.4   Readiness and capability chart

FORCE-FIELD ANALYSIS

Force-field analysis is another technique which can be used at the diagnostic stage of problem-solving, especially in situations where people's attitudes and reactions are important. It uses Lewin's concept of dynamic equilibrium (familiar in another form to chemists and physicists), which explains the apparent immobility of a social system as the result of the opposing forces acting on it balancing each other exactly. The forces can be needs, drives, aspirations, fears and other feelings generated either within oneself or in interpersonal, intergroup or organizational-environmental situations affected by a proposed change from the present to the desired condition. Not all the forces impeding change are inertial; they could be political or ideological forces.

Some of the forces tend to drive the point of equilibrium towards the desired condition; others restrain such movement. Force-field analysis is the identification of the forces, their direction and their strength. Relative strength can be shown by the length of an arrow, in a diagram such as Figure 17.5. In using the diagram, each arrow is labelled with the force it represents.

It is implicit in the theory underlying the model that, in general, movement towards the desired condition can most readily be achieved by reducing or removing the restraining forces. Intensifying the driving forces before reducing the restrained forces tends to build up a counter-reaction which increases the tension without moving the point of equilibrium.

The technique is usually used in groups, with the diagram drawn on a flipchart. The steps in the process are

(1) define specifically the change that is desired and ensure mutual understanding;
(2) consider all the forces at work in the present situation; do not consider possible or hoped-for events or solutions. Try to understand the forces felt by the people or groups affected by the change – not by the group doing the analysis; and
(3) draw arrows of length proportional to the strength of the forces and label them. If insufficient information is available to estimate the strength, decide how it can be obtained.

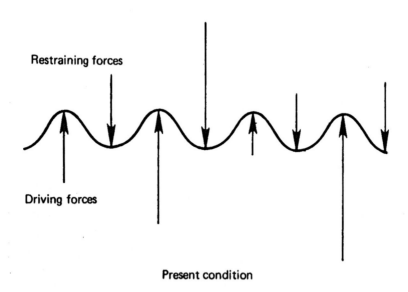

Figure 17.5   Force-field analysis

In the Barrow case study, the main driving forces were identified as leadership and skills development, professional development with a focus on teaching and learning, fostering resilience and partnership development.

PERSONAL APPLICATION

Draw a force-field diagram for a change needed to move your school towards a desired future scenario.

PROBLEMS TO BE TACKLED

The next step in the process is to examine carefully the present, projected and desired scenarios with a view to pinpointing the main problems that have to be solved, in order that the present scenario may be shaped towards the desired future, instead of drifting towards the 'doom' scenario. Consider the different demands and responses in the three scenarios. Are the people and the systems likely to change (e.g. retirement of head, reform of A-levels, less union militancy, etc.)? Subjective, though informed, judgements will have to be made about the relative importance of the problems that will have to be tackled: some may go away, others may get worse.

If you write down a long list of every problem that you can conceive, then you will almost certainly become discouraged by the enormity of the task ahead. Big and little problems will be mixed, and until you have thought about solutions you will not know where on earth to start.

So, the next step is to look for patterns of problems that may overlap or interconnect in some way. Think in terms of clusters of problems with a related theme. For example, there might be a cluster of problems connected with 'internal communication', or with 'maintaining everyone's commitment to their jobs while the change is being effected'. Sometimes you will come across a 'domino effect': when one problem in a cluster has been solved, the solution to all the others will fall into place fairly easily. For instance, if the English department shows that mixed-ability teaching actually produces better exam results, it may be easier for other departments to follow suit.

Another helpful sorting technique is to identify and write down the types of change that you need to make, e.g. changes in

(1) policy;
(2) working procedures;
(3) staff training; and
(4) equipment and layout.

Some problems will have to be tackled before others; some will take longer to solve: so set some priorities. Whittle down the list to a manageable number of problem clusters, logically arranged and ranked in order of priority. Set the less urgent problems on one side, to tackle later.

PERSONAL APPLICATION

If you are some way down the road of tackling an organizational change, write down each problem on 'Post-it' adhesive slips (for easy sorting). Choose and label a problem cluster; arrange the problems on a flipchart in order of priority; identify any domino effects and important interactions.

RESOURCES FOR CHANGE

If you have followed through the approach so far, you will have a clearer idea of what has to be done to effect the change you want, but possibly some misgivings about your ability to achieve it, and only a hazy idea of how to go about solving the problems that you have identified as important. To be clear about what the problems are, however, is to point yourself down the right road to solving them. A vague appreciation of the problems is liable to divert you and others down false trails.

Some introspection is now needed to find out what is going for you. Managers initiating change bring several things to the change effort. Their qualities have already been mentioned (Chapter 15), i.e. knowledge, skills, personality characteristics, situational awareness, style, etc. Their practical experience, and success or failure in past change efforts, are relevant. Their position in the organization brings some influence. Their motivation is of key importance. Questions to ask oneself are as follows:

(1) Do I need to seek additional training to help me make the change?
(2) Which key people have I the power to influence directly?
(3) Can I influence others through indirect leverage, e.g. through the chair of governors?
(4) Have I any control over the reward system (e.g. career opportunities)?
(5) What can I offer in return for support?
(6) What are my real reasons for wanting change:
    (a) *Organizational*
        to improve effectiveness?
        to reduce cost?
        to improve the teachers' lot?
        to educate the pupils better?
    (b) *Personal*
        to impress others?
        to advance my career?
        to reduce pressures on me?
        to foster my professional interests?

The balance between these last two sets of motives, (a) and (b), is always assessed by others and if it is perceived (however unfairly) as tilted towards personal interests, it can lead to a rejection of the change.

And the final question to yourself:

(7) Am I really determined to bring about the change, irrespective of other demands on my time? If not, why not? What would clinch my determination? If not me, who else would take the lead?

Looking beyond yourself into the wider organization, have you got a critical mass of key skills? ICI once developed this by sending 2,000 managers on Coverdale training; BCLP put ninety of their teaching force (20 per cent) on critical skills programmes. People who have shared a common experience become a powerful resource for change. One of us (Everard) visited China in 1982 and was told that the government was cascading 3 million managers through a standard management training programme in two years, in order to trigger off economic progress. It seems to have worked!

PERSONAL APPLICATION

Put these questions to yourself in relation to the change you want to bring about.

Individuals or task groups unfamiliar with problem-solving may need special help from people particularly skilled as 'facilitators'. These can be internal, such as trained TVEI co-ordinators, or external consultants, such as industrial training managers (Chapter 18). The sort of things they do are shown in Figure 17.6.

DISCUSSION TOPICS

(1) Politics is the art of the possible. Would more things become possible if politicians involved with education followed a systematic approach to change?

(2) What effect would you expect the development of competence in managing change systematically to have on the quality of life of teachers? Why?

(3) Given the extent to which society is changing, are there any implications for the school curriculum arising from this and the preceding two chapters?

FURTHER READING

Beckhard, R. and Pritchard, W. (1992) *Changing the Essence: The Art of Creating and Leading Fundamental Change in Organisations*, Jossey-Bass Wiley, Bognor Regis.

Plant, R. (1987) *Managing Change and Making it Stick*, HarperCollins, London.

Whitney, D. and Trosten-Bloom, A. (2003) *The Power of Appreciative Inquiry: A Practical Guide to Positive Change*, Berrett-Koehler, San Francisco.

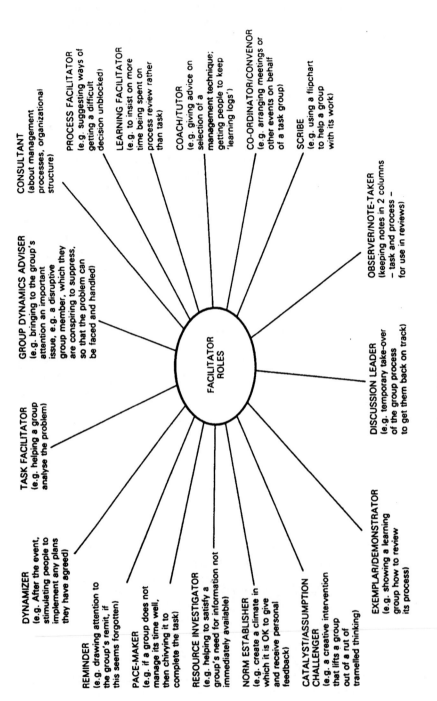

CONSULTANT
(about management processes, organizational structure)

PROCESS FACILITATOR
(e.g. suggesting ways of getting a difficult decision unblocked)

LEARNING FACILITATOR
(e.g. to insist on more time being spent on process review rather than task)

COACH/TUTOR
(e.g. giving advice on selection of a management technique; getting people to keep 'learning logs')

CO-ORDINATOR/CONVENOR
(e.g. arranging meetings or other events on behalf of a task group)

SCRIBE
(e.g. using a flipchart to help a group with its work)

GROUP DYNAMICS ADVISER
(e.g. bringing to the group's attention an important issue, e.g. a disruptive group member, which they are conspiring to suppress, so that the problem can be faced and handled)

OBSERVER/NOTE-TAKER
(keeping notes in 2 columns – task and process – for use in reviews)

TASK FACILITATOR
(e.g. helping a group analyse the problem)

FACILITATOR ROLES

DISCUSSION LEADER
(e.g. temporary take-over of the group process to get them back on track)

DYNAMIZER
(e.g. After the event, stimulating people to implement any plans they have agreed)

REMINDER
(e.g. drawing attention to the group's remit, if this seems forgotten)

PACE-MAKER
(e.g. if a group does not manage its time well, then chivying it to complete the task)

RESOURCE INVESTIGATOR
(e.g. helping to satisfy a group's need for information not immediately available)

NORM ESTABLISHER
(e.g. create a climate in which it is OK to give and receive personal feedback)

CATALYST/ASSUMPTION CHALLENGER
(e.g. a creative intervention that lifts a group out of a rut of tramelled thinking)

EXEMPLAR/DEMONSTRATOR
(e.g. showing a learning group how to review its process)

Figure 17.6 Facilitator roles

18

Transition Management

TRANSITION MANAGEMENT STRUCTURE

The important point to appreciate in managing the *change* process is that the management structures, style, etc., needed are distinctly different from those that work best in managing the status quo. Separate arrangements are needed for the two tasks, although the same people are usually involved in each, albeit in different roles. Failure to provide an adequate structure for managing a complex change programme is frequently the reason for an unsuccessful programme. For example, a major extension of a school into another building could involve the creation of a middle and lower school, affecting both the subject departments and the pastoral system. The transition management structure would have to secure the necessary changes in the work and roles of the operating managers and to co-ordinate the new arrangements. If this were delegated to the day-to-day operating management of the school, the change would not be likely to be smooth.

A suitable transition management structure is likely to need

(1) the authority to mobilize the resources necessary to keep the change moving;
(2) the respect of the existing operating leadership and of the proponents of the change;
(3) the interpersonal skills needed to persuade people rather than coerce them; and
(4) the time required to do the necessary planning and implementation.

The choice of a suitable structure depends on the nature of the change to be managed. Some of the possibilities for managing the transition state are as follows:

(1) The head could become the project manager, possibly assisted by an external adviser or consultant. This may be particularly helpful if the change will have an impact on many external boundaries, since it is usually the head who manages the school boundaries. On the other hand, he or she may not have the time to invest in managing the current

state, preparing to manage the future state, and managing the transition which could easily take 50–100 hours out of the working year.

(2) A project manager could be appointed, such as a deputy head. This is appropriate when there are many internal boundaries to be managed.

(3) An existing group of managers, such as a committee of heads of house, can be given the transition management task, in addition to their normal operational roles. This is only likely to be effective if they operate as a well-knit team.

(4) A group of representatives of constituencies could be chosen, such as representatives of unions and management. This may be useful for changes that are politically charged.

(5) A group of natural leaders could be selected. This might be done, for example, if the formal leadership was lacking in credibility, and it provides an excellent opportunity for staff development. However, they would need to be assured of the necessary clout and to earn the respect of the operating leadership.

(6) A diagonal slice of people at different hierarchical levels in different departments could be used. This structure might be chosen, for example, in cases where the existing hierarchy was the main source of resistance to the change.

(7) A special task force can be set up, selected from staff whom the head feels he or she can trust – a sort of 'kitchen cabinet', responding to him or her informally and candidly. This may be the best structure when it is important for the head to exert direct control, but is unable to devote the necessary time personally to the transition management. However, it may give rise to political problems.

Sometimes a combination of these possibilities is best, with the structure changing at various stages in the change programme. For example, an interservice group formed at a local conference called to improve implementation of the Education Act 1981 considered its own composition at its first meeting and changed it, bringing in two parents. Interestingly, it was chaired not by the most senior official in the group, or even someone from the education service, but by a social worker with good process skills.

A sure recipe for failure in a school is for the head to exclude him or herself by failing to display active interest and support: he or she must maintain a close working partnership with the transition management team, if not a member of it.

One general point is that it is very difficult for a stable organization to change itself, i.e. for the regular structures of the organization to be the structures used to manage the change. The creation of networked temporary systems using novel approaches is more likely to be effective, as an example from BCLP shows.

Case study from BCLP: networking systems

Enid Fraser, Headteacher of Parkview Community College of Technology in Barrow, was very keen to investigate and address the dynamics of the school's leadership team as a catalyst for improving practice. She also accepted the role of co-leader of one of the NCSL's pilot Leadership Learning Groups. An intensive residential in collaboration with Brathay and John Byrne, a former Unilever Senior Manager who had also worked with NCSL, led to a series of individual and group interventions with the leadership team, facilitated by John. In a parallel initiative, Enid was trained in peer-coaching skills using the GROW (Goals, Reality, Options, Will) model by Brathay Consultant Gary Cooke. The activities of the Leadership Learning Group formed a key element in a successful Networked Learning Community (NLC) proposal, again with Enid Fraser acting as a prospective co-leader.

The changes have included the broadening and restructuring of the senior leadership team, the introduction of peer coaching as a change management tool, a radical move from a horizontal to a vertical tutor group system and a very visible commitment to leading change through networks and partnerships – in the form of BCLP, the Leadership Learning Group, a Networked Learning Community (the South Cumbria Learning Innovation Partnership) and an Enterprise Learning Pathfinder Pro-gramme based on the same membership and core curriculum priorities (critical skills development) as the NLC.

A further development is the use of collaborative peer coaching by Enid and the headteachers of the other three Leadership Incentive Grant (LIG) secondary schools in Barrow as a vehicle for identifying priorities for change and targets for action. This model uses BCLP staff, trained in peer coaching, as observers in triads. The observers then provide feedback on questioning techniques, issues arising and the effectiveness of the coaching in allowing colleagues being coached to identify key actions and deadlines relating to priority issues.

In summary, Enid has used a combination of partnership working, development and application of new skills, redeployment of key staff and the integrating framework of the NLC's six levels of learning to generate worthwhile change through a range of linked strategies:

National College of School Leadership
Networked Learning Community
Six levels of learning (where positive impact is expected to occur)

(1) Pupil/student learning
(2) Adult (initially teaching/non-teaching staff) learning
(3) Leadership learning (at all levels within the organisation)
(4) Within-school learning
(5) School-to-school learning
(6) Network-to-network learning.

BCLP's role has been to create opportunities – through co-ordinating and co-leading in the Leadership Learning Group and NLC bids, developing partnership working with John Byrne and Brathay, supporting the peer-coaching triads, and securing additional funding to develop the peer coaching to include teachers with leadership roles at all levels within BCLP and NLC schools.

By the same token it can be enormously helpful to bring in an external consultant or 'facilitator' to the transition management structure, such as an LEA adviser, a local training manager or a college lecturer with appropriate experience (Gray, 1988; Weindling, 1989); few major organizational changes in ICI were ever accomplished by the former divisions pulling themselves up by their own bootstraps. More and more LEAs and schools are using consultants. Even if a consultant is used, it is also important to provide training for people in the transition management structure. Fullan (1982) recommends no less than 27 days of training per staff member per year, and warns that too little training can be dangerous, because it brings problems to the surface without solving them. This may be a counsel of perfection, but industrial experience would suggest that a lead operator in the management of change should have about a month's training. Unfortunately, current provision of such training in the public sector is far from adequate in quality or quantity.

Whatever option is chosen for setting up a transition management structure, there needs to be some system for informing, consulting and involving people affected by the change. Any change creates anxieties, and the transition managers have to explain fully what is happening, in order to build up wide 'ownership' of the change and to motivate people to let it happen and make it work. The communication must be two-way, so that the managers are provided with reliable information about the real impact of the change. At one school visited by one of the authors, an otherwise very capable transition manager (a new deputy head) seemed to be short of intelligence about how the change was really perceived by the scale 1 and 2 teachers, so he assumed an unrealistic degree of commitment to the change. The shrewd manager pokes 'climate thermometers' into the organization at several levels, since he or she wants to deal with things as they really are, and not as they are intended to be.

PERSONAL APPLICATION

Consider a potential major change problem involving your school. What transition management structure would you set up to handle it? What problems would your choice create? How would you handle them?

TASKS FOR THE TRANSITION MANAGEMENT

The kind of tasks that will fall to the transition management structure will depend on the nature of the change. Consider, for example, the amalgamation of two schools, with representatives of each school and of the LEA managing it:

(1) Plans need to be developed to manage
    (a)   the period of the change;
    (b)   any unaffected systems (e.g. a youth wing on one site);
    (c)   organizational integration and operational effectiveness during the change (i.e. managing the 'present state'); and
    (d)   the future situation, when amalgamation is complete.
(2) Because change can be unsettling to people, their apprehension has to be recognized and assuaged as far as possible. Rumours may spread, so clear information about the future state and its effect on people inside and outside the school must be supplied.
(3) Planning needs to cover changes in structures, roles, tasks, people and formal and informal systems. Many attempts at change go wrong when these elements are treated in isolation, so make sure that there is consistency and integration.
(4) The person leading the change needs to be visible, and available to give guidance and support, especially in connection with any conflicts that arise. Any negative energy (frustration, anxiety, threat) needs to be managed so as to encourage constructive behaviour.
(5) People need help in understanding the nature of change. There will always be uncertainty, since at the outset only broad outlines can be set, and the details usually require the involvement of many people.
(6) Communications and information systems need to be effective and to operate in both directions, since: (a) role expectations will need clarifying; (b) norms and assumptions need to be brought into the open and examined; and (c) implications for workloads and job satisfaction need to be understood. Especially important are sensitive areas such as job security and rewards.
(7) Empathy with those affected by the change is important: the 'death' of one of the schools in an amalgamation may induce a sensation akin to mourning, and people need time to disengage from the present state and adjust to the future. In these circumstances some counselling may be needed.

These needs can place a high demand on management and lead to emotional strain if they are not planned for in advance. Admittedly, the amalgamation of two schools is a somewhat extreme example of change, but it is surprising how people can be disturbed and upset by even relatively modest changes, if they feel threatened or disadvantaged in any way. As Fullan says (1982, p. 120), you have to understand the subjective world of the role incumbents as a necessary precondition for engaging in any change effort with them: you must understand what reality is to those in each role. To do this, personal contact is essential, with time for discussion and reassurance.

It is therefore of critical importance that organizational arrangements to provide the time and skill required are carefully thought out and designed. These arrangements then need to be communicated so that everyone concerned understands how the change is being managed.

DEVELOPING A PLAN

Using a 'crisis management' approach to cope with change is not to be recommended, as it is extremely stressful for all concerned. It is far better to draw up a strategic plan to deal with the process of change. Burnes (2000) states that successful organizations spend 90 per cent of the time planning and organizing change and 10 per cent implementing it. Effective planning does not come naturally to many teachers, although anyone who has constructed a school timetable will obviously have valuable expertise. In the authors' experience teachers tend to confuse decisions or intentions with plans, so that specificity is lacking.

A process plan is like a road map for the change effort. It contains detailed statements on who is to do what by when; it clarifies objectives and sets mileposts along the path to their achievement. It unambiguously specifies the means of its own implementation, and it incorporates ways of checking and monitoring progress. The characteristics of an effective plan can be summarized as follows. It is

(1) *purposeful:* the activities are clearly linked to the change goals and priorities;
(2) *task specific:* the types of activities involved are clearly identified rather than broadly generalized, and responsibility for carrying them out is unambiguously assigned;
(3) *temporal:* target dates are specified and achievement is monitored;
(4) *integrated:* the discrete activities are linked to show interdependencies and sequencing networks;
(5) *adaptable:* there are contingency plans and ways of adapting to unexpected problems, such as time slippage and unforeseen resistance; and
(6) *cost-effective:* in terms of the investment of both time and people.

There is one further point. The people who are assigned responsibility for implementing the various activities in the plan usually have their normal work to perform as well: the change activities are an added extra. Management may see the additional responsibilities as an enrichment of their normal work. However, if the change activities do not bring with them a pressure to achieve targets equal to that which applies to operational work, then they will not be regarded as fundamental to the job. So if change activities are inadequately recognized or rewarded, those involved will give a higher priority, in the direction of their energy, to the area which provides the intrinsic rewards, e.g. classroom teaching. Therefore management should be explicit in regarding work on change as part of the primary work of the people concerned, and attempt to recognize, reward or punish it accordingly. In some circumstances this may involve negotiation and the temporary transfer, curtailment or postponement of operational work.

PERSONAL APPLICATION

Reflect carefully on the adequacy of any plans for major change or other projects with which you have been associated. What went wrong? Which of the characteristics of an effective plan were wanting? Can you generalize about the shortcomings that most often recur? What can you resolve to do about it?

HIERARCHY OF OBJECTIVES

There are two main approaches to the development of tension and energy in organizations. The first is the use of controls and the second is the use of purpose, goals and objectives. Controls are effective only if they are backed by a rigorously used reward and punishment system, which can lead to the development of negative energy if mishandled. Purpose, goals and objectives generate tension by developing hope for achievement and of a better condition in the future. However, once a goal is achieved, tension is relaxed and there is no further generation of energy. In order to maintain tension continuously, it is necessary to establish a hierarchy of objectives and to update them regularly.

It is possible to identify four levels of objectives:

Aspirations. These tend to be very long term, bordering on the idealistic. Such gleams in the eye generate little energy or excitement. Replacement of O-levels and CSE by a single exam was for years such an aspiration, before they merged into GCSE.

Strategic. These are time bound and are expressions of what has to be done by year X (say, five or more years away) if we are to reach our aspirations. A school faced with falling rolls and a drift of population away from the area might well set a strategic objective to become a community school catering for a wider age range, in order to survive.

Tactical. These focus on a point in time, usually not more than half-way between the present and the time when the strategic objective is to be attained. Agreement on a tactical goal seen as realistic is the main device for generating tension and energy. It has to make clear where the responsibility lies for the achievement of the goal.

First steps. These are immediate things that have to be done in order to make further action legitimate, such as an announcement that a working party will be set up to initiate the change process.

It is important to consider objectives at one level in the context of those at other levels in order to ensure coherence and consistency of approach.

Diagrams are often helpful in showing how the various objectives interlink. As far as possible, objectives should be SMART:

- Specific
- Measurable
- Achievable
- Realistic
- Time-bound.

GAINING COMMITMENT

Experience in organizational change has shown that in addition to developing the plan for carrying out the change, the planners must determine who in the organization must be committed to the change and to carrying it out, if the change is actually to take place. Traditionally, managements consider this from a political stance, talking of the need to 'get a few people on board', 'get the governors' approval', 'have the unions' agreement' or 'have the majority of the teachers going along'. We would like to suggest, however, that in addition to these intuitive political judgements about who needs to be committed, there should be a systematic analysis of the system to determine those subsystems, individuals and groups whose commitment to the idea, to providing resources (e.g. money and time) and to carrying out and persevering with the change is necessary. Then the manager has to develop a plan to gain the necessary commitment; this is sometimes called 'responsible scheming', which sounds better than 'manipulation'.

The steps in developing a commitment plan are as follows:

(1) Identify target individuals whose commitment is needed.
(2) Define the 'critical mass' needed to ensure the effectiveness of the change, i.e. the minimum number of people who must be committed.
(3) Assess the present level of commitment, of each individual in the critical mass, to the change.
(4) Develop a plan for getting the necessary commitment from the critical mass.
(5) Develop a monitoring plan to assess progress.

Step 3 can be helped by judging where each individual is on a scale of commitment, such as

(1) ready to *oppose* the change;
(2) willing to *let* it happen;
(3) willing to *help* it happen; and
(4) willing to *make* it happen.

Second, a judgement can be made on the same scale of where each individual needs to be for success. Plotting the position on a chart helps (Figure 18.1).

Step 4 is a crucial one to which there are various approaches. Force-field

Individual	Oppose	Let	Help	Make
Head			O	——— X
First deputy head		X	———————	O
Union representative	X	——— O		
LEA adviser		XO		

X = present position
XO = desired position

Figure 18.1 Commitment chart

analysis (Chapter 17) can help. Another way is to apply the Gleicher formula, which can also be useful in assessing any system's readiness to change:

$$C = f(ABD) > X$$

where

C = change, which is a function (f) of:
A = extent of dissatisfaction with the status quo (present state)
B = clarity of vision of where we want to be (future state)
D = feasibility of the first practical steps for getting there
X = cost of the change, in both financial and psychological terms.

Sometimes managers can gain commitment to change by fanning dissatisfaction with the status quo, or with the 'doom' scenario to which this will lead if nothing is done. Or they can paint an attractive and enticing picture of the future state, convincing people that it is something worth striving for. Often, however, it is the practical steps involved in the change which need spelling out, so that people can see just how it will work for them. The net cost of the change can be reduced by trying to ensure that it gives ultimate personal advantage to those affected by it, to offset the extra efforts required in breaking the old mould. Enlightened self-interest always helps. Professional development, or an improved chance of career advancement, are two such benefits.

Other approaches to gaining commitment are as follows:

(1) *Use of power:* although there are still heads who rule with a rod of iron, coercive power is a decreasingly effective strategy for gaining real commitment. But there are times when it helps to overcome initial resistance, enough to give way to more acceptable and enduring methods of winning hearts and minds.
(2) *Involvement:* a participative style of management helps, but sometimes takes a long time to produce results. A way round this dilemma is to think of involvement as applying to three distinct levels – shaping the decision, shaping the implementation and shaping the pace of change. Significant commitment can be obtained at the second and third levels.

(3) *Problem-solving activities:* significant parts of the system are not always aware that there is a problem. By involving them in trying to identify and clarify a problem or need, one can increase their appreciation of the problem and, often, gain their commitment to change.

(4) *Educational activities:* sometimes a training course or educational event will provide the kind of awareness and commitment which policy statements or directives cannot accomplish.

(5) *Treating 'hurting' systems:* one way of moving the process forward is to begin work with those subsystems that are 'hurting'. Change is more likely to occur, and the 'critical mass' is more likely to develop, with such subsystems.

(6) *Change the reward system* to *value different behaviour:* consider both extrinsic and intrinsic rewards; they need not be financial.

(7) *Functioning as a role model:* changed behaviour by the leader is sometimes required in order to get others to change theirs.

(8) *Forced collaboration mechanisms:* in order to get commitment, it is sometimes necessary to require people to work together and to take on certain managerial roles.

(9) *Persuasion:* the techniques used by reputable salespeople are worth considering; these are described on pages 224–5.

The process of selecting a mechanism to involve those whose commitment is essential is often best helped by analysing the forces that get in the way of change. Thus if one can find an activity that unfreezes frozen attitudes, one may be helping the process of creating the conditions necessary for allowing new attitudes to form, with a consequent increase in energy and commitment. This is better than forcing the change on those who are resistant to it.

Finally, when it comes down to dealing with particular individuals, you may have to be ready to spar with the negative thinkers who habitually resist change. Derek Waters, who trained many ILEA primary-school heads, has a useful list of common objections (Figure 18.2) which he gets his courses to role play. There are effective rejoinders to all these snipers' bullets. Try thinking of some and keep them up your sleeve!

RESPONSIBILITY CHARTING

In carrying out any plan, or determining how the future state is to be managed, it is vital to ensure that the key people (or 'actors') understand how they are going to be involved. The allocation of work responsibilities can be assisted by a technique called 'responsibility charting'. It aims to clarify role relationships, as a means of reducing ambiguity, wasted energy and adverse emotional reactions. The basic process is as follows:

(1) I can't see that working with the teachers here.

(2) I can just hear what our parents would say about that – especially after the trouble with the mathematics work last summer.

(3) It won't work in a large (small ... county/voluntary ... urban/rural) school.

(4) I'm sure we haven't got the space (resources/materials/time) for that.

(5) You realize the French (Germans) abandoned that idea five years ago?

(6) How do you think the new governing body are going to react? You remember what they said about the sex education programme!

(7) I wouldn't want the local newspaper to get a hold of this one.

(8) Isn't that an untested theory?

(9) Isn't that an American idea?

(10) You're not putting that idea forward seriously, are you?

(11) Yes, it does sound as though it would work. But you do realize what it would do to the language work programme, don't you?

(12) Isn't that the approach they used to advocate that environmental studies should be tackled back in the sixties?

(13) I can see it would be a good idea, but why change – for so small a gain?

(14) It's a fine plan – but I wonder if it is just a little too advanced for us at this point in our development?

(15) We're different here.

(16) It sounds like a very fashionable thing to do.

(17) If it's so good, why hasn't someone else tried it?

(18) From a practical point of view it does seem all right; but what about the wider implications?

(19) Hardly what I would call a professional approach to our problems.

(20) Is this your own idea?

(21) I'm sorry, but I don't see the connection with what you are suggesting and what most of us perceive as our real needs.

(22) I can think of some much better ways to spend the money.

(23) Perhaps we ought to wait for a more opportune time.

(24) With respect, I don't think you have been here long enough to understand our set-up and how we prefer to work.

(25) I hope you don't expect the infants (juniors) to join in this new scheme.

(26) We have tried this before.

(27) The caretaker will have some very definite views about these plans.

(28) I really can't keep wasting my time like this.

(29) Wasn't that something Keith Joseph tried to introduce?

(30) Well, we would like to do that, but the Education Reform Act makes it impossible!

(31) And how are we going to do this with two teachers short in that department?

(32) What?

(33) You must have stayed up half the night thinking that one out. (Consider your reply most carefully, if you actually did stay up half the night.)

Figure 18.2 Verbal barriers to change (used with permission of Derek Waters)

1. The vertical axis

Using a form designed as shown in Figure 18.3, two or more people whose roles inter-relate or who manage groups that have some interdependence (e.g. a head of year and a head of department) develop a list of actions, decisions or activities (e.g. disciplining pupils, recording disciplinary incidents, using common equipment) and record them on the vertical axis of the form.

2. The horizontal axis

Then, working *individually*, each person identifies the 'actors' who have some kind of behaviour towards each action or decision, and lists these actors on the horizontal axis of the form. Actors can include

(1) those directly involved;
(2) those immediately above them in the hierarchy;
(3) groups as well as individuals (e.g. the senior management team); and
(4) people outside as well as inside the organization (e.g. the chair of governors).

3. Charting behaviours individually

Still working individually, the required behaviour of each actor towards a particular activity is charted, using the following categories:

R = *Responsibility* for seeing that decisions or actions occur.
A = *Approval* of actions, with a right to veto them.
S = *Support* of actions or decisions by provision of resources, but with no right of veto.
I = *Informed* of action or decisions, but with no right to veto.

4. Reaching a consensus

Now working as a group, all the actors (or as many as possible) share their individual perceptions, possibly by circulating the form or by using flipchart displays. Where there is agreement, the only further work is to agree the nature of any support action. The purpose of the meeting is to produce an agreed version of the responsibility chart by a consensus decision. A majority vote will not do: differences have to be ironed out and resolved. The end result must be that each actor treats the decision as though it were ideal.

True clarity will not be achieved if more than one R exists for an activity. Agreement on where the R should be assigned for any activity is the first step in the discussion, and the actor concerned (who will be an individual) will certainly have to agree with subsequent categorizations. There are three approaches which may help, if agreement cannot be reached on who has the R:

CODE: R – Responsibility (initiates)
       A – Approval (right to veto)
       S – Support (put resources against)
       I – Inform (to be informed)

ACTORS → DECISIONS ↓							

Figure 18.3 Responsibility chart

(1) Break the problem down into smaller parts.
(2) Move the R up one level in the organization by including a new actor.
(3) Move the decision about the allocation of the R up one level.

Once the R has been placed, other letters can be agreed. A ground rule is that a decision must be made on which *single* letter goes into the box.

Another problem that will occur is that agreement may only be reached on some activity by assigning a large number of As. This, however, is unrealistic, because it leads to a situation in which there is great difficulty in getting decisions that allow progress on the work. Discussion is then needed on how to change some As into Ss or Is.

5. Circulating the chart

Having developed the chart, the group then tests it out with any actors not present at the meeting (indeed no major actor should have been absent) and circulates it to colleagues as a vehicle for communicating operating practice.

6. Using the chart

The actors use the chart to check what their appropriate behaviour is and to call the attention of other actors to behaviour that is out of line with what was agreed.

The usefulness of responsibility-charting lies not only in the end product of an agreed chart but also in developing understanding of people's different roles, and a better appreciation of different feelings and attitudes towards the operation.

PERSONAL APPLICATION

With the help of one or two colleagues with whom you have to work on some operation, draw up a responsibility chart following these guidelines. Afterwards, review how the process worked and in what other contexts it could be applied with advantage.

MONITORING AND EVALUATING CHANGE

One of the problems with change is ensuring that it is followed through. With something as discrete as the amalgamation of two schools, it is relatively easy to know when the change is complete. However, some changes, such as 'improving school leadership' are ill-defined. To move from the present to the future state, the system has to be unfrozen, changed and fully stabilized in the new state. We need, therefore, to have yardsticks by which we can recognize when the organization has got to where it wants to be, and which we can use to set a ratchet to prevent backsliding. The last thing we want is a façade of change, followed by the system gradually sinking back into its old ways of working. As Sir John Harvey-Jones has observed (2003, p. 114):

> Ultimately change is only anchored firmly when individuals have changed their perceptions and values, and it is important to be realistic about the time that this may take. Five years is absolute par for the course of changing attitudes and even that is only achievable if one is moving well within the establishment grain of thinking.

To help stabilize the system in the new state, we need to develop success criteria or measures that will tell us that the change has been effective and has become truly assimilated. The 'future scenario' description may yield some useful clues to the measures that might be adopted, if it is specific enough. Some means of gathering reliable information and analysing it should be set up as part of the overall plan for change (not as an afterthought), and may have to extend beyond the point when the change can be said to be complete, so as to make sure that it endures. The means of measuring success might take the form of a checklist of procedures, a questionnaire about role responsibilities, an analysis of exam results or an attitude survey to be completed by those most likely to know if the change has been successful – perhaps the pupils. It will focus on the actual outcomes of the change.

It is necessary to assign responsibility to named individuals for monitoring the critical factors that measure success and for managing the processes needed to take corrective action in case of a shortfall. Responsibility-charting is useful for this. Processes that influence several of the success criteria and are known to have been inadequate in the past merit particular attention.

The existence and purpose of the evaluation or review plan, and the intention to use it for correcting any tendency for the system to regress, should be communicated to those involved, because this will help in the process of stabilization of the change. It will signal the completion of the transition stage and the arrival of the 'future state'. Success makes obsolete the behaviour that led to success: new behaviour is now needed, appropriate to the future state having been attained.

A further reason for this review is to check on unforeseen consequences of the change, so that any new problems thrown up are properly managed, and new opportunities made the subject of further change.

The results of the review should be carefully studied so that the management knows and celebrates what activities have been successful. Organizations can consciously learn how to manage change more effectively, but only if they review the process, consolidate the successful practices and plan to overcome any difficulties next time round.

The whole organization is entitled to receive some kind of report from management about the success of the change, and this may well be linked with expressions of thanks for their co-operation. This is all part of the attempt to mould the reward system so that change efforts and development are valued and recognized as much as operational work.

Finally, there is the possibility that other schools will be able to benefit from your experience, e.g. through your contributing a paper to a conference or to the technical press.

DISCUSSION TOPIC

Assuming that you are involved in some major change within your school, arising from a school development plan, an Ofsted inspection or implementing the requirements of new legislation, consider the extent to which there is evidence of the approaches outlined in the last two chapters being applied, explicitly or implicitly. Can you, with colleagues, open up opportunities to contribute to implementing the change by using the knowledge you have picked up in this book? If not, how else do you propose to demonstrate that you have gained in competence by having read Part III of the book?

FURTHER READING

Aspinwall, K., Simkins, T., Wilkinson, J.F. and McAuley, M.J. (1992) *Managing Evaluation in Education*, Routledge, London.

Fullan, M. (2003) *Change Forces with a Vengeance*, RoutledgeFalmer, London.

Senge, P., Kleiner, A., Roberts, C., Ross, R., Roth, G. and Smith, B. (1999) *The Dance of Change: The Challenge to Sustaining Momentum in Learning Organisations*, Doubleday Currency, New York.

Glossary

(Abbreviations and acronyms which may not be familiar to readers outside the UK are set out below.)

BCLP: Barrow Community Learning Partnership, an agency for effecting cultural change in Barrow schools and the local community.

BEMAS (renamed BELMAS): British Education (Leadership) Management and Administration Society, a professional body for education managers and those who develop them (www.belmas.org.uk).

CNAA: the Council for National Academic Awards was an official validating body set up to grant higher academic awards to students.

CSCS: the Centre for the Study of Comprehensive Schools, based at University of Leicester, Moulton College, Moulton, Northampton NN3 7RR, is a national organization set up in 1980 to collect, study and disseminate good practice in comprehensive schools (www.cscs.org.uk).

DfES: the Department for Education and Skills (formerly the DfEE, the Department for Education and Employment, DfE, the Department for Education, and before that the DES, the Department of Education and Science) is the government department centrally responsible for education in England (but not Scotland, Wales or Northern Ireland) (www.dfes.gov.uk).

ERA: the Education Reform Act 1988. A major piece of legislation, introducing a National Curriculum, mandatory testing, local management of schools (LMS) and the right of schools to opt out of the local authority system.

GNVQ: General National Vocational Qualifications are a form of accreditation of what candidates can do, as opposed to what they know.

HIP: Headteachers' Induction Programme (formerly HEADLAMP). A government initiative to train newly appointed headteachers.

HSC/HSE: Health and Safety Commission/Executive, the national UK body that oversees health and safety in the workplace.

HoD: head of department. Secondary schools are structured according to subject discipline, with the various departments headed by senior practising teachers. In Scotland the term 'principal teacher' is more common. Some schools also have faculties which group together related subjects. Where the context so requires, the term HoD should be taken to include also heads of faculties.

ICI: Imperial Chemical Industries plc is a British multinational chemical company which for many years had a reputation for progressive management and for helping science teachers to improve their teaching materials. It has also been active in transferring some of its management practices to schools.

ILEA: the Inner London Education Authority was an elected body responsible for providing and co-ordinating all the public-sector education in inner London. Disbanded under ERA, its principal functions are now provided by the boroughs.

INSET: in-service education and training is provided mainly by public sector educational institutions, universities, LEAs *(q.v.)* and the DfES *(q.v.)*.

LEA: local education authorities are bodies of elected representatives responding to county, metropolitan district and borough councils. The permanent officials are usually headed by a director of education or chief education officer responsible for the administration of the authority. Their powers were curtailed by ERA *(q.v.)*. Most teachers are employees of an LEA.

LMS: local management of schools. A provision of ERA *(q.v.)*, which devolves much power and authority from LEAs to individual schools.

LPSH: Leadership Programme for Serving Headteachers.

LSC: Learning and Skills Council, the government agency that took over from the Further Education Funding Council and the Training and Enterprise Councils for funding vocational education and training in England.

MCI: the Management Charter Initiative was the 'lead body' that developed national occupational standards of competence in management, on which National (and Scottish) Vocational Qualifications are based. Now replaced by the Management Standards Centre (www.management-standards.org.uk).

MSC: see TEED.

NAHT: the National Association of Head Teachers is the largest professional association of heads and deputies in the UK, covering both the primary and the secondary sector.

NCSL: the National College for School Leadership has taken over from TTA (*q.v.*) responsibility for raising standards in school management and leadership (www.ncsl.org.uk).

NPQH: National Professional Qualification for Headship (for aspiring heads).

NTL: the National Training Laboratories are an American organization which has successfully pioneered the development and application to management and organization of the behavioural sciences, especially humanistic psychology, since the Second World War. Its nearest UK equivalent is the Tavistock Institute for Human Relations. Both are proponents of experiential, as distinct from didactic, learning methods.

NUT: the National Union of Teachers is the largest and most powerful teachers' union in the UK. It is affiliated to the TUC (Trades Union Congress).

NVQ: National Vocational Qualifications (in Scotland, SVQ) attest to competence in the workplace against national standards. Overseen originally by NCVQ (NC = National Council), and replaced in 1997 by QCA (*q.v.*) and in Scotland by SCOTVEC (Scottish Vocational Education Council).

OD: organization development has no satisfactory definition. It is used to denote an approach to the improvement of the effectiveness of organizations and of the individuals that staff them. This approach makes systematic use of the behavioural sciences (applied psychology, sociology, social anthropology, etc.) to diagnose situations and solve the problems that emerge. Although not synonymous with the management of change, OD is very much associated with it.

Ofsted: the Office for Standards in Education is the inspecting authority for English schools (formerly conducted by HMI – Her Majesty's Inspectorate – www.ofsted.gov.uk).

QCA: Qualifications and Curriculum Authority, formed in 1997 by amalgamating NCVQ and the Schools Curriculum and Assessment Authority (www.qca.org.uk).

ROSLA: raising of the school leaving age. In UK schools compulsory education continues to the age of 16 – formerly 15, and before that, 14.

SED/SEED: the Scottish (Executive) Education Department discharges the responsibilities which in England are handled by the DfES (*q.v.*). The two education systems differ in some major respects, so it is often misleading to speak of 'British' education.

SEN: special educational needs. A phrase used to refer to the needs of children with handicap and disability, provision for whom is covered by the Education Act 1981, which followed the Warnock Report on the subject.

SHA: the Secondary Heads Association is the main professional association for (specifically) secondary headteachers, deputy and assistant headteachers.

TEED: the Training, Enterprise and Education Directorate of the former Employment Department (later amalgamated with the former Department for Education) succeeded the Training Agency, which in turn succeeded the Manpower Services Commission (MSC). It exerted pressure on the education system to respond more effectively to national economic needs.

TTA: Teacher Training Agency, set up under the Education Act 1994 to oversee nationally the initial and in-service training of teachers. The NCSL (*q.v.*) has now taken over responsibility for headteachers.

TVEI: the Training and Vocational Education Initiative was a government-funded scheme aimed at shifting the focus of secondary education towards practical and vocational activities, and thus to counter the 'academic drift' which followed the Fisher Education Act 1917 making the universities responsible for the main examination system.

Useful Websites

www.dfes.gov.uk/a-z/into.html A to Z of school leadership and management issues.

www.dti.gov.uk/mbp *Managers and Leaders: Raising our Game.* Government's response to Report of the Council for Excellence in Management and Leadership (www.managementandleadershipcouncil.org).

www.leeds.ac.uk/educol/slm.htm Search site for school leadership and management issues.

www.management-standards.org Management and Leadership Standards.

www.ncsl.org.uk National College for School Leadership.

www.teachernet.gov.uk DfES guidance.

References and Further Reading

Adler, S., Laney, J. and Packer, M. (1993) *Managing Women*, Open University Press, Buckingham.

Babington Smith, B. and Sharp, A. (1990) *Manager and Team Development*, Heinemann, Oxford.

Ball, C. (ed.) (1994) *Start Right: The Importance of Early Learning*, Royal Society of Arts, London.

Barber, M., Evans, A. and Johnson, M. (1995) *An Evaluation of the National Scheme of School Teacher Appraisal*, HMSO, London.

Bartlett, J. (1987) *Familiar Quotations*, Citadel Press, Sacramento..

Bayliss, V. (1999) *Opening Minds: Education for the 21st Century*, Royal Society of Arts, London.

Bayliss, V. (2003a) *Opening Minds: Taking Stock*, Royal Society of Arts, London.

Bayliss, V (2003b) Opening Minds, *RSA Journal*, June 2003, pp. 30–33.

Beck, C. (1990) *Better Schools: A Values Perspective*, Falmer Press, Lewes.

Beckhard, R. and Harris, R.T. (1987) *Organizational Transitions. Managing Complex Change* (2nd edn), Addison-Wesley, Woking.

Beer, S. (1981) *Brain of the Firm*, John Wiley, London.

Belbin, R.M. (1981) *Management Teams: Why They Succeed or Fail*, Heinemann, Oxford.

Belbin, R.M. (1995) *Team Roles at Work*, Butterworth-Heinemann, Oxford.

Berne, E. (1968) *Games People Play: The Psychology of Human Relationships*, Penguin, Harmondsworth.

Black, P. and William, D. (1998) *Inside the Black Box*, King's College, London.

Black, P. *et al.* (2002) *Working Inside the Black Box*, King's College, London.

Blake, R.R. and Mouton, J.S. (1994) *The Managerial Grid*, Gulf Publishing, Houston, Tex.

Bolam, T., Smith, G. and Cantor, H. (1979) *LEA Advisers and the Mechanisms of Innovation*, Routledge, London.

Bowring-Carr, C. and West-Burnham, J. (1994) *Managing Quality in Schools: A Training Manual*, Longman, Harlow.

Boyatzis, R.E. (1982) *The Competent Manager*, Wiley, New York.

Boydell, T. and Leary, M. (1994) From management development to managing development, *Transition*, Vol. 94, no. 9, p. 8.

Burgoyne, J.G. (1976) *A Taxonomy of Managerial Qualities as Learning Goals for Management Education. Development and Initial Testing*, Centre for the Study of Management Learning, Lancaster.

Burnes, B. (2000) *Managing Change*, Prentice Hall, London.

Burns, T. and Stalker, G.M. (1994) *The Management of Innovation*, Oxford University Press, Oxford.

Butcher, K. (1995) Private communication.

Buzan, A. (2003) *Use Your Head*, BBC Consumer Publishing, London.

Caldwell, B. and Spinks, J.M. (1998) *Beyond the Self-Managed School*, RoutledgeFalmer, London.

CBI (1998) *Greater Expectations (Priorities for the Future Curriculum)*, Confederation of British Industry, London.

Council for National Academic Awards (1984) *Handbook*, CNAA, London.

Cyert, R.M. and March, J.G. (1992) *A Behavioral Theory of the Firm*, Blackwell, Oxford.

Davies, B. and Ellison, L. (2003) *Strategic Direction and Development of the School: Key Frameworks for School Development Planning*, RoutledgeFalmer, London.

Dean, J. (1985) *Managing the Secondary School*, Routledge, London.

Dearing, R. (1995) *Review of 16–19 Qualifications: Interim Report*, School Curriculum and Assessment Authority, London.

DES (1988) *School Governors. A Guide to the Law*, HMSO, London.

DfES (1998) *A Good Practice Guide: Health and Safety of Pupils on Educational Visits* (with 2002 supplements on www.teachernet.gov.uk/visits), Department for Education and Skills, London.

DfES (2003) *Teachers' Pay and Conditions Document*, HMSO, London.

DfES/DTI (2002) *Managers and Leaders: Raising our Game*, www.dti.gov.uk/mbp/bpgt.

Dickmann, H. and Stanford-Blair, N. (2002) *Connecting Leadership to the Brain*, Corwin Press, Thousand Oaks, California.

Emery, F.E. (1969) *Systems Thinking*, Penguin, Harmondsworth.

Esp, D. (1993) *Competences for School Managers*, Kogan Page, London.

Evans, J., Everard, K.B., Friend, J., Glaser, A., Norwich, B. and Welton, J. (1989) *Decision-making for Special Educational Needs*, Tecmedia, Loughborough.

Everard, K.B. (1980) The Christian layman in management, *Industrial and Commercial Training*, Vol. 12, no. 4, p. 140.

Everard, K.B. (1984) *Management in Comprehensive Schools: What Can Be Learned from Industry?* (2nd edn), Centre for the Study of Comprehensive Schools, University of Leicester, Northampton.

Everard, K.B. (1986) *Developing Management in Schools*, Blackwell, Oxford.

Everard, K.B. (1989a) Competences in education and education management, *Management in Education*, Vol. 3, no. 3, pp. 14–20.

Everard, K.B. (1989b) Organization development in educational institutions, in N. Entwistle (ed.) *Handbook of Educational Ideas and Practices*, Routledge, London.

Everard, K.B. (1993) *A Guide to Handling Some Values Issues*, National Association for Values in Education and Training (NAVET), Aberdeen.

Everard, K.B. (1995a) Teambuilding – a powerful tool for educational development, *Educational Change and Development*, Vol. 15, no. 2, pp. 21–4.

Everard, K.B. (1995b) Values as central to competent professional practice, in H. Busher and R. Saran (eds) *Managing Teachers as Professionals in Schools*, Kogan Page, London.

Fayol, H. (1967) *Industrial and General Administration*, Pitman, New York.

Fidler, B. and Cooper, R. (eds) (1992) *Staff Appraisal and Staff Management in Schools and Colleges: A Guide to Implementation*, Longman, Harlow.

Fullan, M. (1982) *The Meaning of Educational Change*, Teachers College Press, New York, and Institute for Studies in Education, Ontario.

Fullan, M. (1993) *Change Forces*, RoutledgeFalmer, London.

Fullan, M. (2001) *The New Meaning of Educational Change*, RoutledgeFalmer, London.

Fullan, M. (2003) *The Moral Imperative of School Leadership*, Corwin, London.

Fullan, M. (2003) *Change Forces with a Vengeance*, RoutledgeFalmer, London.

Fullan, M., Miles, M.B. and Taylor, B. (1980) Organization development in schools: the state of the art, *Review of Educational Research*, Vol. 50, no. 1, pp. 121–84.

Garratt, B. (1987) *The Learning Organisation*, Profile Books, London.

Glatter, R., Preedy, M., Riches, C. and Masterton, M. (eds) (1988) *Understanding School Management*, Open University Press, Milton Keynes.

Goldsmith, W. and Clutterbuck, D. (1984) *The Winning Streak: Britain's Top Companies Reveal their Formulas for Success*, Weidenfeld & Nicolson, London.

Goleman, D. (1996) *Emotional Intelligence: Why it Can Matter More than IQ*, Bloomsbury, London.

Goleman, D. (1998) *Working with Emotional Intelligence*, Bloomsbury, London.

Gray, H.L. (ed.) (1982) *The Management of Educational Institutions: Theory, Research and Consultancy*, Falmer Press, Lewes.

Gray, H.L. (ed.) (1988) *Management Consultancy in Schools*, Continuum International Publishing, London.

Handy, C.B. (1993) *Understanding Organizations* (4th edn), Penguin, Harmondsworth.

Harris, T.A. (1995) *I'm OK, You're OK*, Arrow, London.

Harrison, R. (1972) How to describe your organization, *Harvard Business Review*, Sept.–Oct.

Harvey-Jones, J.H. (2003) *Making it Happen: Reflections on Leadership*, Profile Books, London.

Health and Safety Executive (1992) *Safety Assessment Principles for Nuclear Plants*, HMSO, London.

Her Majesty's Inspectorate (1977) *Ten Good Schools*, HMSO, London.

Hersey, P., Blanchard, K.H. and Johnson, D.E. (1996) *Management of Organizational Resources Utilizing Human Resources*, Prentice-Hall, Englewood Cliffs, NJ.

Herzberg, F. (1975) *Work and the Nature of Man*, Crosby Lockwood, Reading.

Honey, P. and Mumford, A. (1989) *Manual of Learning Styles*, Honey, Maidenhead.

Hopkins, D. (2001) *Think Tank Report to Governing Council*, National College of School Leadership, www.ncsl.org.uk.

HSE/IOSH/CCC (2000) *Preparing Young People for a Safer Life*, Health and Safety Executive, Institute of Occupational Safety and Cheshire County Council, London.

Huxley, J. (1984) How ICI pulled itself into shape, *The Sunday Times*, 29 July, p. 57.

Hymer, B. and Michel, D. (2002) *Gifted and Talented Learners: Creating a Policy for Inclusion*, NACE/Fulton, London.

Jameson, H. and Watson, M. (1998) *Starting and Running a Nursery: The Business of Early Years Care*, Stanley Thornes, Cheltenham.

Jirasinghe, D. and Lyons, G. (1996) *The Competent Head: A Job Analysis of Heads' Tasks and Personality Factors*, Falmer Press, London.

Johnson, G. and Scholes, K. (2001) *Exploring Corporate Strategy*, Financial Times Prentice-Hall, London.

Jones, A. (1987) *Leadership for Tomorrow's Schools*, Simon and Schuster, London.

Kelly, M. (1995) Action first – thinking later, *Management in Education*, Vol. 9, no. 2, pp. 10–12.

Kolb, D.A. (1984) *Experiential Learning: Experience as the Source of Learning and Development*, Prentice-Hall, Englewood Cliffs, NJ.

Lavelle, M. (1984) The role of consultancy and OD in innovation in education, *School Organization*, Vol. 4, no. 2, p. 161.

Lawrence, P.R. and Lorsch, J.W. (1969) *Organization and Environment*, R.D. Irwin, New York.

Leithwood, K. (1995) Leadership for school restructuring, in K. Leithwood, J. Chapman, D. Corsan, P. Hallinger and A. Hart (eds) *International Handbook of Educational Leadership and Administration*, Vol. 2, Kluwer, Dordrecht and London.

Leithwood and Montgomery (1986) quoted in Schmoker, M. (1999) *Results: The Key to School Improvement* (2nd edn), Association for Supervision and Curriculum Development, Alexandria, Va.

Lyus, V. (1998) *Management in Early Years*, Hodder and Stoughton, London.

MacGilchrist, B., Myers, K. and Reed, J. (1997) *The Intelligent School*, Paul Chapman Publishing, London.

Mant, A. (1983) *The Leaders We Deserve*, Blackwell, Oxford.

Maslow, A.H. (1943) A theory of human motivation, *Psychological Review*, Vol. 50, pp. 370–96.

Maw, J., Fielding, M., Mitchell, P., White, J., Young, P., Ouston, J. and White, P. (1984) *Education plc?*, Institute of Education, University of London.

McClelland, D.C. (1985) *The Achieving Society*, Simon and Schuster, London.

McGregor, D. (1985) *The Human Side of Enterprise*, McGraw-Hill, New York.

Mortimore, P. and MacBeath, J. (2003) School Effectiveness and Improvement, in M. Preedy, R. Glatter and C. Wise (eds) *Strategic Leadership and Educational Improvement*, Paul Chapman Publishing, London.

Mortimore, P., Sammons, P., Stoll, L., Lewis, D. and Ecob, R. (1988) Key factors in effective junior schooling, in Glatter *et al.* (eds) *op. cit.*

Myers, S.M. (1991) *Every Employee a Manager*, Pfeiffer, New York.

NACETT (1995) *Report on Progress towards the National Targets*, National Advisory Council for Education and Training Targets, London.

NCE (1995a) *Learning to Succeed*, National Commission on Education, London.

NCE (1995b) *Success Against the Odds*, National Commission on Education, London.

NCVQ (1995) *NVQ Criteria and Guidance*, National Council for Vocational Qualifications, London.

Ofsted (1995) *Inspection Quality 1994/1995*, Office for Standards in Education, London.

Ofsted (2003) *Leadership and Management: What Inspection Tells Us*, Office for Standards in Education, London.

Ormston, M. and Shaw, M. (1994) *Inspection: A Preparation Guide for Schools* (2nd edn), Longman, Harlow.

Ouston, J. (ed.) (1993) *Women in Education Management*, Longman, Harlow.

Parsons, C., Welsh, P., Day, C. and Harris, A. (2000) Targeting performance management: some reflections on the leadership programme for serving headteachers, *Management in Education*, Vol. 14, no. 5, pp. 11–13.

Peter, L. (1996) *Quotations for Our Times*, Souvenir Press, London.

Peters, T.J. and Waterman, R.H. (1995) *In Search of Excellence*, HarperCollins, New York and London.

Pettigrew, A.M. (1985) *The Awakening Giant: Continuity and Change in Imperial Chemical Industries*, Blackwell, Oxford.

Plant, R. (1987) *Managing Change and Making it Stick*, HarperCollins, London.

QCA (1999) *Early Years Education, Childcare and Playwork: A Framework of Nationally Accredited Qualifications*, Qualifications and Curriculum Authority, London.

QCA/HSE (1999) *The New General Teaching Requirement for Health and Safety*, Qualifications and Curriculum Authority and Health and Safety Executive, London.

Rackham, N., Honey, P. and Colbert, M. (1971) *Developing Interactive Skills*, Wellens Publishing, Northampton.

Reddin, W.J. (1971) *Managerial Effectiveness*, McGraw-Hill, New York.

Rice, A.K. (1971) *The Enterprise and the Environment*, Tavistock, London.

Rutter, M., Maugham, B., Mortimore, P. and Ouston, J. (1979) *Fifteen Thousand Hours*, Open Books Publishing, Cudworth.

Schmoker, M. (1999) *Results: The Key to School Improvement* (2nd edn), Association for Supervision and Curriculum Development, Alexandria, Va.

Schmuck, R., Runkel, P., Arends, J. and Arends, R. (1977) *The Second Handbook of Organizational Development in Schools*, Mayfield, Palo Alto, Calif.

School Management Task Force (1990) *Developing School Management – The Way Forward*, HMSO, London.

School Teachers Review Body (1995) *Fourth Report*, HMSO, London.

Sergiovanni, T. (1996) *Leadership for the Schoolhouse*, Jossey-Bass, San Fransisco.

Seymour, R. and West-Burnham, J. (1989/90) Learning styles and education management: parts 1 and 2, *International Journal of Educational Management*, Vol. 3, no. 4, pp. 19–25, and Vol. 4, no. 4, pp. 22–6.

Sloan, A. (1986) *My Years with General Motors*, Sidgwick & Jackson, London.

Stewart, V. (1983) *Change: The Challenge for Management*, McGraw-Hill, London.

Stoll, L. (2003) School Culture and Improvement, in M. Preedy, R. Glatter and C. Wise (eds) *Strategic Leadership and Educational Improvement*, Paul Chapman Publishing, London.

Stoll, L. and Fink, D. (1996) *Changing Our Schools: Linking School Effectiveness and School Improvement*, Open University Press, Buckingham.

Stoll, L. and Myers, K. (eds) (1997) *No Quick Fixes: Perspectives on Schools in Difficulty*, RoutledgeFalmer.

Tannenbaum, R. and Schmidt, W.H. (1958) How to choose a leadership pattern, *Harvard Business Review*, Vol. 36, pp. 95–101.

Taylor, F.W. (1947) *Principles of Scientific Management*, Dover Publications, New York.

Taylor, J. (1984) Bridging the gap: a county council's approach to the management development of head teachers, *BACIE Journal*, March/April, p. 67.

Taylor, M. (1992) *Coverdale on Management* (2nd edn), Butterworth-Heinemann, Oxford.

Trist, E.L. (1960) *Socio-technical Systems*, Tavistock Institute of Human Relations, London.

Tuckman, B.W. (1965) Development sequences in small groups, *Psychological Bulletin*, Vol. 63, pp. 384–99.

Urwick, L. (1964) *Making of Scientific Management*, Pitman, London.

Weindling, D. (1989) The process of school improvement, *School Organization*, Vol. 9, no. 1, pp. 53–4.

West-Burnham, J. (1977) *Managing Quality in Schools*, Falmer Press, London.

Whalley, M. (2004) *Management in Early Childhood Settings*, Sage, London.

Woods, D. and Orlick, S. (1994) *School Review and Inspection*, Kogan Page, London.

YMCA (2000) *Children's Work Handbook* (2nd ed.), Young Men's Christian Association Publications Department, Walthamstow.

Index